FASHIONS IN MANAGEMENT RESEARCH

For Mum and Dad

Fashions in Management Research

An empirical analysis

PATRICK THOMAS
CHI Research, Inc.
Haddon Heights
New Jersey
U.S.A.

Ashgate

Aldershot • Brookfield USA • Singapore • Sydney

Published by
Ashgate Publishing Ltd
Gower House
Croft Road
Aldershot
Hants GU11 3HR
England

Ashgate Publishing Company
Old Post Road
Brookfield
Vermont 05036
USA

British Library Cataloguing in Publication Data
Thomas, Patrick
    Fashions in management research : an empirical analysis
    1.Management - Research
    I.Title
    658'.0072

Library of Congress Catalog Card Number: 99-72659

ISBN 1 84014 730 X

Printed and bound by Athenaeum Press, Ltd.,
Gateshead, Tyne & Wear.

Contents

List of Figures

List of Tables

Acknowledgements

Carrying out the research for this book was a long task, and one which I could not have completed without the help of many people. I would like to express my gratitude to David Watkins and Keith Spicer for their support, both academic and personal, throughout the project; their contribution to its completion cannot be overstated. In addition, I would like to thank everybody who has supported me during the project, particularly my family and friends.

I would also like to thank Southampton Institute for the financial and practical support it provided during the research for this book.

1 Introduction

The Growth of Management Research

Organisations, whether social, economic or political, occupy a central position within many societies in the latter part of the twentieth century. Individuals interact with organisations on a regular basis in order to fulfil a variety of requirements, including employment; education; health care; and food and clothing. The increasing proliferation of organisations within many spheres of activity has engendered a concomitant growth in the analysis of their operation. Research into the operation of organisations is often defined as 'organisational research' or 'management research'. The latter definition reflects the fact that the success of modern, large-scale organisations, and the policies employed to achieve this success, are often largely the responsibility of professional managers.

Management research is one of the fastest growing areas of academic study. The interest in this area is reflected in the growing number of academic journals devoted to the study of organisations. In 1965, about twenty journals were primarily concerned with the analysis of organisations. This number had increased to well over one hundred journals in 1994, highlighting the increasing amount of research undertaken in this area. One interesting aspect of the growth in the number of journals is that it has not been restricted to peripheral serials. Among the journals generally regarded as the core publications within management research, only one had started publication before 1956 (*Harvard Business Review*). Of the other leading journals in this area, *Administrative Science Quarterly* was first published in 1958; *Academy of Management Review* in 1976; and *Strategic Management Journal* in 1980. The high level of influence achieved by these relatively new journals over a short period of time reflects the dynamic nature of management research as a discipline.

Concerns Facing Management Researchers

The expansion in management research literature has led to an increasing desire for an evaluation of its role. There are two main concerns currently

1

facing the management research community. The first of these is the *quality* of research output. As a recent *Economic and Social Research Council* (ESRC) report stated, 'the value and quality of some management research has been questioned by academics, funders and users alike' (ESRC, 1994, iv). The concern with research quality is not only driven by high-minded ideals. The emphasis placed on quality also derives from the desire to attract greater funding for management research. Between 1990 and 1992, 17% of proposals from management researchers for ESRC research grants were successful. This compares unfavourably with an overall success rate of 26% for the social sciences (ESRC, 1994, 10). The main reason put forward for the low acceptance rate for management research proposals was their inherent 'lack of quality' (ESRC, 1994, 1). Given the increasing competition for research funding throughout higher education, it is seen as essential for the quality of management research to be improved.

The second concern facing management researchers is that of *relevance* - the applicability of management research to management practice. The ESRC report states that 'management research still does not make enough impact on users and thus on management practice' (ESRC, 1994, 5). Since management research is, by its nature, an applied discipline, it is clearly damaging for it to have little influence on management practitioners. The ESRC report concludes that management research faces a 'double challenge' (ESRC, 1994, 17): its output must be of high academic quality, but also relevant to management practitioners.

Role of Management Fashions

It has been argued that one of the main problems in meeting this 'double challenge' is the increasing influence of management fashions (Thompson and Davidson, 1994). Many management theories have been depicted as little more than fashions which are popular for a time, but have no positive impact on management practice in the longer term. Wickens (1995) contends that management researchers and practitioners have become 'fad surfers', switching their attention from one theory to the next as they come in and out of fashion. A similar depiction of management researchers may also be identified in the work of Alvarez (1993).

A number of problems have been identified with the supposed proliferation of management fashions. The first of these is that management fashions may cause the diffusion of inefficient techniques at the expense of efficient ones (Abrahamson, 1991). A second problem is that many fashionable approaches only address one aspect of the problems facing managers (Wickens, 1995). The recommendations they offer thus appear to be attractively simple, but will not provide long-term solutions because of their failure to account for the complex nature of organisations. This leads to potentially the most damaging aspect of management fashions - that their failure to achieve what they promise causes management practitioners to dismiss management research as irrelevant. One senior manager, interviewed by Watson (1993), reported that

> We do all the right things. I mean just look at it. We've had the lot: total quality management, a winning culture, customer focus, continuous improvement, business improvement plans, decentralisation, business action teams, harmonisation, blah, blah, blah. Every bloody consultant in the world has given us advice. And what does it add up to? We ought to be one of these so-called 'excellent' companies. But I don't think we are.

Although care must be taken in the interpretation of the views of a single manager, this quotation highlights the challenge faced by management research. If the beliefs of this manager (i.e. that new management techniques result in few practical benefits) become widespread among practising managers, this may adversely affect the attitude held towards management research, and therefore reduce the influence of this research upon management practice.

Fashionable management theories are thus regarded as having a potentially deleterious impact upon the image and influence of management research. As a result, the issue of management fashions has attracted increasing interest over recent years (ironically, it may be that the study of management fashions is itself a fashion within management research). A number of writers have analysed various aspects of management fashions (e.g. Abrahamson, 1991, 1996; Gill and Whittle, 1992; Kieser, 1997). The work of these theorists is discussed extensively in the following chapter. One characteristic which is common to their work is that it is not based upon extensive empirical research, but is largely theoretical in content.

Purpose of this Book

This book offers an alternative approach to the study of management fashions. It represents the first attempt to offer a large scale *empirical analysis* of fashions within management research literature. As such, it may be regarded as complementary to existing theoretical analyses of management fashions. Research into management fashions is still a relatively new phenomenon. This book therefore offers an exploratory empirical study of this area. The models which emerge from the analysis may be regarded as the first empirically tested models of fashions in management literature. There are three main objectives of this book, as outlined below:

1. To develop an empirical method of identifying those theories within management research which are subject to the pressures of fashion. This method must delineate those management ideas whose influence is relatively transient; and those ideas which have a lasting and profound influence upon management research.
2. To study various characteristics of management research, in order to identify factors that explain why particular management theories are susceptible to the influence of fashion.
3. To develop theories of the operation of fashions within management research. These theories emerge from the results of the research undertaken to address the first two objectives of the book. The resultant theories may then be compared with those emergent from previous studies of management fashions, which are based upon theoretical, rather than empirical, analysis.

Management fashions are therefore to be identified on the basis of their transient influence upon management research. A method of empirically measuring the influence of management literature over time is thus required. The method employed was founded upon the techniques developed within the field of study defined as 'bibliometrics'. The discipline of bibliometrics studies the characteristics of research fields through analysis of their published literature. For the purpose of this book, the branch of bibliometrics which was of particular relevance was 'citation analysis', which studies the development and structure of academic disciplines through the pattern of citations received by published research items. Citation analysis facilitated evaluations of the influence over time of particular items of published management research.

Two distinct research fields thus inform this book. The first of these contains existing studies of fashions in general, and fashions in management research in particular. These studies provide the theoretical and contextual foundations of this book. However, their largely theoretical content precludes their employment as a basis for the empirical research undertaken for this study.

The empirical work in this book is therefore based upon the concepts and techniques developed within citation analysis. This book is not the first to employ citation analysis in the study of management literature (see Snyder *et al* [1995] for a discussion of previous studies). However, this book offers the first attempt to undertake a longitudinal analysis of the published literature within management research (and one of the first to do so in social science).

A Plan of the Book

This book contains nine chapters, in addition to the introduction. The content of these chapters is outlined briefly below, in order to offer a summary of the substance of the book.

Chapter 2 -   discusses the development of general theories of fashion, which are largely derived from the study of art, costume, architecture and literature. It also assesses the extent to which theories of fashion developed for the analysis of these areas can be applied to management literature. Leading on from this discussion is an evaluation of existing theories of management fashions; and the generation of a suggested technique for analysing these fashions empirically.

Chapter 3 -   the empirical analysis for this research is based largely upon the study of citations received by the work of leading management theorists. This chapter therefore provides an extensive discussion of the potential applications of citation analysis. It also highlights some of the issues associated with citation analysis, which emerge largely from questions surrounding its validity as a research tool.

Chapter 4 -   one identifiable aspect of fashionable ideas is their relative lack of longevity. This chapter therefore studies the issue of literature obsolescence, and analyses reasons why the influence of particular published items declines over time. It also analyses methods through which literature obsolescence can be measured.

Chapters 2, 3 and **4** may be regarded as the *theoretical framework* for this study. The discussion of management fashions in Chapter 2 develops a method of identifying management fashions on the basis of their pattern of influence and longevity. Methods of measuring these variables are then developed in Chapters 3 and 4. Hence, in combination, these three chapters generate a method through which management fashions may be identified.

Chapter 5 -   describes the methods employed in the construction of the sample for the empirical analysis. It highlights a number of problems associated with the sampling procedure, with particular reference to the different publishing practices within scientific and social scientific disciplines.

Chapter 6 -   outlines preliminary attempts to measure the longevity and influence of management literature using parabolic models. Such analysis is problematic due to the erratic nature of citation data, and the inherent instability of the parabolas generated to depict these citation patterns. The results of this analysis are therefore disregarded in the final analysis. However, the analysis offers a number of useful insights which influence the implementation of the main empirical work.

Chapter 7 -   discusses the method employed in the main empirical anlysis for the identification of management fashions. This is based upon the modelling of cumulative citation counts using logistic curves. The models generated offer a measure of the longevity and level of influence of individual published items. The results of this analysis are the foundation for the identification of management fashions.

Chapter 8 -   analyses various factors which may have an influence upon the citation patterns associated with particular published items. Multiple regression techniques are employed to analyse the factors that cause the influence of particular management theories to be transient in nature.

Chapter 9 -   offers a two-dimensional analysis of the longevity and influence of individual published items, in order to produce a more detailed depiction of management research. This work is based upon cluster analysis. Emergent from this analysis is a qualitative assessment of the citation patterns identified, and a discussion of further factors that may promote the proliferation of management fashions.

Chapter 10 -   develops a theory of the operation of management fashions, based upon the findings of the regression and cluster analyses. This theory is then compared with previous depictions of management fashions, with particular attention paid to highlighting any similarities and differences.

2 Theories of Fashion

A Definition of Fashion

As outlined in the introductory chapter, this book is designed to offer a contribution to the ongoing debate regarding so-called 'management fashions'. In order to implement a study of management fashions, it is first necessary to define the concept of 'fashion'. Sperber (1990, 13) defines fashion as

> ..the preoccupation with keeping in step with the times ... following the example of prestigious opinion leaders who crystallise and reinforce the vaguely expressed collective tastes of the public; admiring proposals when they are in 'good taste' and new, and discarding them when they are in 'bad taste' and old.

The aim of this book is to evaluate the extent to which the elements of the fashion process outlined in this definition may be detected within management research; and to identify those factors which may foster the spread of management fashions.

The role and influence of fashion has been the subject of research over many years. Early studies of fashion, notably that by Kroeber (1919), concentrated largely upon the area of costume adornment, although Kroeber contended that his analysis of fashion was also applicable to areas such as Renaissance art, Greek philosophy and Romantic literature. More recent studies of the role of fashion have analysed various subject areas. These include Robinson's (1976) study of men's beards, Barthes' (1983) analysis of women's dresses, and Lauer and Lauer's (1981) research into children's names. The focus of these studies has led Abrahamson (1996) to conclude that the study of fashion has been largely limited to subjects that could be regarded as 'trivial'.

Despite the supposedly 'trivial' nature of their focus, a number of useful theoretical ideas emerge from these studies of fashion. These ideas have been employed in the study of fashions in academic research. Costume adornment may appear an unusual field to employ to inform debate upon academic research. However, it has been argued that the two areas are characterised by similar pressures. The pertinence of theories of fashion to the study of scientific research is supported by Sperber's (1990, ix) assertion that

> ... styles or models of scientific thought rise to and fall from prominence just as shifting hemlines and chrome fenders are brought onto and cast off center stage, that their fate is governed by the operation of collective tastes and sentiments that are shifting, amorphous, pervasive, and usually unacknowledged by the audience

Terms such as 'fashion' and 'fad' have also been used by many writers to describe various management techniques (e.g. Abrahamson, 1991, 1996; Gill and Whittle, 1992; Kieser, 1997). This chapter will study the theories of management fashions developed by these writers. These theories will be compared with theories of fashion developed in the study of costume and art, in order to evaluate the extent to which management research is subject to the same pressures of fashion as areas traditionally regarded as 'fashion-led'. Abrahamson (1996, 257) defines a management fashion as

> ... a relatively transitory collective belief, disseminated by management fashion setters, that a management technique leads rational management progress

In developing a theory of management fashions, two distinct issues must be recognised. The first of these refers to the processes through which certain management fashions become influential. There are two aspects of the *fashion process* - the reasons why there is a demand for fashionable management ideas; and the manner in which management fashions are developed and disseminated. The second issue refers to the *impact of fashions* upon the development of management research and practice. These two aspects of management fashion must be analysed separately, since they address essentially different issues.

The Fashion Process

Demand for Fashions

A number of writers have studied the factors which may cause fashions to prevail within a particular area. The theories they espouse emerge mainly from the study of costume and art. There are three main theories which have been developed, each of which shares a common link. They all locate the demand for fashions in the *sociopsychological* demands of the consumer.

The oldest theory of fashions is *trickle-down* theory. This was first postulated by Spencer (1888) and Simmel (1904). Trickle-down theory states that fashions emerge because the lower classes wish to imitate the practices of the upper classes, in order to improve their apparent social status. They therefore copy the styles of clothing preferred by the upper classes. As the upper classes realise that this imitation is occurring, they change their style of clothing, in order to differentiate them from the lower classes. The lower classes then imitate this new style. Hence there is a continuous cycle of changing clothing patterns, each of which may be defined as a fashion.

The second theory of fashion is *collective selection* theory, founded by Blumer (1969). This theory contends that fashions satisfy a number of needs in individuals. The first of these is that they provide a method through which individuals can make sense of an infinitely complex world, by narrowing the choices available to them. Fashions are regarded as restricting the options available to individuals, and so increase their feeling of security. Fashions also satisfy the need of individuals for change. They offer a means through which traditional ideas may be discarded in favour of new ideas. Fashions therefore play a major role in defining the so-called *zeitgeist* (Blumer, 1969).

The third theory of fashion is the *marionette* theory (Berger, 1992). This theory regards fashions as an inevitable product of the capitalist mode of production. Capitalism depends upon a continual demand for new products by consumers. These consumers are manipulated by advertising into desiring those products which are most modern, and thus become 'marionettes' of the advertisers. As a result, products are continually discarded as they become outmoded, thus increasing the rate at which particular fashions emerge and fade from prominence.

Demand for Management Fashions

Socio-Psychological Factors   In the study of management, particular emphasis has been placed by previous writers upon the trickle-down and collective selection theories of fashion. Sapir (1937) contended that fashions satisfy competing psychological needs among managers. He depicted managers as desirous of individuality and novelty on the one hand (thus building upon the trickle-down theory), and conformity and security on the other (an argument based upon collective selection theory). Fashionable management techniques thus offer managers the opportunity to appear up-to-date and novel, while removing the risk of them being regarded as deviant.

The importance of fashionable techniques to managers has been emphasised by a number of writers. Gill and Whittle (1992) offer a psychoanalytical explanation for the implementation of management fashions. They picture managers as members of a 'dependency culture', seeking security in the implementation of widely accepted management techniques. Eccles and Nohria (1992) offer a similar analysis, arguing that frustration on the part of managers leads them to seek quasi-magical solutions to their problems. When these solutions do not work, their despair is magnified. This leaves them vulnerable to the next technique suggested as a solution to their problems. Support for sociopsychological explanations of the management fashion process has also been offered in the popular management press. *Business Week* (1986) ascribed management fashions to childlike excitement on the part of managers, while *Harvard Business Review* (1994) compared them to manias and outbreaks of mass hysteria.

The psychological reliance of managers upon management fashions may be located in the expectations made of them. Meyer and Rowan (1977) contend that organisational stakeholders expect the managers of their organisations to act in a rational manner. Hence, there exists a *norm of rationality* to which managers must conform. Managers also often face a *norm of progress*. Abrahamson (1996) points to the need for managers to appear to be using the latest management techniques. This is a reflection of the collective selection theory of fashion, in which fashions are employed as a justification for disregarding previous ideas. This leads Lasch (1991) to conclude that norms of progress in management do not have a utopian end. Instead they offer the prospect of never-ending progress, without a definable goal.

In satisfying these norms, one problem facing managers is that, as March and Olsen (1976) argue, many organisations are 'organised anarchies'. They are characterised by uncertainty and conflict over the goals of the organisation, and the best methods to employ in order to achieve these goals. Similarly, Granovetter (1979) argues that different management techniques offer improvements to a wide range of organisational characteristics. These include criteria such as quality, speed, flexibility, and customer satisfaction. Problems are often encountered in the adoption of these techniques, since the criteria for evaluation are neither fixed nor universal. The demands of managers will also vary between organisations, and within the same organisation over time.

Two competing forces must therefore be reconciled. Organisational stakeholders expect managers to select and adopt techniques on the basis of rationality and progress. However, there exists no mechanism through which these ideals can be universally evaluated. The way in which the two forces are reconciled is through the employment of fashionable ideas, and the *management rhetorics* associated with these ideas. Rhetorics are spoken and written discourses that justify the application of particular techniques (Kieser, 1997). They are developed by opinion leaders in management to depict the apparent rationality of new techniques (Clark and Salaman, 1996). Rhetorics are often based upon the construction of anecdotes and myths around the success of organisations which have adopted them (Hannabus, 1987) and are regarded as a 'feel-good' and 'feel powerful' discourse (Thompson and Davidson, 1994), which may be employed by managers to justify their adoption of particular techniques. By adopting new techniques, the organisation can construct an image of being both enlightened and up-to-date (Gill and Whittle, 1992).

Managers cannot therefore rationally evaluate the different decisions facing them. In order to meet the expectations of stakeholders, they must *appear* to be acting in a rational and progressive manner. Fashionable techniques and rhetorics offer a tool for managers to achieve this apparent rationality, since they provide a recognised technique which managers can employ as a justification for their actions.

Techno-Economic Factors The concentration upon sociopsychological causes of the fashion process has its roots in the study of costume adornment. Writers such as Sperber have suggested that the techniques employed to study clothing fashions can be applied in the study of all disciplines. However, writers studying management research have disputed this. Abrahamson (1996) claimed that there is a major difference between the study of costume and the study of management. He argued that the former is dominated by the necessity of appearing to be beautiful and modern. This requirement is driven by psychological and social factors. However, fashions in management research are more complex. They are based upon economic and technical change, as well as social and psychological factors. Abrahamson thus locates the causes of fashions in two areas - socio-psychological and techno-economic.

Research undertaken by Barley and Kunda (1992) highlighted the importance of techno-economic factors in the adoption of management fashions. Their research revealed that macroeconomic changes often lead to modifications in the objectives of organisations. This alters the techniques required by managers. The techniques which reflect most accurately the requirements of managers will be those that become fashionable. Similarly,

Blau (1971) argued that fashions are caused by inherent contradictions in the management of organisations. The example of centralisation and decentralisation in organisations may illustrate this point. As organisations become more centralised, their constituent parts become less autonomous, which may lead to frustration and lack of flexibility. Managers seek solutions to these problems. Techniques offering greater autonomy through decentralisation may thus become popular. However, decentralisation brings with it a lack of control. This may lead managers to become interested in approaches which increase control, the result of which is greater centralisation. The original problems associated with centralisation thus return. This apparently infinite cycle of adoption and rejection has been described as akin to changes in the length of women's skirts (Mintzberg, 1979).

Edwards (1979) offers an alternative, Marxist depiction of the fashion process. He argues that particular management techniques become fashionable in the face of unrest from workers. They are designed as a 'sop' which will encourage workers to co-operate with managers. However, this is only successful in the short term, since the underlying inequality of the employment relationship remains unchanged. Workers therefore become disillusioned with the techniques, and unrest increases. This leads managers to implement new techniques, and the cycle starts again.

Supply of Management Fashions

Having discussed the reasons why managers demand a succession of solutions to the problems that they face, it is then necessary to analyse how these solutions are developed. In simple terms, having analysed the demand for management fashions, it is appropriate to study the supply of these fashions.

In early studies of the fashion process, the supply of fashions was often associated with so-called 'opinion leaders' (Simmel, 1904; Kroeber, 1919). These opinion leaders are regarded as being responsible for the development and dissemination of fashionable ideas. As such, they can be distinguished from 'opinion followers', who simply adhere to prevailing fashionable ideas.

Sperber (1996) has noted the recent development of a particular type of opinion leader. He points to the increasing prevalence of *academic entrepreneurs* who promote themselves and their work in order to achieve career advancement. Such theorists have attracted a great deal of attention in the study of management. Often referred to as '*management gurus*' (Huczynski, 1993), they are regarded as having a far reaching influence upon management research and practice (Thompson and Davidson, 1994). Having emerged in America, the so-called 'guru' is now becoming an increasingly common feature of European management research (*The Economist*, 11/3/95). Abrahamson (1996) identified a number of potential sources of management gurus. These include consulting firms, the business mass media and business schools. Galbraith (1980) identified an alternative source of management gurus. He argued that the source of most management ideas could be located in the techniques employed by successful management practitioners. The process of fashion setting in management may therefore be regarded as more complex than in many disciplines, due to the wide range of potential opinion leaders.

Abrahamson (1996) identified four stages in the formation and dissemination of fashions by management gurus. The first stage occurs as fashion leaders *create* a number of management techniques, which they define as innovative. These techniques do not have to be original; they must simply differ from current management practice - the practice of recycling previous management techniques under a new guise has been highlighted by previous writers (e.g. Kimberley, 1981). In order to *select* which techniques to develop further, fashion leaders attempt to sense the emergent collective preferences of managers. They then select those techniques which fit in with existing managerial mores. The third stage involves *processing* the ideas developed in order to make them acceptable to managers. In order to achieve this, rhetorics are employed, as discussed earlier. These rhetorics are designed to reflect the preferences of the management community. Finally, the rhetorics are *disseminated* back to managers in the guise of progress, through consultancy firms, seminars and the popular and academic management press.

The important point to note in this process is that fashion leaders do not develop ideas in isolation, and then disseminate them to the management community. Rather, the ideas they develop are a reflection of the mores of their audience. A number of writers have suggested that new techniques and rhetorics are developed by fashion setters because they are demanded by practising managers (DiMaggio and Hirsch, 1976; Peterson, 1979; Blau, 1993). The role of opinion leaders may therefore be more complex than that which is often depicted. At the same time as being instrumental in effecting change, the fashion leader is also led by the existing social consensus. The theorists who become dominant are seen as those who crystallise the existing mores of practising managers. This leads to the belief that the ultimate arbiter of the selection of fashion leaders, and thus fashion, is public opinion (Valency, 1973).

Impact of Management Fashions

The discussion has thus far concentrated upon the reasons why there is a consistent demand for new management techniques (many of which prove to be fashionable in nature); and how this demand is met. This combination of supply and demand of management fashions may be defined as the fashion process (Abrahamson, 1996). Having discussed the processes through which fashions develop, it is then appropriate to analyse the effect fashions have upon a given field of study.

Kroeber (1919) identified two characteristics which may be identified in a field in which the influence of fashions is strong. These are:

1. The *lack of rigour* in the evaluation of new ideas
2. The tendency towards *ahistorical analysis* of new ideas

Kroeber thus contended that ideas are accepted simply because they are regarded as being novel and up-to-date. There is no attempt to evaluate the content or validity of new ideas. Sperber (1990) extended the work of Kroeber to the study of academic research, and found that these two characteristics could also be located in academic fields in which there were strong fashionable pressures. The extent to which these impacts may be associated with management research is assessed below.

Lack of Academic Rigour

A number of writers have addressed the issue of the theoretical robustness of management techniques. Aktouf (1992) argued that many academic theories in management lack adequate theoretical assumptions and background. From an empirical perspective, Freeman (1986) found that the quality of data employed in management research was often insufficiently robust in statistical terms. It has therefore been argued that, in both theoretical and empirical terms, some areas of management research at present lack academic rigour.

The lack of academic rigour in management techniques may be the result of fashionable, so-called 'pop management' theories. It has been argued that the ideas put forward within 'pop management' have little academic underpinning (Thompson and Davidson, 1994). This is seen as a conscious policy, since it makes the ideas more acceptable to management practitioners (Gill and Whittle, 1992). However, the benefits of the new approaches are hard to define theoretically, with the result that their influence cannot be confirmed or falsified (Thompson and Davidson, 1994; cf. Popper, 1959). This makes management research appear atheoretical when compared to other social science disciplines (ESRC, 1994).

The removal of academic content from 'pop management' means that the resulting theories often offer little more than simplistic 'turnkey' solutions to organisational problems (Darwent, 1988). These frequently consist of checklists detailing the actions seen as essential for organisational success. In order to attract the attention of managers, the solutions have to offer quick, simple solutions. However, as Mitroff and Mohrman (1987, 69) argue

> [managers] easily fell prey to every new management fad promising a painless solution, especially when it was presented in a neat, bright package. But all simple formulas are eventually bound to fail. By definition, simple formulas cannot cope with complexity, and complexity is what today's world is all about.

This oversimplification has potentially damaging implications for the influence of management research. However, as outlined above, the problem is not caused solely by researchers and consultants. 'Turnkey' solutions to organisational problems are often developed because they are what practising managers demand (ESRC, 1994, 16).

The prevalence of rhetorics in management research (Abrahamson, 1996) may also suggest that atheoretical debate is prevalent in this area. The lack of theoretical debate is identified by Sperber (1990) as symptomatic of the presence of fashions.

Ahistorical Thought

The presence of ahistorical bias in research leads to the concentration upon those ideas which have been recently developed. The corollary of this is that many techniques are only influential in the short term, due to the constantly changing interests and demands of the audience. The extent to which a transient pattern of influence can be associated within management techniques may offer a guide to the existence of ahistorical thought within management research.

A number of management techniques have been described as transient in their influence. Gill and Whittle (1992) identified three such approaches - Management By Objectives (MBO), Organisational Development (OD), and

Total Quality Management (TQM). They argued that these approaches had been fashionable, but had failed to meet the promises they made. Similarly, Abrahamson (1991) found that a number of approaches had been dismissed by other writers as 'management fads', including: strategic-planning units; job enrichment; T-groups and matrix structures; quality circles; decentralisation; and joint ventures. The basis of this dismissal is often left undefined. Other writers have studied management fashions on a small scale using empirical methods. A survey undertaken by Castorina and Wood (1988) revealed that more than 80% of leading companies which had introduced quality circles in the early 1980s had abandoned them by the end of that decade. This suggests that the influence of quality circles was essentially transient. Abrahamson (1996) also employed an empirical approach (article counting) to analyse the influence of literature on employee stock ownership. He found that the interest in this area was cyclic, as the subject repeatedly gained and lost influence and popularity. This reflects Kimberley's (1981) argument (outlined earlier) that management techniques are often rediscovered and repackaged at a later date.

Summary of Previous Studies

In the previous section, the theories developed in the analysis of fashions in costume adornment were applied to the study of management. In analysing fashion processes in management, the causes of fashion were discovered to be more complex than those hypothesised as a result of the study of costume. This is due to the influence of techno-economic factors, and also the complexity of the fashion setting community. The outcomes of fashions in management research were also analysed. The lack of academic rigour and tendency towards ahistorical thought (identified by Sperber (1990) as signifiers of a field in which fashions are prevalent) were identified in previous evaluations of management research.

The discussion above suggests that the role and influence of fashion discovered in the study of management research is broadly similar to that identified in traditional studies of fashion in costume. It can therefore be inferred that the employment of the concept of 'fashion' may be valid in the study of management research.

Developing a Methodology for Identifying Management Fashions

The discussion in the previous section established the salience of the concept of fashion to the study of management research. However, one issue that was not addressed was how fashions can be identified. A number of writers have defined particular techniques as management fashions. However, these definitions were based largely upon anecdotal evidence, and small-scale empirical analysis. The purpose of this book is to identify and analyse empirically those areas of management research which are characterised by the prevalence of fashions. It is therefore necessary to develop a methodology through which fashions can be identified. The manner in which this was achieved is discussed in this section.

One of the major problems in identifying and analysing the role and influence of fashion is the nature of the concept being measured. Fashion is an inherently nebulous concept, which does not lend itself to simple analysis. Kroeber (1919) recognised that, due to its complexity, fashion is an essentially qualitative phenomenon. However, he argued that the only way it could be measured in a meaningful way, on a significant scale, is through the use of quantitative techniques. In order to apply these techniques, it is clear that the concept of fashion must be reduced to a set of constructs which are open to quantitative analysis. This inevitably restricts those aspects of fashion that can be measured.

Building upon the analysis of fashions in the previous section, two possible methods of identification were suggested. These reflect the two aspects of the fashion concept (i.e. the fashion process and the outcomes of that process). The first approach is to focus upon the fashion process. In order to achieve this, the *diffusion model* suggested by Abrahamson (1991) was analysed. This model concentrates upon the mechanisms through which the fashion process operates in management. The second method of identifying fashions is to concentrate upon their outcomes. The model analysed to achieve this was the *life cycle model* developed by Gill and Whittle (1992). The focus of this model is the outcome of the fashion process.

These two models were analysed in detail to discern their possible application in the current study. Particular attention was paid to the extent to which the models could be employed as a foundation for empirical analysis.

Diffusion Model

Abrahamson (1991) put forward four theoretical perspectives explaining the diffusion (or rejection) of particular management techniques. These can be seen in Figure 2.1. A definition of the factors which explain the diffusion (or rejection) of particular techniques within each perspective is offered below. Further analysis was undertaken into those perspectives suggesting that the influence of management techniques is essentially transient.

Efficient Choice Perspective It is assumed that organisations (and their managers) have little uncertainty about their objectives, and have sound knowledge of the benefits to be gained through the adoption of a particular new technique.

Diffusion: environmental changes cause 'performance gaps' across organisations. Performance gaps can be defined as discrepancies between organisational performance, and the goals that are perceived as attainable. These gaps may be caused by changes in the economic, social and political environment, or by changes in the technical knowledge available to an organisation (e.g. new management techniques). Organisations will act in such a way as to close the perceived performance gaps, and thus adopt those techniques necessary to this process.

Rejection: organisations will reject those techniques which will not close the performance gaps. Since organisations are assumed to have sound knowledge of the outcomes from the adoption of particular techniques, they can reject in advance those which do not offer the improvements desired.

	Imitation Processes do not Impel Diffusion and Rejection	Imitation Processes Impel Diffusion and Rejection
Organisations within a Group Determine the Diffusion and Rejection within this Group	**Efficient Choice Perspective**	**Fad Perspective**
Organisations outside a Group Determine the Diffusion and Rejection within this Group	**Forced Selection Perspective**	**Fashion Perspective**

Figure 2.1 Influences upon diffusion/rejection of management techniques (Abrahamson, 1991)

Forced-Selection Perspective It is assumed that there are a number of external institutions which have a strong influence over the way in which organisations operate. These may include government departments and national labour unions. The institutions may be interested in imposing certain techniques, irrespective of their efficiency.

Diffusion: techniques are diffused according to the interests of powerful external groups. For example, the labour boards in America forced the adoption of personnel administration techniques during World War II (Baron *et al*, 1986). Diffusion is thus the result of interests other than those of the organisation.

Rejection: in the same way that powerful external groups can enforce the diffusion of techniques, they can also cause rejection in order to further their interests. New approaches may be rejected because they have a detrimental effect upon the interests of a particular group. For example, labour unions may block the introduction of new working methods because they fear that the new techniques will reduce employment.

The two perspectives above share the assumption that agents, whether organisations or external institutions, have a clear understanding of their objectives, and of the environment in which they operate. The perspectives regarding management research offered in the following section dispute this assumption. Rather, management objectives are depicted as amorphous and ever-changing (cf. March and Olsen, 1976). An alternative assumption is thus introduced. This states that organisational actors are uncertain of their goals and their environment. In this situation, it is assumed that they will imitate others in order to increase their sense of certainty. It is this assumption which forms the basis of the two perspectives outlined below.

Fashion Perspective This perspective assumes that under conditions of uncertainty, organisations will imitate techniques employed by agents seen to be 'fashionable'. These 'fashion-setters' may include consultancy firms, the business media, and prominent management researchers (Abrahamson, 1996).

Diffusion: techniques do not diffuse by popular demand. Rather, certain approaches are put forward by fashion-setters. Their diffusion is supported through the development of organisations' awareness. The extent to which techniques diffuse thus depends upon the medium through which they are disseminated, and the extent to which the opinions of particular fashion-setters are trusted by organisations.

Rejection: new approaches often replace existing efficient systems simply because they are fashionable. However, the influence of new techniques is often temporary. As the novelty wears off, the lack of improvements offered by many management techniques becomes apparent. This leads managers to seek new techniques in order to address organisational problems. Rejection in this example therefore involves the implementation of techniques, followed by their rejection. This may be contrasted with the Efficient Choice and Forced Selection perspectives, in which techniques are rejected in advance.

Fad Perspective The fad perspective differs from the fashion perspective because it assumes that organisations imitate other organisations within the same group, rather than external agents. Hence techniques are adopted which have been used in other organisations in the same industry, rather than techniques which have been suggested by external consultants. Research has shown that those organisations with the highest reputations are imitated most often (DiMaggio and Powell, 1983).

Diffusion: techniques may diffuse for a number of reasons. Organisations may adopt new techniques in order to appear to conform to accepted norms (Carroll and Hannan, 1989); in order to reduce ambiguity concerning innovation (Rogers, 1983); or to ensure that any benefits from the techniques do not offer other organisations a competitive advantage (Arthur, 1988). The way in which fads diffuse has often been described using the literature concerning epidemiology - the study of contagious diseases (Bailey, 1975). Two factors are identified which influence the extent to which ideas diffuse. The first of these is *heterophily* - the degree to which organisations differ in their characteristics. Clearly the greater the similarity between organisations, the more likely it is that an idea will be diffused from one to the other. The second factor is *disconnectedness* - the extent to which an organisation is connected with others in the communication network. The more isolated an organisation is, the less likely it is to adopt ideas put forward elsewhere (cf. Crane, 1972). A further element must be included in the analysis of diffusion. As more organisations adopt a given approach, those which remain feel increasing pressure to follow them, through fear of becoming uncompetitive. Granovetter (1978) developed a model showing how the likelihood of individuals adopting a given idea grows as the number of previous adopters increases. This model can also be applied to the study of organisations. The model suggests that organisations may therefore be subject to 'bandwagon pressures' to adopt particular techniques.

Rejection: the bandwagon pressures outlined above may also cause a technique to be rejected. Originators of an approach will see that any advantage they have gained has been dissipated due to the assimilation of the idea by competitors. They will therefore reject the approach, and look for a new technique to provide a competitive advantage. As increasing numbers of organisations reject the technique, the remaining organisations will feel pressurised to reject it, because of the feeling that it must be inefficient. The technique is therefore finally rejected, as interest moves to a new approach.

Within this model, the main difference between fads and fashions is the popularising agent. Abrahamson (1991) argued that fashions are popularised by agents external to organisations, while fads result from the imitation of leading organisations. However, the discussion on fashion setters in management (offered earlier in this chapter) suggests that the two perspectives may not be mutually exclusive. The relationship between leading management writers and innovative organisations is such that the original source of new techniques is often difficult to identify. Galbraith (1980) argued that innovative techniques are developed by managers, and then popularised by external agents who observe these managers. This suggests that the source of new techniques (which represents the difference between the 'fad' and the 'fashion' perspectives suggested by Abrahamson) may be impossible to identify. For the purposes of this study, the fad and fashion perspectives may therefore be encapsulated in a single category, defined as *management fashions*.

Application of the Diffusion Model

The difference between management fashions (as defined above) and other perspectives in Abrahamson's model lies in the reasons for adoption by organisations. These reasons may be analysed with reference to the discussion of the demand for management fashions offered earlier. This discussion suggested that there are two possible causes of management fashions - techno-economic and socio-psychological. The first of these reflects the influence of factors, external to an organisation, which may lead to its adoption of particular techniques. It is these factors which are identified by the efficient choice and forced selection perspectives as the main catalysts for the adoption of management techniques. The efficient choice perspective suggests that techniques are adopted due to perceived performance gaps. These gaps are often caused by changes in the environment in which organisations operate. The forced selection perspective contends that it is external actors which force the adoption of particular management techniques.

The second cause of the diffusion of fashions is socio-psychological. In this explanation of the fashion process, particular ideas and techniques are adopted by individuals as a result of psychological needs and/or social pressures. The fashion and fad perspectives developed by Abrahamson (encapsulated in a single 'management fashion' perspective in this book) reflect these pressures. As discussed earlier, fashionable management techniques offer security and novelty, both of which are sought by managers. They also offer an appearance of rationality to methods employed by managers. This satisfies the social pressures from organisational stakeholders that managers will operate on a rational basis.

From this discussion of Abrahamson's model, it would appear that management fashions should be relatively simple to identify. All that needs to be determined is the reasons why particular techniques are employed. The model suggests that if techniques are adopted due to socio-psychological pressures upon managers, then they can be defined as management fashions. This approach therefore necessitates a survey of practising managers, in order to analyse their reasons for the adoption of particular techniques. It thus has the advantage of being based upon the direct experience of practising managers, who presumably have the greatest experience of the implementation of management techniques. They should therefore possess well-developed insights into the diffusion of fashionable management techniques.

However, such an approach is fraught with difficulties. A number of problems, common to management research in general, may be identified. These include: gaining access to sufficient organisations to develop robust theories (Beynon, 1988; Easterby-Smith *et al*, 1991); hostility to the research on the part of respondents (Argyris, 1968); and awareness of respondents regarding the purpose of the study, such that they offer responses that they regard as desirable in order to appear co-operative (Oppenheim, 1992). These problems are regarded as endemic to the management research process. However, there are additional problems associated with the current study due to the nature of its focus. These are outlined below:

1. In analysing the reasons for the adoption of particular management techniques, access is required to those organisational actors who are instrumental in the adoption process. These actors will tend to be senior managers and executives. However, as Punch (1986) argues, it is often very difficult to gain access to these actors, making the analysis problematic.

2. By its nature, the examination of reasons for the adoption of management techniques is retrospective. The issue being studied is therefore why particular techniques *were* adopted. This requires a retrospective evaluation on the part of respondents. As Dunkerley (1988) argues, this evaluation will inevitably be distorted by the subjective memories of the respondent.

3. As discussed earlier, a major characteristic of management research is the presence of rhetorics. These rhetorics generate a discourse in which the adoption of techniques is justified by reference to progress and rationality, rather than psychological and social pressures. It may therefore be difficult to isolate the actual causes of adoption from those suggested to managers by management rhetorics (Kieser, 1997).

The issues outlined above suggest that there may be problems encountered in the employment of Abrahamson's model for the identification of management fashions. It is therefore necessary to analyse alternative techniques through which management fashions may be identified.

Life Cycle Model

The second possible method for identifying academic fashions is through their influence upon their subject. As discussed earlier, this influence manifests itself in a lack of academic rigour in the analysis of new ideas; and in a tendency towards ahistorical thought. The issue of ahistorical thought is of particular interest to this book. Kieser (1997) argues that management fashions follow a pattern of influence which can be described as 'bell shaped', in that these fashions are popularised and discarded within a relatively short time period.

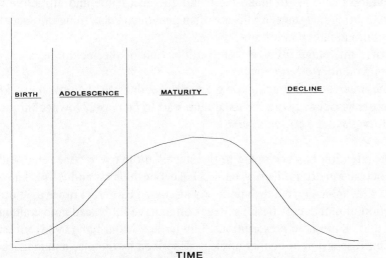

Figure 2.2 Life cycle model of management panaceas
(Gill and Whittle, 1992)

The pattern of influence of management fashions has also been studied by Gill and Whittle (1992) using a life cycle model. The idea of the life cycle has been used in the study of a number of subjects. These have included the organisational life cycle (Kimberly *et al*, 1980) and the product life cycle

(Lancaster and Massingham, 1993). The life cycle depicted in these approaches has four discernible stages - birth, adolescence, maturity and decline. Gill and Whittle suggested that this model could be applied to areas of management research, in particular those techniques defined as 'management panaceas'. These panaceas can be equated with the management fashions defined in the evaluation of the diffusion model (i.e. those ideas categorised as management fads or fashions), since they offer short-term solutions to organisational problems. However, their influence is transient. The schematic model developed by Gill and Whittle can be seen in Figure 2.2 (previous page).

The four stages in the life cycle of a fashionable management technique can briefly be defined as follows (Gill and Whittle, 1992):-

1. Birth: the seminal work is written. This may be the work of the originator of the approach, or a popularising text by a leading management writer.
2. Adolescence: the technique is promoted by consultants and researchers. They develop packages to make the technique accessible and attractive to managers. During this stage, myths are often generated concerning the success of the technique in certain organisations.
3. Maturity: this stage involves the routinisation of the technique as it is applied to a number of organisations.
4. Decline: interest in the technique gradually declines, as the novelty wears off and costs associated with the technique start to increase. New techniques emerge to replace the current one.

Particular attention has been paid to the stages in the cycle concerned with adolescence and maturity. During adolescence, consultants produce packaged versions of the management technique. As discussed earlier, in order to attract the attention of managers, these packages often have little academic content, and rely upon simplistic prescriptions. Lawler and Mohrman (1985) reflect this in their discussion of quality circles - described by them as a managerial fad. They wrote that, for a fixed price, organisations can buy a quality circle package 'off the peg'. Inevitably, such a package will fail to take into account the individual characteristics of each organisation, thus reducing its ability to effect significant organisational improvements. The reasons for the eventual decline of a particular approach may thus be rooted in the manner in which it is popularised.

The decline may also be influenced by the way a technique is implemented. This forms part of the maturity phase in the life cycle model.

A number of writers have argued that techniques have failed because of problems in their implementation. These may be caused by a failure to understand fully the technique being introduced (Hodgson, 1987); increasing costs associated with the technique (Lawler and Mohrman, 1985); inappropriateness of a technique for a particular organisation (Hackman, 1975); or opposition from workers and/or managers (Lawler and Mohrman, 1985). If a technique fails in its implementation, it will inevitably be discarded. A decline in the interest in a particular technique will set in where the problems associated with implementation are experienced by a large number of organisations.

Application of the Life Cycle Model

Gill and Whittle (1992) contend that management fashions may be identified because their influence approximates to a life cycle pattern. However, there may be a problem with this contention since, as Kroeber (1919) argues, all social phenomena are characterised by a life cycle. These life cycles are simply of different lengths. This suggests that all management techniques, even those which cannot be defined as fashions, will eventually be disregarded.

Hence, a modification must be made to Gill and Whittle's model. Management fashions cannot be identified because their influence follows a life cycle pattern, since all management ideas theoretically conform to this pattern. Instead, fashions may be identified by the length of the life cycle associated with a particular idea. Management panaceas will be characterised by a life cycle pattern of influence which is relatively short (Gill and Whittle tentatively suggest forty years for the entire life cycle). Alternatively, techniques which offer lasting improvements to organisational performance will be influential over a longer period. If the length of time over which particular management techniques are influential can be identified, it may thus be possible to identify which of these techniques may be defined as management fashions.

This approach offers two main advantages. The first is that it avoids the problems associated with implementing surveys of practising managers, discussed in the evaluation of the potential application of the diffusion model. The second advantage of the life cycle model is that it is based upon the measurement of time. Time represents a quantifiable unit of measurement, which is suggested by Kroeber (1919) as the prerequisite for the empirical analysis of fashions.

After consideration of the advantages and problems associated with the two approaches to the identification of fashions, it appeared that the outcomes of the fashion process offered greater potential for empirical analysis. *The analysis in this book therefore concentrates upon the outcomes of the fashion process.* As such, it mirrors the work of Kroeber. Although his work offers hypotheses concerning the causes of the fashion process, the empirical work which forms the basis of his study focuses upon the outcomes of that process.

Measurement of Influence

The method employed in this book to identify fashions is based upon the measurement of the influence of management theories and techniques over time. Fashions are identified through the transient nature of their influence. The main problem encountered in the implementation of this approach lies in the requirement for the definition and measurement of 'influence'. The definition employed must not only encapsulate the concept of 'influence', but must also facilitate empirical analysis. This may be problematic due to the complexity of 'influence' as an idea. Various methods have been suggested to address this problem. These methods offer various surrogates through which influence may be measured. The common link between these surrogates is that they can be measured quantitatively.

Gill and Whittle (1992) suggest that the amount of resources devoted to particular management ideas should be measured over time. This approach is based upon the assumption that the level of resources devoted to the study of particular ideas may be employed as a surrogate for influence of those ideas. A number of problems with the measurement of resources can be identified. These include problems with isolating which resources to include in any measurement; how to compare resourcing across different countries; and the changing monetary values associated with resourcing over time.

An alternative method of measuring influence is to concentrate upon the published literature. Huczynski (1993) points to the importance of the literature in the dissemination of management techniques. Hence, as Abrahamson (1996) argues, the published literature offers archival data which may be employed in the study of fashions. Abrahamson (1996) and Kieser (1997) both implemented empirical research into management fashions based upon the published literature. Their research was implemented on a small scale, and its results were not analysed in any depth.

The technique employed by Abrahamson (1996) and Kieser (1997) was article counting. This measures the number of articles published on a particular subject over time. The number of articles is thus employed as a surrogate for the level of influence. A more commonly employed method of studying the published literature concentrates upon the citations appended to published work. In this approach, citations are regarded as denoting the influence of earlier work upon published research. *Hence, the length of time over which a published item is cited may be considered to be a surrogate for its period of influence.*

The literature pertaining to citation analysis was thus analysed in order to determine how it could be employed in the identification and measurement of management fashions. A discussion of this analysis is offered in the following chapter. Particular attention is paid to the issue of whether citations may be regarded as a valid surrogate for the influence of published research.

Note Regarding the Focus of this Study

The purpose of this book is to analyse the role and influence of management research. From the discussion in this chapter, it emerges that management research has two distinct audiences - management practitioners and management researchers. Recent work in this area (Abrahamson, 1991, 1996; Gill and Whittle, 1992; Kieser, 1997) has concentrated largely upon the impact of management fashions upon practitioners. By concentrating upon citations received by published management literature, this book focuses *explicitly* upon the influence of management fashions upon the management research community (since it is researchers who offer citations). This point must be noted, since it has implications for the manner in which the results of the study may be analysed and interpreted.

3 Measuring the Influence of Research using Citations

Introduction

As outlined in the previous chapter, the empirical work for this study is based upon analysis of the citations appended to academic literature. In order to implement this analysis, it is first necessary to study the issues surrounding the employment of citation analysis.

Citation analysis represents a major branch of the area of study often referred to as *bibliometrics*. Bibliometric techniques study academic research by analysing the media through which this research is disseminated. The employment of bibliometric techniques for analysing academic literature has gained increasing prominence in recent years. The majority of the work undertaken has studied natural science research. However, there is a growing interest in the potential employment of bibliometric techniques within the social sciences.

This chapter will outline the techniques employed in the bibliometric analysis of academic literature, as well as highlighting the areas of debate concerning the validity of these techniques in various contexts. Particular attention will be paid to the applicability of bibliometric techniques (notably citation analysis) developed in the study of scientific disciplines, to the analysis of the social sciences.

Foundation of Citation Analysis

Citation analysis concentrates upon the citations received by academic publications. Hence the unit of analysis is the citation. In order to implement citation analysis, it is thus important that there is a clear understanding of the role and significance of academic citations.

Researchers receive recognition largely as a result of academic publications. In particular, recognition is awarded to those researchers whose work can be defined as original in some way. This need for originality is often reflected by the use of the metaphor of a track race (Gaston, 1971), but it is one where only the winner receives a prize (Cronin, 1984). As long ago as 1902, Rutherford wrote to his mother 'I have to keep going, as there are always people on my track. I have to publish my present work as rapidly as possible in order to keep in the race' (quoted in: Crowther, 1952, 54). Original work is thus regarded as the intellectual property of the researchers concerned. In order to use the results of this work, future researchers must pay in terms of a 'coin of recognition' (Merton, 1968), usually in the form of a citation. *A citation is thus seen as an acknowledgement of a debt to previous work.*

The relationship described above, where a writer acknowledges a debt to the positive contribution of previous research, represents the formal foundation of citation analysis (Johnson and Podsakoff, 1994). Various functions of citations emerge from this relationship. Cronin (1981b) argues that citations can be regarded as 'frozen footsteps' which show the way in which disciplines have developed. A similar contention is made by Allen *et al* (1994), who regard citations as a form of external memory of academic disciplines. If this depiction of citations is accepted, citation analysis may be regarded as *a technique through which the development and structure of academic research may be studied.*

The relationship between citing and cited papers outlined above also facilitates a second application of citation analysis. In acknowledging the use of previous research, a citation establishes the 'property rights' of previous scholars over the cited work (Mitra, 1970). Acknowledgements of this type have been employed as a surrogate for the influence of published work. Hence *the greater the number of citations received by a particular published item, the more influential it is assumed to be.*

Citations have thus been employed to analyse both the historical development of particular disciplines, and the relative influence of particular authors, institutions and publications within this development. However, before using citation analysis, a number of issues must be addressed, concerned chiefly with the role of citations described above. These issues may be regarded as operating at three levels:

1. The role and nature of citations
2. The research process within which citations are generated
3. The academic community within which the research process is located

These levels are clearly interdependent. The role and nature of citations will be influenced by the research process, which in turn is dependent upon the norms and practices of the wider research community. The three areas of concern will be addressed in the following section, with particular emphasis placed upon the ways in which the different issues are inter-related.

Role of Citations

The depiction of citations as the acknowledgement of a positive debt to previous work is seen as overly simplistic by many writers. These writers argue that there are many reasons for citing previous work, and these reasons need to be acknowledged in the employment of citation analysis.

There are two main methods through which the role of citations has been analysed. The first of these is to concentrate upon the citations themselves. Cronin (1981a) implemented an innovative study based upon this approach. The citations were removed from an unpublished research paper, and the remaining text distributed to scholars in the field. These researchers were asked to add references where they believed them to be necessary. There was some similarity in the citations included by the different authors, but insufficient to suggest that citing practices may be regarded as uniform. An alternative study was implemented by Small (1980). He carried out a study of fifty texts regarded as being highly influential in their particular field (chemistry). The references offered to each of these papers were then analysed, in order to identify the purposes for which they were offered. In around 87% of cases the references which were offered referred to the same aspect of the cited paper. A comparative study was carried out into another scientific field (recombinant DNA), and again a high proportion of citations to particular papers were offered for the same purpose (around 76%). These studies appear to offer evidence for the existence of uniform elements in citer motivations. However, some non-uniform elements still exist, as reflected in the lack of complete congruence between the purposes for which particular papers are cited.

These non-uniform elements may emerge from the variety of reasons behind the offering of citations. Moravcsik and Murugesan (1975) implemented a study of the reasons why citations are generated and, as a result, developed a four-fold classification upon which citations may be evaluated:

1. *Conceptual / Operational* - are particular references offered to previous work for theoretical purposes (citations as conceptual), or because of the methodological content of the earlier work (citations as operational)?
2. *Organic / Perfunctory* - do particular citations reflect the central importance

of the cited item to the construction of the citing work (citations as organic), or are they passing references to work in a similar area (citations as perfunctory)?

3. *Evolutionary / Juxtapositional* - does the citing paper build on previous work (citation as evolutionary), or does it offer an alternative approach to similar research problems (citation as juxtapositional)?

4. *Confirmative / Negational* - are particular citations included in order to support the work undertaken by previous researchers (citation as confirmative), or as a method of highlighting shortcomings in previous work (citation as negational)?

The classification of citations offered by Moravcsik and Murugesan highlights the heterogenous nature of their role. This heterogeneity has been also reported by a number of studies employing a second approach to the study of the role of citations. These studies do not directly analyse citations. Instead, they are based upon surveys of academics, and aim to understand the motivations behind the citation process. Studies by Brooks (1986), Vinkler (1987) and Liu (1993b) have established the complex nature of citer motivations. This complexity is reflected in the study by Weinstock (1971), who outlined fifteen reasons for citation. These include providing background reading, giving credit to related work, substantiating claims, and criticising previous work. Similar findings were reported by a number of other writers, including Lipetz (1965), Duncan *et al* (1981) and Swales (1990). An alternative conception of citations was offered by Small (1978), who argued that citations are often 'symbolic', in that the cited work is employed as a symbol for a particular theory or technique.

The nature of the relationship between citing and cited papers thus appears to be more complex than that depicted in the original definitions. This is reflected in the study by Frost (1979), who found that two commonly quoted functions of citation, the acknowledgement of a debt to previous work, and building on previously published ideas, were lacking in the reasons for citing put forward by researchers. Given that these functions of citations represent the formal foundation of citation analysis, the validity of such analysis must be questioned.

However, evidence has also been provided to support the validity of citation analysis. One study offering such evidence was implemented by Shadish *et al* (1995). Their study was based upon a questionnaire sent to authors in psychology, requesting information on the motivations behind their citation practices. Twenty eight different motivations for citation were given by the respondents. This could support the contention that the citation process is characterised by a degree of heterogeneity which is too high to support the validity of citation analysis. However, this conclusion may be misguided. Four of the motivations accounted for over 50% of citations offered. These were:

1. Supporting an assertion (18% of citations offered)
2. Revealing source of techniques or theories employed (16%)
3. Citing a classic paper in the field (9%)
4. Symbolic citation for a particular genre of studies (8%)

These four motivations all reflect the positive contribution of the cited work. Hence, although the motivation for citation is complex, this need not necessarily be regarded as injurious to the validity of citation analysis. The work of Moravcsik and Murugesan (1975) may also be regarded as offering support for this view. This can be established with reference to their four-fold classification of citations (see above). The influence of a cited document upon the citing work is not affected by the question of whether the citation is offered for conceptual or operational purposes. The same can be said with regard to the issue of evolutionary and juxtapositional citations. However, a similar assumption cannot be made when considering the other two classifications. The influence of a cited document will clearly be affected by the extent to which citations offered to it are organic or perfunctory. Similarly, negational citations should not be regarded as equivalent to those which are confirmative, since the former are referring to shortcomings in previous research, rather than highlighting its positive contribution to the development of the discipline.

For the purposes of the analysis in this book, a more detailed study of the issues of peripheral and negative citations was therefore necessary. Discussion of these two issues is offered below. A further issue, that of non-citation, was also analysed.

Levels of Influence

As discussed above, a complication is introduced to the analysis of citations when the *strength of the relationship* between citing and cited documents is considered. Bonzi (1981) defined four levels of influence represented by a citation. These range from a situation where the cited document is not specifically mentioned (as in statements such as 'several studies have shown that'), through to citations representing a number of direct references in the text. This raises an important question since, as Voos and Dagaev (1976) argue, citation indexing operates on the assumption that all citations are of *prima facie* the same value. The study by Moravcsik and Murugesan (1975), which introduced the concept of organic and perfunctory citations, showed that 41% of citations in 'Physics Letters' were perfunctory. A similar result was disclosed by Prabha (1983), who found that in business administration literature, less than one third of the works cited were regarded as essential by the citing authors. This has led to calls for authors to be more selective in the citations that they offer (Cronin, 1981b), in the hope that the citations offered would be restricted to work of central importance to the construction of the citing paper.

The research outlined above studies the strength of the relationship between citing and cited documents. Research has also been undertaken into the nature of the links denoted by the citations provided. Harter *et al* (1993) implemented a study of the semantic similarity of citing and cited documents, and found only a weak semantic link between the documents in many cases. Similar studies have been carried out by Small (1980) and Swanson (1987), concentrating on logical, rather than semantic linkages. Small found a high degree of similarity of content between papers linked by citations in the study of DNA. However, the work undertaken by Swanson contradicts this finding. He found that there was only a weak logical relationship between pairs of citing and cited papers within a particular medical field. The contradictory nature of these findings may be the result of the different disciplines being studied, and the employment of dissimilar measurement techniques.

The studies above appear to highlight the different types of relationship denoted by citations, in terms of both the strength and character of these relationships. This lack of a simple relationship between citing and cited documents may be problematic in the employment of citation analysis.

Negative Citations

As discussed earlier, *negative citations* are also seen as a potential problem facing citation analysis. Within many studies, all citations are counted as having equal value (Voos and Dagaev, 1976), and there is often little analysis of why particular citations have been offered. A paper containing erroneous information may be highly cited due to later writers highlighting the mistakes made. Since the influence of a paper is defined by the number of citations it receives, such a paper would be defined as having a major influence on the research community due to its inherent quality (Johnson and Podsakoff,

1994). A well known recent example was the work published on cold fusion by Martin Fleischmann and Stanley Pons, which represented the most highly cited work of that particular year (Coghlan, 1991).

Clearly, negative citations can have a detrimental effect upon the accuracy of citation analysis in the measurement of research quality. However, their influence should not be overemphasised. Chubin and Moitra (1975) found no totally negative citations in the papers they studied, with 5% of citations being defined as partially negative. The research by Moravcsik and Murugesan (1975) found 14% of citations to be negative, with no distinction made between totally and partially negative citations. These figures reflect the argument of Meadows (1974) that the typical response to erroneous work is to ignore it, rather than to cite it negatively. This argument is supported by Shadish *et al* (1995), who found no evidence to support the notion that 'bad' work continues to be cited over a significant time period. Hence negative citations should not have a great influence upon the employment of citation analysis. Negative citation may also have a positive impact on a research field, in that challenging but flawed work, such as that by Fleischmann and Pons, may generate increased interest in a particular research area.

Non - citation

A further issue, that of *non-citation*, was of interest to this study. Non-citation occurs where authors fail to offer certain citations that the content of their work demands. Various studies have suggested the existence of non-citation. Prabha's (1983) study of business literature found evidence to support the suggestion that not all the influences upon a particular work had been cited, while there were citations included to work which had not been consulted specifically in the construction of the citing document. MacRoberts and MacRoberts (1988) put forward similar evidence, thus supporting the assertion of Davies (1970), who stated that 'not all that is cited is read, that not all that is read is cited'. This finding is supported by a survey of journal editors carried out by Cronin (1982b). These editors pointed to a lack of correlation between the papers that had apparently been read in the development and implementation of particular research projects, and those that were cited. They also pointed to a natural bias in the citation process. This bias in the citing process may be caused by the desire to promote certain ideas, and could lead to the systematic non-citation of opposing schools of thought (Delamont, 1989).

A more common explanation of non-citation is that of *eponymy*. This occurs where certain ideas become so well established that they no longer require a citation to locate their origin (Cole and Cole, 1971). In their study of the role of eponymy, Baird and Oppenheim (1994) quote the example of Einstein's paper in which his Theory of Relativity first appeared. They argue that there is no requirement for later researchers to cite this paper, since its contents are so well established. Thomas (1992) implemented a more extensive study of the role of eponymy. This study revealed that the number of citations to classic works may decrease over time, while the name of the author of the work remains evident in the text of later research papers. Thomas thus concluded that the classic works *are* being employed in later research. However, the authors of later research (and the editors of the journals to which they submit their work) do not see the need to offer a citations to the classic works.

There have also been arguments offered suggesting that the impact of eponymy upon citation practices is minimal. Referring to the example of Einstein, Cole and Cole (1972) counted the number of citations he received in the 1970 *Science Citation Index*. Einstein's work was well established by this time, and should therefore have been subject to the influence of eponymy. Cole and Cole found 271 citations to his work in 1970, and pointed to this as evidence of the lack of influence of eponymy upon citation rates. However, this conclusion may be invalid. Given the central position of Einstein within the physical sciences, 271 citations appears to underestimate the number of papers which depend in some way upon his work. The research of Cole and Cole could thus be regarded instead as evidence that Einstein's work was used more often than it was cited, thus suggesting the existence of non-citation. With reference to the current study, the issue of non-citation was of particular concern, given this book's focus upon *seminal* management research publications. Care therefore had to be taken to recognise the potential non-citation of classic management literature.

Summary of the Role of Citations

The discussion above concentrates upon the relationship between citing and cited documents. This facilitates analysis of the role played by citations. It was discovered that citations are used to represent various relationships between documents. This undermines the assumption that citations simply denote the positive contribution of the cited work. Given that this assumption represents the foundation of citation analysis, the validity of this technique must be questioned. The various roles of citations were thus analysed in greater depth. Many of these roles were found to have no deleterious effect upon the validity of citation analysis. However, three areas of particular concern were identified - negative citation, non-citation, and the level of influence denoted by individual citations. Studies have shown that negative citation should not present too many problems over time. Greater difficulties were encountered when considering non-citation and levels of influence. Non-citation is, by its nature, extremely difficult to analyse on anything other than a small scale, since it requires in-depth analysis of the content of individual papers. It is therefore difficult to estimate how much influence non-citation has upon citing practices. Analyses of the levels of influence denoted by citations may encounter similar problems of scale. Large scale studies of this issue are beyond the practical scope of many researchers, since they require the analysis of individual citations. However, there have been some studies of both non-citation and the levels of influence denoted by citations, albeit on a small scale. These studies have suggested that citations may indeed reflect different levels of influence. There is also evidence of non-citation. The presence of these two influences means that simplistic depictions of citations must be approached with care.

The Research Process

The analysis has thus far concentrated upon the different reasons for offering citations, and the levels of influence that these citations denote. There has been no attempt to outline the contexts within which citations are generated. These contexts must be studied since, as Cronin argues 'citation is not something which happens in a void, and citations are not separable from the contexts and conditions of their generation' (Cronin, 1984, 86). The validity and relevance of citation analysis is thus dependent not only upon the nature of citations, but also upon the processes through which academic research is generated. It was therefore necessary to analyse the nature of the research process, and the effect of this process upon citing practices.

Nature of the Research Process

In traditional analyses of the research process, it is depicted as a rational practice driven by high-minded ideals such as the search for knowledge and innate curiosity on the part of the researcher. In this view, therefore, scientists have four motivations for undertaking research - universalism, organised scepticism, communism and disinterestedness (Merton, 1973). These motivations become universal through the norms which regulate the research process, leading to the description of this approach as the 'normative' view of academic research.

The accuracy of this depiction of research has been increasingly questioned, particularly with reference to scientific disciplines. As Cronin contends, 'it may be necessary to look beyond the "storybook" image of science as a selfless and dispassionate search after truth' (Cronin, 1984, 1). The suggestion here is that the subjective beliefs and attitudes of the researcher will influence the research process. Kuhn represents this relationship between the objective and subjective facets of research in terms of the internalist and externalist views of science (Kuhn, 1968). The internalist view considers only the substance of science as knowledge, thus corresponding to the objective depiction of research; while the externalist view concentrates upon the social processes through which scientific knowledge is generated, thus reflecting the subjective nature of the research process (cf. Latour, 1987). Mitroff (1972) also studied the relationship between the objective and subjective aspects of the research process. He concluded that it is too simple to say that the research process (in science) is either totally objective or totally subjective. If this hypothesis is accurate then a number of implications arise for citation analysis. These arise from the lack of objectivity associated with the content of published research.

The problems identified with the normative view of the scientific research process may also be regarded as applicable to the study of management research. A number of writers have highlighted the need for analysis of the externalist view of the management research process. As Mann (1992) argues, the way in which researchers develop and focus their work will be influenced by their own attitudes and beliefs. These beliefs are, in turn, affected by the norms of the research community (Aspinwall, 1992). Hence the research undertaken will reflect not only the ideas of the individual researcher, but also the interests of the research establishment.

The attitudes and beliefs of researchers may therefore affect the objectivity of the work that they publish. This objectivity may also be influenced by the nature of research papers themselves. It has been suggested that academic papers are inherently fraudulent, since they offer an inaccurate picture of the research process (Medawar, 1964). Textbooks set out research as a linear, rational activity with definite procedures and objectives. However, there has been criticism of this description, with the idea of research as a neutral, rational activity proving particularly contentious. Various writers have argued that the 'garbage can model' (put forward by Cohen *et al* (1972) to show the lack of rationality in the operation of organisations), is the most appropriate description of research activity. As Bryman (1988, 8) argues, 'the very fact that the application of such a model to research in the social sciences can be countenanced may be treated as evidence of the disillusionment with an explication of the research process in terms of a rational, goal-directed, linear activity.' This reflects Starr's (1983) argument that the role of research papers is to represent chaos in an orderly fashion.

The discussion thus far suggests that the research process is both chaotic and susceptible to the influence of subjectivity on the part of researchers. However, no suggestion has been made that the research process is any way biased or distorted. A number of authors have questioned this depiction of the research process as unbiased, preferring to emphasise its political nature (e.g. Pettigrew, 1985). This is supported by Krohn, who argues that 'behind noble motives, "love of truth" or "curiosity", can be detected the down-to-earth motives of seeking recognition, prestige and career advancement' (Krohn, 1980, xviii). In this depiction of the research process, researchers are regarded as being driven chiefly by the desire to achieve prominence within the academic community. In order to achieve this prominence, they must aim to become part of the 'persuasive community' (Allen *et al*, 1994). Members of this community set the research agenda for a discipline through the work that they publish. The work published by the members of the persuasive community thus tends towards 'acceptance status' (Latour and Woolgar, 1979). This status is restricted to those pieces of research that become so widely accepted within the academic community that they come to be regarded as standards or classics in their particular discipline. The research process is thus regarded as being driven largely by the desire of researchers for increased prestige. This desire is most evident in examples of fraud. Studies by Broad and Wade (1982) and Kochan and Budd (1992) outline examples of fraud in science. They argue that evidence of fraud is the clearest evidence available for the existence of motivations among scientists other than the disinterested dissemination of knowledge.

Effect of the Research Process on Citing Practices

The nature of the research process will have a number of implications for the procedures through which citations are generated. This has led to the call for 'citation context studies' (Small, 1978) to analyse the pressures upon the citation process. The nature of these 'citation contexts' differs according to the manner in which the research process is depicted. In particular, the extent to which the research process is regarded as subjective and driven by the ambitions of researchers will influence the role accorded to citations.

It is generally accepted that the opinions and ideas of individual researchers influence referencing practices. Ravetz (1971) argues that citation is seen as a low priority issue by many researchers, when compared to the other problems facing them. In this view, therefore, the main problem facing citation analysis is the relative lack of importance attached to citations within the research process. As Cronin argues, 'anecdotal evidence seems to favour the idea that many authors cite in reflexive fashion, without necessarily dwelling on the implications of the practice' (Cronin, 1984, 5). The lack of concern for the implications of the citing process was also reported by Kaplan (1965), who stated that researchers are given guidelines on how to present citations, but are offered little training in the meanings conveyed by the citations that they provide. These studies therefore suggest that the subjectivity of researchers will affect the extent to which the citation process can be regarded as rational. This view of citation represents it as a somewhat crude device which is of little concern to the majority of researchers (Ravetz, 1971). However, it is regarded as a process which is relatively unbiased on the part of citing authors.

A number of writers go further in their analysis of citation contexts. They point specifically to the effect of the ambitions of active researchers upon citing practices. May (1967, 890) argues that 'the author selects citations to serve his scientific, political and personal goals, and not to describe his intellectual ancestry'. This may involve errors of omission (such as excluding citations to similar research) or errors of commission (what Mitra (1970) describes as the malpractices of window dressing, padding and sprinkling citations to add credibility). Brooks (1985) carried out a study on the reasons why citations are offered. This research revealed that the most important reason for citation was 'persuasiveness' - the desire to convince the reader of the arguments and techniques put forward. By citing previous work which supported the present research, it was hoped that the reader would be convinced as to the accuracy and applicability of the citing paper. The suggestion that citations are used to boost the credibility of the published work is supported by Bavelas (1978), who argues that citations are offered partly to establish that the author is familiar with the field being studied. A study by MacRoberts and MacRoberts (1988) reported similar results. They found that self-citations are often offered in order to establish that the author has previous experience in the field, thus showing that the present work is not that of a novice to the area.

Self-Citation

The issue of *self-citation* has attracted a great deal of attention within bibliometric studies. It is regarded as one of the main obstacles to the accuracy of citation analysis. In order to increase the level of acceptance of their work, researchers must first ensure its prominence. One way of achieving this is by ensuring that the work is cited as widely as possible. This will increase the number of researchers who are aware of a particular published item. One method through which researchers can develop increased visibility for their research is through citing the work themselves. It has been argued that self-citation not only increases the visibility of particular research, it also may be employed by researchers to further their careers. With the increasing use of citation counts to measure research quality (which will be discussed later) there has been growing concern that authors may attempt to enhance their citation score (and thus their research rating) through assiduous self-citation of their previous work. However, the effect of self-citations should not be overstated. Most techniques employing citations to measure research quality treat self-citations in such a way as to prevent their influence becoming too great (Doreian, 1988; Thomas, 1995). Also, as Pendlebury argues, the refereeing processes at leading journals will tend to lead to the rejection of papers which reveal over-dependence upon the author's previous work (quoted in *Science*, 14/5/93). This will force these authors to publish in journals with lower prestige, thus reducing their probability of being cited by other researchers (Schubert and Braun, 1993).

The concerns surrounding self-citation have been extended to 'citation circles'. These are defined as groups of academics who agree to cite the work of others in the circle, in order to enhance the citation ratings of all researchers in the group. This is seen as potentially highly damaging to citation analysis, since it cannot be detected as easily as self-citation. However, there is little evidence of the existence of such circles, so that they remain something of a myth in the research community (Coghlan, 1991).

It can also be argued that writers do not cite themselves purely to increase their profile within the research community. As Sandison (1989) argues, researchers often refer to their own work because it is the research with which they are most familiar. Self citations may also become necessary where a researcher is working in a small, highly specialised field. In this situation, the only work which is relevant to the researcher may be that undertaken earlier in his/her publishing career.

The Halo Effect

The discussion earlier in this chapter suggests that the chief ambition of researchers is to gain prominence within the academic community. Previous research has suggested that this prominence may be self-perpetuating in some respects, particularly in terms of citations. Research undertaken by Cole and Cole (1972) discovered that the scientific community is highly stratified. There exist a small number of institutions which attract the most influential researchers, and also receive the vast majority of external research funding. Cole and Cole found that this structure had important implications for citing practices. Leading researchers almost exclusively cited research undertaken at other 'elite' institutions. Prominent researchers also received citations from researchers outside the elite group. Researchers from lower profile institutions were found to receive very few citations from leading researchers, and relatively few citations from other academics working outside the elite.

This pattern of citations has led to suggestions that a 'halo effect' may be detected in citation practices (Cole and Cole, 1972). This refers to the offering of citations to particular work due to the identity of the cited work's author (or institutional base), rather than because of its content. As a result of this 'halo effect' eminent scholars will tend to receive a large number of citations due to their reputation within a field. The 'halo effect' has been described as a specific example of the 'Matthew Effect', which states that 'more comes to those that have' (Merton, 1968).

The structure of research outlined above leads Cole and Cole to raise the issue of the size of the scientific community. They argue that the 'tail' of institutions could be removed, without affecting adversely the research undertaken by the scientific community as a whole. This contention explicitly rejects the so-called 'Ortega hypothesis' (discussed in Cole and Cole, 1972) which states that leading scientists can only make progress as a result of the efforts of the small scale, cumulative advances made by researchers outside the elite. Cole and Cole's contention is also supported by Price (1963), who found that there were a small number of highly productive scientists (as measured by the number of papers published), with a much larger 'tail' of researchers producing little published research.

This depiction of the scientific community was also found to offer an accurate reflection of the structure of management research in the UK (Thomas and Watkins, 1995). Similar implications may therefore be identified for the size and structure of the British management research community.

Summary of the Research Process

There are a number of pressures that affect the manner in which research is undertaken. These pressures are derived, in part, from the desire of individual researchers for career advancement. This desire affects both the questions which will be addressed by researchers, and the manner in which they go about this process. Hence the depiction of research as the disinterested search for greater knowledge may be misleading. In turn, this may have implications for the citing practices within any discipline. The problems associated with issues such as self citation and the 'halo effect' can be traced directly to the presence of pressures upon citing practices other than the simple desire to reveal the influences upon a given piece of research.

The role of citations may also be affected by the nature of the research process itself. Citation analysis is founded upon the assumption that citations are offered on the basis of rational consideration on the part of the citing author. However, the two aspects of this assumption (rationality and consideration) may be idealistic. Previous research has shown that citations are not a major concern within the research process, and that the amount of consideration they receive is minimal. The issue of rationality is also regarded as problematic. It can be argued that the research process itself is not based upon rational grounds, so that the citing process cannot be assumed to operate on a rational basis.

This section thus calls into question the nature of the contexts in which citations are generated. It appears that there are a number of problems associated with these contexts. These problems have a number of implications for the validity of citation analysis. A discussion of these implications is offered later in this chapter, as part of a more general analysis of the validity of citation analysis.

The Academic Community

The discussion of the research process concentrated upon the influence of this process upon the generation of citations. However, it is also necessary to analyse how the research process is influenced in turn by the norms and practices of the academic community. It is this community which forms the context in which research takes place. The manner in which research is implemented and disseminated differs according to the norms of the discipline being considered. As discussed earlier, the majority of the studies employing citation analysis have concentrated upon the natural and physical sciences. In applying these techniques to social science, it is therefore necessary to analyse any differences discovered in the citation processes in science and social science. These may emerge from a number of sources.

Nature of Information Seeking

The first of these sources is the way in which researchers search for information. This will influence which information is located by researchers, and thus which published items these researchers may cite. Ellis *et al* (1993) defined eight categories of information seeking among scientists. These categories are employed by researchers at various stages in the research process in order to access different types of information. In studying the information seeking practices of social science authors, little difference was noted when compared with scientific authors. However, the emphasis between the two groups differed. In particular, authors in science spent a significant amount of time verifying their work against previously published results. This process was largely absent in the research process in social science. The different information requirements of scientific and social scientific researchers may therefore lead to a disparity between the citation practices associated with science and social science disciplines.

Informal Research Networks

In addition to studying the manner in which researchers seek information, it is also necessary to analyse the norms governing the processes of information dissemination in science and social science. An early study by Crane (1972) established the concept of the *invisible college*. This refers to a network of researchers who disseminate information to each other on an informal basis. Information may be transferred through media such as personal communications, pre-prints of papers and informal meetings at academic conferences. A study by Garvey *et al* (1971) discovered that informal networks were marginally more widespread in science than social science. They found that 83% of science authors had disseminated information prior to publication, compared with 72% in the social sciences. This may reflect the tightly-knit nature of the scientific community (Garvey *et al*, 1971). However, it may also be the result of the wider range of sources used by social scientists in the preparation of their research (Cronin, 1982a). This broader scope means that researchers cannot rely upon a single network for developing and disseminating their work, since its content will be of interest to a number of different audiences.

One impact of the existence of informal networks for disseminating information is a reduction of the requirement to publish in scholarly journals. Garvey *et al* (1971) found that 60% of authors had no intention of publishing their work in journal form. The main reason given for this was that the work was adequately available elsewhere. In science, technical reports and conference proceedings were regarded as alternative media for disseminating research findings. Social scientists, on the other hand, concentrated upon publishing books alongside articles in academic journals. The importance of book publication in the social sciences was also reflected in the study carried out by Bath University (1980).

This pattern of information dissemination has important implications for the employment of citation analysis. Journal publication is the main source of data employed in most citation analyses. Thus any move away from journal publication may be problematic for the validity of these studies. For the purposes of this study, the main implication was the *importance of book publication in the diffusion of management research* (a fuller discussion of this issue is offered in Chapter 4).

Editorial Policies

The publishing process outlined above may also be affected by the editorial policies of journals within a particular discipline. It is these policies which will determine which papers are published and, as a result, become part of the established knowledge within a discipline. A number of authors have studied the issue of editorial policies. Shadish *et al* (1995) found that there was a tendency for journals in psychology to reject papers marked by a high degree of creativity and originality. Garvey *et al* (1971) found that the main reasons for rejection of papers in both the physical and social sciences were methodological and theoretical. These two findings may be related. Creative papers are likely to draw their originality from the innovative employment of existing theories and methodologies. This may not meet with the approval of journal editors, thus leading to an increased probability of rejection for the paper. Campanario (1993) points to a number of examples of scientific papers which experienced great difficulty in getting published, yet were later found to be of great importance. These works tended to be those offering innovative ideas or original applications of existing methodologies.

There are two possible effects of this rejection process. The first is that authors may look for alternative methods of disseminating their research, other than journal publication. The second possibility is that authors may submit their work to journals with a lower reputation within the field in which they are researching. Cronin and McKenzie (1992) found this to be a common pattern of journal submission. Creative papers may therefore be restricted to journals with less impact upon a given discipline. This will tend to reduce the number of citations they receive. Such a fate may also be encountered by papers written by authors from developing countries. Cronin and McKenzie (1992) found that authors from the third world experienced difficulty in publishing their work in journals based in countries with well established research communities. This is revealed in the much higher rejection rate for papers written by authors from developing nations.

Norms of Citation

The discussion of the scientific community to this point has revealed that the citation process may be influenced by norms of information dissemination. The generation of citations may also be affected by the accepted citing practices within the discipline being studied. As Peters and van Raan (1994) note, citing practices will differ across disciplines. Cronin (1982b) argues that citing is a 'tacit skill' (cf. Polanyi 1958) which is developed by researchers over time. They do not develop this skill in isolation. Rather, educators have a central role in the inculcation of citation practices to their students (Cronin, 1982b). These norms and practices of citation may also be influenced by changes over time. Nelson (1996) argues that academic research is characterised by an ever increasing number of citations. She defines many of these citations as spurious. The increasing number of citations was also noted by Allen *et al* (1994). They argue that the number of citations within papers increases as the archive of published research grows. This is due to the existence of a greater number of citable items. Allen *et al* also noted that one characteristic of recent decades is the rapid reduction of the age of literature cited.

Summary of the Effect of the Academic Community

Bibliometric studies are based upon analysis of the media through which research is disseminated. As a result, these studies are influenced by the manner in which researchers choose to publicise the results of their work. Where results are transferred informally, they become inaccessible to study using citation analysis. Hence the existence of invisible colleges may militate against the applicability of citation studies. The majority of citation studies have been carried out in scientific disciplines, where informal networks are particularly prevalent. It was therefore expected that the impact of informal networks upon the current research would not be greater than upon previous citation studies, given the social science focus of this book. The issue of informal dissemination of information was therefore not regarded as a major problem facing this study. Of more concern was the issue of the media through which research is published. Most citation studies are based upon items published in scholarly journals. This is partly due to the publication traditions in scientific disciplines. It also occurs because of the focus of the *Science Citation Index* and *Social Science Citation Index* upon articles published in academic journals.

In management research, however, there exists a long-standing tradition of book publication. This had to be taken into consideration in the implementation of the analysis in this book (see Chapter 5 for a fuller discussion of this issue). Another concern for this study was the pattern of rejection of creative research papers. This may lead to an overstatement of the influence of research which employs traditional methods, at the expense of work which may be marked by greater originality.

Studying the Validity of Citation Analysis

A number of issues pertaining to the employment of citation analysis have been discussed in this chapter. Through discussion of these issues, the complex nature of citations becomes apparent. This complexity has led some writers to argue that citation analysis may lack the validity necessary for scientific research. As Cronin argues, 'it is mildly ironic that science, founded on the traditions of quantification and verification, should be content with an explanation of citation, an activity central to the scientific process, which emits a whiff of the metaphysical' (Cronin, 1984, 24). However, the analytical power of citation analysis has meant that a great deal of time has been spent by researchers trying to solve these problems of validity, leading to the development of increasingly sophisticated measurement techniques. These techniques overcome many of the methodological problems encountered by early analyses. Nevertheless, problems still remain, and are responsible for 'hairline cracks in the superstructure' (Cronin, 1981b). This leads to two broad approaches to citation analysis. The first of these is the *pragmatist* view, which argues that citation analysis should be used as efficiently and accurately as possible, while still noting the methodological weaknesses (Kidd, 1990; Seglen, 1994). The *positivist* view, on the other hand, opines that unless these weaknesses can be remedied, citation analysis cannot be regarded as being 'scientific' (Bavelas, 1978).

This debate has also been defined in terms of the *normative* approach to citation, and the *microsociological* view of its role (Liu, 1993a). The normative view argues that citations do, on the whole, represent credit given to previous work. This view is supported by Small, who argues that 'the reasons and motivations for citing appear to be as subtle and as varied as scientific thought itself, but most references do establish valid conceptual links between scientific documents' (Small, 1976, 67). The microsociological view states that the manner in which citations are generated is insufficiently understood to justify the crude employment of citations as a measurement tool. Rather, a theory of citing (Cronin, 1981b) is required before citation analysis can be employed with any confidence. Liu (1993a) argues that a theory of this type is still far from being achieved.

As a result of these problems with the validity of citation analysis, Cronin raises the question 'whether the considerable practical benefits of citation indexing will continue to outweigh the residual misgivings concerning the construct validity of the principle upon which the system rests' (Cronin, 1984, 28). This issue of validity is central to the justification of the use of citation analysis. As outlined above, no satisfactory theory of citing has been developed which ameliorates the problems associated with the heterogenous nature of citations. Particular problems have been encountered with the depiction of citations as the acknowledgement of the positive contribution of the cited work. As a result of this lack of a generalisable theory of citing, the *construct validity* (i.e. the extent to which a technique measures what it purports to) of citation analysis cannot be established. This means that citation analysis must refer instead to the *pragmatic validity* of its findings (Cronin, 1981b). This type of validity refers to the extent to which the results of a technique can be regarded as accurate, irrespective of the validity of the technique itself.

The most commonly employed method of testing the validity of citation analysis is to compare its results with those produced using alternative measurement techniques. In particular, peer review, or 'expert' opinion, is employed as a standard against which the results of citation analysis are evaluated.

This evaluation is often implemented by comparing measures of influence based upon citation analysis with those suggested by surveys of experts in the field. Studies of this type have been carried out at a number of levels:

1. *Individual Researchers* - early studies revealed that there is a relatively high correlation (r= 0.5 to 0.8) between citation rates and 'measures of eminence' (Clark, 1957; Narin 1976). These measures of eminence include Nobel prizes, membership of professional associations and membership of editorial boards. Research has also shown a high correlation between pay and publication in highly cited journals (Gomez-Meija and Balkin, 1992). There has also been support for the idea that citation rates are a reliable guide to pay (Diamond, 1986). The assumption behind these studies is that the most influential scholars within a particular field will tend to be among the most highly paid. The fact that citation counts correlate with pay thus suggests that citations do indeed offer an accurate guide to the influence of particular researchers.

2. *Academic Journals* - a number of studies have reported a strong correlation between measures of journal quality based upon citation analysis, and ratings of these journals based upon the opinion of leading scholars within the particular discipline (e.g. Franke *et al*, 1990; Cooper *et al,* 1993). Johnson and Podsakoff (1994) also highlighted the close relationship between the (subjectively determined) level of influence of management research journals, and the number of citations received by these journals.

3. *Research Institutions* - various studies have revealed the existence of a high correlation between rankings of academic institutions based upon citations and expert opinion (Moed *et al*, 1985; Thomas and Watkins, 1995). A study of American university departments carried out by Roche and Smith (1978) found a high level of agreement between these two methods of ranking institutions. Roche and Smith also found a high correlation between their ranking of departments using citation counts, and the ranking produced by Glenn and Villemez (1970) which employed an alternative bibliometric technique (publication counting).

4. *Research Fields* - the validity of citation analysis has also been measured with reference to the depiction it offers of the development and structure of academic disciplines. This is achieved by comparing the structure suggested by citation analysis with that developed through surveys of scholars in the particular discipline. A number of studies have shown that citations may be employed to develop an accurate depiction of the structure of research fields (Garfield *et al*, 1964; Sullivan *et al*, 1977; Van Raan and Tijssen, 1993). However, greater problems may be encountered in the use of citations to map changes in disciplinary structures over time (Bell and Rothman, 1991).

These studies appear to lend support to the contention of Baird and Oppenheim (1994) that 'whatever measure you take for the eminence of an individual scientist or of a journal or of an institution, citation counts provide strong correlation with that result'. This suggests that citation analysis may be defined as valid in purely pragmatic terms. However, a note of caution must be included. Bavelas (1978) has questioned the studies above, suggesting that citation rates correlate with measures of eminence because later researchers are forced to cite leading authors to show that they are familiar with the field, not necessarily because of an acknowledgement of a debt to the earlier work.

Is Citation Analysis a Valid Research Tool?

The discussion in this chapter has highlighted a number of problems associated with the employment of citation analysis. These centre upon the role accorded to individual citations within these analyses. Problems were encountered with the simplistic definition of a citation as an acknowledgement of a debt to previous research. These problems were analysed at three levels - the individual citation, the research process, and the academic community.

The problems encountered at each of these levels call into question the validity of citation analysis. In particular, the construct validity of citation analysis remains to be established. However, there appears to be empirical evidence to support the pragmatic validity of citation analysis. This is established through the strong correlation between rankings of research based upon citations and rankings based upon 'expert' opinion. It has led to the development of the pragmatist approach to citation analysis, which accepts the inherent problems with this technique, but points to the accuracy of its outcomes.

In response to the debate concerning the validity of citation analysis, this study will follow a broadly pragmatist approach. It is accepted that the citation process is indeed subjective, but this is regarded as inevitable due to the presence of personal motivations and beliefs in the research process. The social and political reasons for dismissing citation analysis are thus noted, but regarded as a natural feature of (social) scientific inquiry. Potentially more damaging is the question of the nature of citations themselves. As outlined above, the strength and nature of the relationship between citing and cited papers is problematic. However, the belief that 'most' (rather than 'all') citations represent a valid conceptual link between papers (Small, 1976) means that results of citation analyses must be approached carefully, but not dismissed out of hand. In particular, it must be noted that the validity of citation analysis is based upon the practical applicability of its results, rather than upon the inherent validity of the technique itself.

However, the lack of convincing evidence to support the view that citation represents the positive contribution of the cited work introduces an important point for the evaluation of the results of citation analyses. This is that citation reflects *only*

1. The use of information contained in the cited paper (Shadish *et al*, 1995); or
2. The use of the cited paper as a symbol of a particular concept or technique (Small, 1978)

Citation does *not* therefore reflect the quality or importance of the cited work (Roche and Smith, 1978). This view is supported by the findings of the research carried out by Porter *et al* (1988). They implemented a survey designed to determine which papers scientific authors regarded as representative of their highest quality work. These quality ratings were then compared against the number of citations received by the various works published by each author included in the study. It was found that the research regarded by authors as their best work was often not that which was cited most often. This may be a reflection of the finding outlined earlier, that creative works are often hard to publish in leading journals. Researchers may rate their most creative work most highly, but this creativity may result in lower rates of citation (Shadish *et al*, 1995).

The contention that citations reflect the use of the cited work, rather than its quality or importance, has important implications for the employment of citation analysis in this study. As outlined in the previous chapter, management fashions are to be identified by the amount of time over which particular theories are influential. Citation analysis offers a platform to achieve this. A citation is assumed to show that the cited work has been *used* by the citing author in the preparation of his/her work. It may be inferred from this that in this usage, the cited work had some influence, however slight, upon the citing author. *Thus, for the purposes of this study, citations may be employed as a surrogate in the measurement of influence. However, this measure of influence cannot be employed to draw conclusions concerning the quality of the work of particular management theorists.*

4 The Aging of Research Literature

Introduction

The primary objective of this book is to identify and analyse fashions in management research literature. As discussed in Chapter 2, management fashions may be identified by the transient nature of their influence upon management research. The purpose of this chapter is to develop a method through which changes in the pattern of influence associated with management literature over time may be analysed. The first part of this chapter analyses the potential causes of changes in the influence of research literature over time. The second part of the chapter evaluates different techniques that may be employed in the measurement and modelling of these changing patterns.

Previous writers have put forward the idea that academic literature has a 'total life' (Egghe and Rao, 1992). In studying the 'lifetime' of a literature, one important point must be noted - academic literature is not characterised by a constant rate of influence, before being disregarded suddenly. Rather the pattern of influence changes over time. A great deal of attention has been paid to the study of these patterns, the primary focus being *the question of whether the number of times a work is cited is influenced by its age.*

Studies analysing changes in patterns of literature usage are chiefly concerned with *obsolescence* in academic literature. For the purposes of the current study, obsolescence can be defined as 'the decline over time in validity or utility of information' (Line, 1970). The important point to note from the definition above is the existence of two possible causes of obsolescence in literature. The first of these is that the content of Aging literature is no longer valid. This lends the term obsolescence its pejorative overtones of particular literature being of little lasting value. However, the second cause of obsolescence - lack of utility - is caused by the lack of usage of particular work by later researchers. This may be caused by a number of factors external to the content of a particular item. Care must therefore be taken in the interpretation of terms such as obsolescence, since they are often regarded as value laden. Indeed, obsolescence could be regarded as a positive phenomenon. As Griffith *et al* argue (1979), Aging of literature could offer evidence that researchers are building cumulatively upon existing knowledge in the research field.

Causes of Obsolescence

In studying obsolescence, it is insufficient simply to describe patterns of decay in the influence of literature. An attempt must be made to study the reasons if (and why) the influence of literature declines over time. A number of possible causes of obsolescence are discussed below.

Content of Literature

Obsolescence may be caused by factors concerned with the content of the published literature. Line and Sandison (1974) offer four possible reasons for the decline in the use of a paper over time, based upon the content of the paper. The first of these is that the content of the work is valid, but is incorporated into later work, which may be referred to instead. The second cause is that the information is valid, but is superseded by later work, such that the later work is of greater interest to later researchers. These two causes do not diminish the importance of the earlier work. Rather, they reflect the cumulative nature of knowledge within a particular field. The third possible reason is that the information in a published work is valid, but in a field in which interest is declining. Again, the validity of the work itself is not in question, since the decline in its usage is caused by the changing interests of the academic community. The final reason for work to be disregarded is that it is no longer valid. As can be seen from this list, only the final cause of obsolescence can be attributed to a lack of validity in a particular published item. This reinforces the argument that obsolescence should not be defined in value-laden terms.

The classifications offered by Line and Sandison were developed as a result of analysis of scientific disciplines. They highlight the fact that literature obsolescence is not necessarily caused by lack of validity. Such a contention may be given even greater support in the study of social science disciplines, due to the different conceptions of 'validity' between science and social science disciplines. In scientific disciplines, lack of validity is often equated with particular work being proved to be incorrect in some way by later research. However, validity in the social sciences may be regarded as a more complex idea. Within social sciences, including management, research may be invalidated not only because it is shown to be incorrect. Its apparent validity may also be adversely affected by changes in the social phenomena that it examines, which cause it to become outdated. Hence literature obsolescence in social science may be caused by factors other than the content of published research. This reinforces the need to avoid equating literature obsolescence with lack of validity.

One issue of particular interest in the study of management research is the distinction between 'classic' and 'ephemeral' literature, as defined by Price (1965). Classic literature is relatively scarce, and is influential for many years. Ephemeral literature, on the other hand, is influential over a relatively short period, and tends to be concerned with the most recent developments in a field. For example, Garfield's (1970) study found that research produced by Nobel Prize winning authors was still cited many years after it has been published. This literature can presumably be defined as classic, both with respect to its prize-winning stature, and the citations it has received. In terms of management research, it may therefore be possible to identify 'classic' publications, since they will be cited over a long period of time.

Nature of Research Field

Various studies have analysed the effect of the characteristics of research fields upon rates of obsolescence. Griffith *et al* (1979) showed that high obsolescence is associated with highly specialised use of literature by a focused group of academics. The rate of obsolescence was found to be lower where the literature is used by a diffuse research community for more generalised purposes. This idea was built upon by De Stefano (1987) in his exploratory study of the application of *adaptive radiation* theories to academic literature. Adaptive radiation addresses issues surrounding the development and survival of species through evolution. The species which survive are those which can adapt to the changing environmental conditions that they encounter. This adaptability is applied by De Stefano to the scientific literature. He argues that literature which is used for diffuse purposes is likely to survive due to its applicability in a range of situations. Applying this theory to management research, it might be expected that theories covering a variety of management issues would be influential over a longer period than theories addressing specialised management questions. However, it should be noted that Wallace (1986) carried out an extensive analysis of the relationship between the breadth of influence of literature and its obsolescence. He found that no linear relationship could be discovered between the two variables.

Academic Background of Research Field

One extension of the study regarding the nature of research fields is the question of the academic traditions within which these fields lie. Particular attention must be given to whether a discipline can be defined as a science, social science or humanities field. With reference to this objective, Price (1970) distinguishes between hard science, soft science, and non-science. The classification of disciplines is based upon the extent to which the terminology and hypotheses of a discipline are clearly definable (i.e. the extent to which they are characterised by unifying paradigms). This raises the question of how social sciences such as management research can be defined within this schema. Very few bibliometric studies go beyond scientific disciplines to consider social sciences and humanities. One study which attempts to analyse these areas was carried out by Heisey (1988). This study employs the same classification as Price. Heisey defines social science as a soft science, and humanities as non-science. This delineation is based upon the contention that humanities are entirely non-cumulative in their patterns of knowledge acquisition, whereas social sciences contain some cumulative elements (Heisey, 1988).

Price (1970) hypothesised that the citation patterns associated with different academic traditions would be dissimilar. He postulated that hard sciences would be characterised by a large number of recent citations. This is due to the depiction of knowledge acquisition in these disciplines as being cumulative, so that scholars cite mainly recent papers representing the research front. Softer sciences, it was assumed, would contain a smaller number of recent citations. The presence of a greater diversity of paradigms within soft science means that citations may be offered to range of different traditions, which have been developed at different times, rather than contemporaneously. Finally non-science is defined as having a complete absence of paradigms. The literature cited in non-science fields therefore has the lowest number of recent citations, since information of any age is equally relevant in addressing research issues.

The hypotheses suggested by Price have been tested by a number of writers. Heisey (1988) argued that hard sciences are characterised by the presence of a definable research front. The constantly changing position of this research front leads to a higher rate of obsolescence as research problems are continually addressed and then solved or disregarded. Glänzel and Schoepflin (1995) also found that the Aging of literature is slower in social science than in science. This supported findings reported by Egghe and Rao (1992), who discovered that the average 'lifetime' of social science literature is longer than the 'life' of literature in mathematics by around 35%. A comparison of mean citation ages is also instructive. Peters *et al* (1988) found that the 'citation peak' for a scientific article occurs between three and five years. This can be compared with Heisey's (1988) finding that the mean citation age in an individual social science (archaeology) is 9.5 years, and the mean in a single humanities discipline (biblical studies) is over 21 years. Although the studies by Peters *et al* and Heisey are limited in scope, and their measures of age not directly comparable, they appear to offer tentative support for Price's hypothesis.

It is important to note the differences between science, social science and non-science disciplines in the study of management research. In particular, it might be expected that the more 'scientific' an area of management research is, the faster its literature is likely to obsolesce.

Growth of Research Field

In studying obsolescence in the literature of a given discipline, one important factor which must be analysed is the rate at which the discipline grows. The rate of growth is regarded as having an influence upon obsolescence rates. This is based upon the belief that a rapidly growing field is characterised by rapid change in research interests and problems (Menard (1971)). Older literature is therefore used relatively infrequently, increasing the rate of obsolescence (Line and Sandison, 1974). Hence it might be expected that the highest rate of obsolescence would be associated with fields exhibiting rapid growth. This is similar to the depictions of management research discussed in Chapter 2.

Various writers have studied the relationship between growth and obsolescence. There are two main objectives within these studies. The first is the attempt to analyse the accuracy of the hypothesis outlined above. The results of these studies are somewhat contradictory. Experimental evidence presented by Rao and Meera (1992) (quoted in Egghe, 1993) offers support for the hypothesis that rapid growth in a research field is positively related to the rate of obsolescence. This result is supported by part of the research undertaken by Egghe (1993). However, contrary evidence was also reported by Egghe, suggesting that faster growth is associated with slower rates of obsolescence. Wallace (1986) also studied the relationship between growth and obsolescence, but the findings were ambiguous. The reason for the different conclusions drawn in these studies may be located in the techniques employed for the measurement of obsolescence (a discussion of these techniques is offered later in this chapter). The relationship between growth and obsolescence therefore remains empirically unproven.

The second reason for studying the relationship between growth and obsolescence is based upon practical considerations. In particular, the question of how obsolescence should be measured within a growing field has attracted a great deal of attention. This question is addressed at length later in this chapter.

Publishing Media

As discussed in Chapter 3, one of the main characteristics of scientific research is the primacy of journal output. This has led to a concentration on the output of journals as a basis for bibliometric analyses. However, the concentration on journal publication is insufficient within disciplines outside science, due to the importance of books in the development of research fields (Heisey, 1988). Despite this problem, little research has been carried out on book publications. Those studies that have been implemented tend to concentrate on a small sample of books, normally selected on the basis of convenience (e.g. Egghe and Rao, 1992). It is necessary for the current research to carry out analysis into the obsolescence of both books and journals, given the importance of both media in the dissemination of management research. In this analysis, note must be made of previous research which found that rate of obsolescence for books and journals differs markedly (Sandison, 1971; Bath University, 1980). Both of these studies showed that books are cited for a longer period than journals. This finding will be tested within the current research.

Use of Information by Scholars

Obsolescence may also be caused by factors concerning the nature of information usage within the academic community. Sandison (1971) defines two types of information usage. The first of these is basic searching of the literature. This is carried out by scholars who are unfamiliar with a particular field. Their searches will involve all literature, including older texts which may form the foundations of a particular area. The second type of usage involves the updating of knowledge by scholars who are already working within a given field. They will tend to use the literature in order to keep up with the latest developments in the field. They are less likely to refer to older texts, because they are already familiar with their content. Both basic and updating searches involve recently published literature, while older literature will tend to be used only by those who are unfamiliar with a particular field. Given that citation is a function of literature usage, this pattern will tend to lead to a higher citation rate for more recent literature.

The pattern of literature usage may also be affected by two pressures inherent to the research process. The first of these is the pressure to refer to classic works. In this way researchers can show that they are familiar with the field and its development. Secondly, there is a pressure to cite recent works, in order to show that the research undertaken is up-to-date and builds upon recent developments in the field. Of the two pressures, the second is regarded as dominant, thus increasing the tendency to cite recent works (Line and Sandison, 1974).

Factors Reducing Rate of Obsolescence

As can be seen from the list above, a decline in citations to a particular work over time may be caused by a number of factors. Many of these are external to the actual content of a particular work. Line and Sandison (1974) also offer three possible reasons why literature may be cited *more often* as it ages. The first of these is that the information in a paper is considered invalid at the time of publication, only to be revealed as valid at a later date by further developments in the same area. An increase in the number of citations received over time may also occur where the content of a paper is valid, but is not exploited due to a lack of adequate theory or technology. As the theoretical and technological aspects of a field develop, the work is then exploited at a later date. The third cause suggested by Line and Sandison is that the work is valid, and lies within a research field attracting increasing interest.

A further possible cause that may be added to this list was outlined by Cole and Cole (1967). They found that early work by an author which is disregarded at the time of publication is cited more often after later work by the same author becomes definitive within a research field. Two possible causes are hypothesised for this pattern. The first of these is that the early work is re-evaluated on the basis of later work, and is found to be of greater importance than was previously thought. The second cause suggests a more dubious intent on the part of citing authors. Cole and Cole argue that increased citations to early work may be caused by 'ceremonial citation' by researchers anxious to show that they are familiar with the work of a leading author in the field.

The existence of these factors which may cause citation rates to increase over time leads Sandison (1971) to argue that there is no inherent reason why older literature should always be of declining interest. Hence in studying the changing usage of literature over time, no theoretical assumptions can be made that there will necessarily exist a pattern of declining citations. Instead, research should be carried out without these assumptions, with the result that empirical results alone will determine the presence or absence of obsolescence within the literature of a particular discipline.

Measuring Literature Obsolescence

As outlined above, the existence of obsolescence in any discipline, and the rate at which it occurs, can only be measured empirically. It would be desirable to be able to effect these empirical measurements in isolation from external influences. There are two external influences which are of particular importance. The first of these is the size and structure of the citing audience (i.e. the nature of the current research community). The second variable is the size and structure of the literature cited by current researchers. The 'pure' case of obsolescence measurement, as described by Griffith *et al* (1979) would involve observation of all the uses of a single set of literature over time by an unchanging academic community. The size of both the citing and cited literature would therefore be fixed. This bibliometric version of the economists' *ceteris paribus* (all other things remaining equal) clearly bears little relation to the reality of the development of research fields. In practice, both the literature and the research community will change in size and structure over time. Hence the 'pure' case is an ideal rather than practical approach to the measurement of obsolescence. As a result 'impure' methods must be employed (Griffith *et al*, 1979). These 'impure' techniques attempt to fix the size of the citing *or* the cited audience (since it is not possible in reality to fix both audiences).

There are thus two main techniques employed in the study of obsolescence. The first of these is the *synchronous* approach. This technique involves the selection of a single year as a basis for analysis. A sample of the literature from that year is constructed. The most common method of sampling is to concentrate upon the contents of leading journals within a particular field. The references contained within these journals are then collected, and analysed in terms of their age. For example, if 1990 is chosen as the base year, citations to 1985 are counted as five years old, 1980 as ten years old, and so on. Having analysed all the references in this way, it is then possible to construct a profile of the age of citations offered within a particular discipline. Synchronous studies have been employed by a number of writers within bibliometrics (Oliver, 1971; Griffith *et al*, 1979; Dequeiroz and Lancaster, 1981; Matricciani, 1994).

Synchronous studies generate a cross sectional approach to the study of obsolescence, in that they offer a guide to the age of literature cited at one particular point in time. The citing literature is fixed, while the cited literature is variable. A potential problem may be encountered with this approach, since the base year selected could be atypical, with the result that analysis offers an inaccurate depiction of a research field. As a result of this, a number of writers have suggested the use of a more complex variant of the synchronous techniques outlined above (Wallace, 1986; Stinson and Lancaster, 1987). This *diasynchronous* approach involves sampling literature from a number of years, rather than concentrating upon a single year as a basis for analysis. The processes involved in the diasynchronous approach are otherwise similar to those employed in synchronous measurements of obsolescence. The main advantage of diasynchronous techniques is that they remove the problems associated with individual years being atypical.

Diachronous techniques are the logical opposite of synchronous approaches. Synchronous approaches fix the citing literature, and study the literature cited within the selected items. Diachronous techniques are based upon the opposite process. A set of articles is selected from a given year. These items form the basis for the analysis. The citations to the items are then collected over a given period of time. The set of cited items is therefore fixed, but the list of citing items is theoretically infinite.

Diachronous techniques are generally regarded as offering a more accurate depiction of the concept of obsolescence. They measure directly the influence of individual articles over time, and thus the rate at which they are disregarded. This leads to Line and Sandison's (1974) argument that diachronous studies are inherently more interesting than those employing synchronous techniques, and Stinson and Lancaster's (1987) assertion that diachronous techniques appear to be more 'correct'. However, very few diachronous studies have ever been carried out.

The lack of diachronous studies is due mainly to practical difficulties in their implementation. Wallace (1986) identified a number of problems associated with diachronous techniques, concluding that they are complex, time consuming and expensive. Diachronous techniques also require large sample sizes studied over long time periods to offer statistical validity. The problems of practical implementation mean that diachronous approaches were regarded as infeasible before the advent of electronic citation indexes and specialist databases (Stinson and Lancaster, 1987). These studies remain complex and time consuming even with the aid of technological developments. The problems associated with diachronous techniques lie in the nature of the citing literature. In synchronous techniques, the cited literature within a particular year can be defined. This means that it is possible to determine the sample size required for any project, and the feasibility of a particular analysis. Diachronous techniques do not offer these guarantees. The citing literature is boundless, with the result that sampling, and the measurement of obsolescence, are problematic.

Due to practical considerations, researchers often appear to avoid diachronous approaches to obsolescence. One alternative approach is the employment of synchronous techniques for analysing obsolescence irrespective of the specific research questions. This approach is based upon the idea that synchronous and diachronous techniques are logically congruent. However, this assumption is erroneous. Synchronous approaches to obsolescence measure the age of literature cited at a particular point in time. They can therefore be employed to measure the nature of the influences upon current research, particularly in terms of their age. However, this is not logically equivalent to studying the influence over time of particular items of literature within a research field. For example, as Sandison (1983) argues, it is incorrect to take the observation that fewer old books are used, and assume that this means that all old books are used less frequently. The first observation is a typical outcome from the application of a synchronous measurement of obsolescence, while the latter represents an issue which can only be studied diachronously. The logical distinction between the two techniques is vital because, as Line and Sandison (1974) observe, one of the most common problems with studies of obsolescence is the employment of synchronous techniques to address problems for which diachronous studies are more appropriate.

Having established that synchronous and diachronous approaches are not logically congruent, the question then arises as to whether the results of the two approaches differ. It could be argued that, despite theoretical shortcomings, synchronous techniques may be employed for diachronous purposes if the results of the two approaches are equivalent. However, this possibility is not supported by empirical evidence. Various studies have shown that the results of synchronous and diachronous measurements of obsolescence differ for the same data set (Stinson and Lancaster, 1987; Egghe, 1993). Care must therefore be taken in selecting the technique employed in any analysis of obsolescence.

In terms of the empirical analysis for this book, the simplest method of measuring the obsolescence of management research would have been synchronous. This would have facilitated analysis of the influences upon current management research, thus offering insights into the rate of obsolescence of the totality of management research. However, no analysis would be possible concerning the influence of particular management theories. Given the focus of the current research upon the longevity of influence of individual theories, data collected using a synchronous technique would therefore have been inadequate to address the research problems specified.

The specific research questions involved in the current study meant that a *diachronous technique had to be employed in the measurement of obsolescence*. There were inevitable problems associated with this, chiefly due to practical considerations. The problems encountered are documented throughout the book.

Models and Measures of Obsolescence

Having identified a technique for measuring literature obsolescence, it was necessary to develop a method for modelling the resultant obsolescence patterns. A number of previous studies have attempted to map the obsolescence of academic literature. These studies have concentrated largely upon the identification of those mathematical curves which best represent citation patterns over time.

Many studies have put forward the idea that citation patterns follow a *negative exponential* pattern. This pattern is characterised by published items receiving a large number of citations in the period immediately after they appear. There is then a rapid reduction in the number of citations they receive in the next few years, followed by a gradual decline to the point where they are virtually disregarded. The pattern of cumulative citations to the literature thus follows an exponential pattern. A number of writers have postulated the pertinence of the negative exponential for modelling citation patterns over time (Dequeiroz and Lancaster, 1981; Gupta, 1984; Wallace, 1986). These studies suggest that the exponential model offers both theoretical and empirical accuracy.

Early attempts to measure obsolescence employed the negative exponential model so widely that it became an assumption in most studies (Sandison, 1971). However, more recent research has called into question this acceptance of the negative exponential model (Sandison, 1983), and this scepticism has been supported by empirical evidence (e.g. Egghe and Rao, 1992). The main problem discovered with the negative exponential concerned its depiction of the early years after publication. A negative exponential has a maximum value in the immediate period after publication. However, this was found to offer an inaccurate depiction of citations to academic literature. Rather the pattern found by a number of writers was one of initial growth in citations, followed by a decline which approximated to an exponential (e.g. Avramescu, 1979; Griffith *et al*, 1979; Stinson and Lancaster, 1987).

Various studies have attempted to address the problems discovered in the application of exponential models of obsolescence. Some have attempted to modify their analysis, while retaining the exponential model in some form (e.g. Glänzel and Schoepflin, 1995). Other writers, such as Stinson and Lancaster (1987) have suggested that a negative exponential may still be employed provided that the years immediately after publication are removed from the analysis.

However, a number of writers have suggested alternative models for the measurement of obsolescence. The first of these is the *lognormal model*. This is a positively skewed distribution with an extended right hand tail (Cooper and Weekes, 1983). In the study of obsolescence, this model suggests an initial increase in the number of citations, followed by a more gradual decline. There remains a tail of citations lasting over an unspecified (theoretically infinite) time period. This model has been suggested by a number of writers (e.g. Heisey, 1988; Egghe and Rao, 1992; Matricciani, 1994). It is also supported informally by the depiction of citation patterns offered by Line and Sandison (1974). They suggest that there is an initial burst of citations, followed by a constant rate of citation at a low level. This could be regarded as analogous to the lognormal model.

The *logistic curve* has also been suggested for the measurement of obsolescence. This curve is used to depict *cumulative* citation rates. The logistic curve is characterised by a relatively slow growth rate at first, followed by a period of rapid increase. The rate of increase slows down until it approximates to zero. The logistic curve thus tends to infinity (Cooper and Weekes, 1983). As in the case of the lognormal curve, the application of the logistic curve is due in part to its empirical accuracy. Previous research has suggested that it offers an accurate depiction of citation patterns over time (Egghe, 1993).

The logistic curve is also of interest due to its apparent congruence with depictions of the growth of research fields. Crane (1972) employed logistic curves in order to depict disciplinary growth. Four distinct phases of growth can be identified using this model. During the initial stages of development a research field is characterised by a lack of organisation. Researchers operate in isolation, often unaware of similar research being undertaken elsewhere. As the results of the research are published, awareness increases and more researchers are attracted to the field (if it appears promising). This leads to a more formal exploration of the area, often with greater access to resources. At this time (the second stage in the model), early work in the field becomes regarded as paradigmatic, and is cited regularly. The third stage in the development of a field is entered as the major problems in the area are solved, such that the majority of remaining work represents elaboration of previous research. The growth rate of the field begins to decline, as financial support and the number of new researchers is reduced. Finally, interest in the field declines sharply as the potential for making significant new discoveries is perceived as minimal.

Crane's model of disciplinary growth has been employed in more recent research, notably by Gupta *et al* (1995). Logistic models have also been used to study issues in bibliometrics. Price (1963) suggested a logistic curve for the depiction of the growth of publications in a research field; while Dequeiroz and Lancaster's (1981) study suggests a similar pattern of growth in the citations within a research field.

A number of other models for the depiction of obsolescence have been suggested by empirical citation studies. Mathematical curves have been modelled upon the influence of research fields, based upon both simple and cumulative influence data. Simple data has been employed to map parabolas onto patterns of influence (Matricciani, 1994); while cumulative data has been employed to model patterns of influence using S-curves (Gupta *et al*, 1995) and power law curves (Egghe, 1993).

Selection of Models for Analysis

Two distributions were identified as possible models for the study of obsolescence within management literature. The first of these was the *parabola*. This was selected in order to test the pertinence of the contention of Gill and Whittle (1992) that the pattern of influence of management theories is broadly parabolic. More extensive analysis was implemented using *logistic curves*. The selection of this model was based upon two considerations. The first of these was the call for further empirical studies of citation patterns using logistic curves (Egghe and Rao, 1992). Secondly, the four periods in Crane's general model of disciplinary growth can be compared directly with Gill and Whittle's analysis of the four stages in the popularisation of management theories. This suggests that the logistic model may be most appropriate for the depiction of citation patterns within management research.

In employing logistic curves, two potential problems must be noted (Gupta *et al*, 1995). The first of these is that logistic curves cannot model a system which is growing very rapidly, since a field of this type will not be characterised by logistic growth patterns. This problem is noted, but is not regarded as problematic for the current research. As discussed earlier, management research can be defined as a social science which is, by its nature, applied. Both of these characteristics (i.e. management is both a *social* and an *applied* science) tend to reduce the rate at which the field develops (Gupta, 1984), suggesting that rapid growth is not likely to be encountered in the study of management research. The second problem is that logistic curves cannot be employed in any meaningful way until the inflection point in the curve has been reached. This problem is discussed at greater length in the implementation of the empirical study in this book.

Accounting for Literature Growth

The effect of disciplinary growth upon the rate of obsolescence was discussed earlier in this chapter. Disciplinary growth, and in particular the growth of the associated literature, also raises practical considerations for the measurement of obsolescence. Particular attention has been paid to the question of whether measures of obsolescence should be corrected for growth in the size of the literature. For example, if interest in a published item remains constant over time, but the size of the citing literature is growing constantly, citations to the item will theoretically grow at the same rate as the citing literature. This would therefore suggest that the item is becoming increasingly influential with time. In reality, the increased citations are a function of the growth in the citing literature. Observed obsolescence may therefore be regarded as a function of two factors - literature obsolescence and disciplinary growth.

The example above reveals the theoretical justification for the correction of citation data to account for changes in the size of the citing literature. The logic presented appears persuasive. However, caution must be applied since the example is purely theoretical. In particular, the example does not account for external influences, such as increases in the number of authors over time and changes in referencing practices.

The first of these has attracted particular interest. In response to Line's (1970) call for the correction of measures of obsolescence to account for literature growth, Brookes (1970) argued that the growth in the number of authors and the growth in the size of the literature would affect the rate of obsolescence in opposite directions. It was therefore unnecessary to correct measures of obsolescence. This argument was supported by Oliver (1971). The justification for this argument is that as the size of the citeable literature grows, the probability that a particular paper will be cited decreases, as all papers are 'competing' for the available citations. However, the growth in the number of authors increases the likelihood of a particular paper being located, thus cancelling out the effect of literature growth. This hypothesis has been attacked by a number of writers. Sandison (1971) argued that Brookes' hypothesis is not justified, a claim he repeated (Sandison, 1987) in response to Stinson and Lancaster's (1987) study of the subject. Brookes hypothesis does appear flawed logically, since the increase in the number of citeable items reduces the chance of each individual author locating a particular published item. This therefore offsets the influence of the increased number of authors offering citations.

The arguments outlined above are mainly concerned with theoretical issues. Advocates of the correction of obsolescence measurements for literature growth appear to dominate this theoretical debate. Whether this is due to the superior logic of their arguments, or the vehemence with which they introduce them (Sandison (1975) went as far as to state that referees should dismiss out of hand studies which did not account for literature growth) is unclear. However, it has meant that later studies have either accepted the need for correction without question (e.g. Dequeiroz and Lancaster, 1981) or have described Brookes' hypothesis as being 'not widely accepted' (Stinson and Lancaster, 1987).

Empirical evidence to support these conflicting arguments is relatively scarce. One study which attempted to rectify this was undertaken by Stinson and Lancaster (1987). Obsolescence was measured using synchronous and diachronous techniques, discounted in various ways. They found different results for synchronous and diachronous measurement techniques. In the synchronous case, there was found to be no requirement to correct for the growth in the literature, while in the diachronous case, correction was found to be necessary. Two aspects of this study may be of greater interest than the specific results. The first is that it offers further evidence that the results of synchronous and diachronous studies cannot be regarded as equivalent. The second point concerns the manner in which the requirement for correction was determined. In order to determine whether particular measurements needed to be corrected, a standard had to be identified against which they could be assessed. The standard selected was the rate of obsolescence calculated using the correction technique advocated by a leading author in the field (Line, 1974). The results of the other techniques were then compared with this standard. The selection of this standard is of great interest. It reveals that, to date, no method for identifying 'true' obsolescence has been developed. Rather, the accuracy of a particular technique is determined in relativistic terms by its convergence with the results of other approaches, particularly those advocated by leading authors in the field. It is therefore difficult to establish empirically the validity of the discounting technique employed in any study (including the current research).

Correction Technique Employed in this Study

As mentioned above, the approach to measuring obsolescence suggested by Line (1974) has been regarded as the standard by later writers. Line employed a diachronous technique, measuring the obsolescence rate using corrected data. The correction factor was the number of publications in the *Science Citation Index*. This technique was also employed by Egghe (1993). Heisey (1988) employed a similar approach in his study, although the correction factor he used was the number of papers within the immediate discipline, rather than the number published across all disciplines. The main problem with the latter approach is the definition of what constitutes the literature of a particular subject (Dequeiroz and Lancaster, 1981).

The current research employs a correction technique developed from that suggested by Line (1974). The use of Line's technique is justified in the first instance by the fact that the current study employs a similar diachronous technique for measuring obsolescence. Secondly, the reliance of management research upon other disciplines makes an approach based upon correction only for intra-disciplinary growth, such as that of Heisey (1988), inadequate for these purposes.

However, the correction technique employed by Line is modified, in an attempt to address two of the main problems facing studies of obsolescence (i.e. increases in the size of the literature, and changes in referencing practices). The method suggested by Line corrects for the growth of the published literature. It also accounts for the increased coverage of the *Science Citation Index*, which has been regarded as having an influence upon the measurement of obsolescence (Line and Sandison, 1974). However, it does not take account of the impact of changes in referencing practices over time. Line and Sandison (1974) argue that this is a major influence upon measurement in diachronous studies. This is supported by Sandison (1971) in his study concerning the probability of an item being cited. He offers a list of influences upon this probability, only two of which are defined as being measurable. These are the number of papers in which a citation can be made (which is covered in Line's approach to correction) and the average number of citations per paper (which is not covered). The issue of the number of citations per paper may be particularly important in management research. Studies of sociology (Line and Carter, 1974) and psychology (Xhignesse and Osgood, 1967) both revealed a pattern of increasing citations per paper over time. The position of these subjects as reference disciplines for management research (ESRC, 1994) may cause these changing referencing practices to be incorporated into the latter discipline.

The current research will not therefore follow Line by correcting the data by the number of published items in the *Social Science Citation Index* (which is more appropriate than the *Science Citation Index* for the current research). Rather the data will be corrected by the number of citations offered in the *Social Science Citation Index*. In this way, both the number of citing items, and the number of citations per item, are accounted for within the correction procedure.

Concluding Remarks

This chapter has reviewed previous research which has studied the issue of literature obsolescence. As a result of this review, it was possible to determine that a diachronous approach had to be employed for the measurement of obsolescence within management research literature. Relevant models of obsolescence were also evaluated, and two (parabolas and logistic curves) were selected as the basis for detailed empirical analysis. Finally, the issue of discounting citation data to account for literature growth was discussed. It appeared that the citation data for the current study may have to be discounted. A technique for discounting the citation data has therefore been developed.

Summary of Theoretical Framework for Study

The aim of this project is to develop a method of empirically identifying and analysing fashions in management research literature. Chapters 2, 3 and 4 outline the theoretical framework for the project. A method has been developed through which management fashions may be identified. This is based upon analysis of the patterns of influence associated with particular management ideas over time. In order to implement such a study, a technique for measuring influence is required. Citation analysis is to be employed for this purpose, using citations as a surrogate for the influence of published management literature. Problems associated with the use of citations for this purpose have been discussed in detail, and the pragmatic validity of citation analysis established. Techniques through which citations may be modelled over time have been reviewed, resulting in the identification of two models (parabolas and logistic curves) which can be employed in the study of the patterns of influence associated with management literature. These models will facilitate the identification and analysis of fashions in management literature.

Having developed the theoretical framework, it is now possible to implement the empirical analysis for this study. The manner in which the empirical analysis was implemented is outlined in the following chapters.

5 Constructing a Sample of Management Literature

Introduction

In order to implement the empirical analysis of management fashions, it was necessary to construct a sample of the published management literature. This chapter describes how this sample was constructed.

Two stages were involved in the sampling process. The first stage involved a pilot citation study based upon a small sub-set of management literature. The publications for this pilot study were selected using established sampling techniques drawn from existing bibliometric research. A number of problems were identified with this approach to sampling, primarily due to the different publishing traditions associated with scientific and social scientific disciplines. The sampling technique was therefore modified to account for the specific nature of social science literature.

A restriction upon the sample must be noted at this stage. The *Social Science Citation Index* classifies citations offered from 1956 onwards. As a result, records of the citations received by works published before 1956 are incomplete, and therefore cannot be accurately modelled. Hence, this study is restricted to management research literature published from 1956 onwards.

Pilot Study

Approach to Sampling for Pilot Study

In studying many disciplines, especially those with extensive literatures, it is unrealistic to include all published items within any study. A number of attempts have been made to address the problem of drawing representative samples from published literature in order to carry out bibliometric analyses. The attempts have concentrated chiefly upon the natural and physical sciences, since these fields have been the main focus of research within bibliometrics.

One characteristic of the scientific community is the extent to which it relies upon academic journals for the dissemination of research (Cronin, 1984). As a result of this, many of the citation studies undertaken concentrate upon the content of academic journals. This is caused partly by practical considerations. Focusing solely upon journal output offers one method for restricting the volume of literature for analysis. In scientific disciplines, it is assumed that this restriction can be applied without excluding a significant amount of literature that is central to the development of a discipline.

The concentration upon journal output has theoretical, as well as practical underpinnings. The journal is seen as the primary communication medium for scientific ideas, and it fulfils four main roles (Cronin, 1984). These are:

1. Provides a means of communicating with interested colleagues
2. Helps guarantee quality through the peer review system
3. Allows individual authors to demonstrate the originality and value of their thinking
4. Facilitates distribution of credit among the scientific community

The first attempt to draw a sample of management literature for the pilot study followed closely the sampling models applied in the study of natural and physical sciences. The sample was therefore constructed solely from articles in journals. This necessitated the selection of journal articles to include in the pilot study. This process involved three stages:

1. Defining those journals concerned with management issues
2. Selecting a set of journals from the list produced in (1) to include in the study
3. Selecting which articles to include in the pilot study from the journals identified in (2)

Identification of Management Journals The first stage in the sampling process was to define those journals primarily concerned with management research. This was achieved with reference to the *Social Sciences Citation Index (SSCI)*. Each year an index is published, supplementary to the *SSCI*, entitled the *Journal Citation Report (JCR)*. The *JCR* offers data on the citations offered and received by all journals in the *SSCI* list. It defines all journals included within it by discipline. Two of the disciplines defined are 'business' and 'management'. It was assumed that the most influential work within management research would be contained within these journals. The study was therefore limited to these journals.

The journal lists employed to construct a sample of management research journals were those in the 1988 *JCR*. The reason for the choice of this data set was to mirror as closely as a previous journal selection study (Pichappan, 1993). Within these lists, there were 50 journals classified within the category entitled business, and 35 journals classified as management. Twenty of these journals appeared in the lists for both business and management. The total number of journals under consideration for the construction of the sample was therefore 65.

Techniques for the Selection of Journals At this point in the sampling procedure, the relevant lists of business and management journals had been defined. Having achieved this, it was then necessary to select a sub-set of these journals to be included within the pilot study. A number of journal selection techniques were studied in order to aid this process. These are outlined below.

Various researchers have focused upon a single journal for their analysis. The journal is often selected because it is regarded as the most influential within a particular discipline. (Gupta, 1984; Westin *et al*, 1994; Chubin and Moitra, 1975). Single journals may also be selected due to their disciplinary positioning. Leydesdorff (1994) selected a single journal for analysis based upon its interdisciplinary position between physics and chemistry. The problem of single journal samples emerges from doubts as to whether the contents of a single journal can accurately reflect an entire discipline (Gottfredson and Garvey, 1980).

Researchers have also based their research upon samples drawn from a range of disciplinary journals. A number of methods have been adopted to select those journals to be included in these multiple journal samples. The first approach is to use journal lists constructed for previous research (Cooper *et al*, 1993; Johnson and Podsakoff, 1994; Doreian and Farraro, 1985). The employment of previously constructed samples has one major advantage - the samples have already been considered suitable by a reviewing process. The disadvantage lies in the assumption that a sample developed for the purposes of one study is necessarily applicable to a later work, which may be on a slightly different area. An uncritical acceptance of previous sampling techniques may also be problematic because any inaccuracies in previous research may be repeated in later work.

An alternative approach to journal selection is peer review, based upon surveys of academics within the relevant discipline (Lee and Evans, 1984; MacMillan and Stern, 1987; Doke and Luke, 1987; Gomez-Meija and Balkin,

1992). This approach has the advantage of being based upon the explicit opinions of researchers within a particular field. However, it may be problematic due to the expense and time of carrying out surveys of relevant academics. Another problem is highlighted by Extejt and Smith (1990), who found evidence to support the notion that scholars offer higher ratings to those journals in which they have published. Hence the peer review of journals may be inherently subjective to some degree.

The problems associated with the peer review process have led to the attempt to find more objective methods of assessing journal influence. One commonly employed approach to this issue has been based upon the use of citations to determine journal influence. Early studies in this area often selected a large body of journals from across a range of disciplines, and analysed the citations therein, in order to identify how often particular journals were cited (Raisig, 1960; Sandison, 1971; Garfield, 1972). The resultant measure offered a guide to the influence of a particular journal upon the entire scholarly research community. This measure is often defined as the 'impact factor' of the journal. The impact factor of each journal is included in the *Journal Citation Reports*. However, as Liebowitz and Palmer (1984) note, researchers tend to be more interested in the influence of a journal upon their immediate research field, rather than academic research in general. Alternative approaches have therefore been developed, which consider only citations from other journals in the immediate research field (Hirst, 1982; He and Pao, 1986; Doreian, 1988; Pichappan, 1993).

Journal Selection Technique Employed in Pilot Study For the purposes of the pilot study, a quantitative approach to journal ranking was employed. The technique chosen was that first suggested by Pichappan (1993), defined as the *Discipline-Contribution Score (DCS)*. This technique was selected as it reflects the relative merit of particular journals, based upon the citations that they receive from other journals within the same discipline. The ranking of journals is thus implemented without the intervention of external factors, specifically citations from journals outside the immediate research area.

The advantage of the employment of DCS scores is that journal ranking will be based on the citing behaviour of researchers in management research, who presumably have the greatest knowledge of the relative merits of management literature. However, it offers no analysis as to the relative impact of management research upon the wider academic community, since citations from outside the subject are excluded from the analysis.

In the calculation of the DCS scores for business and management journals, a number of problems were encountered regarding the measure proposed by Pichappan. These problems were associated primarily with low citation counts, which caused the DCS calculations to become unstable. This led to a modification in the equation used in the calculation of the DCS score (Thomas, 1995).

DCS scores were calculated for the business and management journals included in the 1988 *Journal Citation Reports* lists, using the modified DCS equation. The DCS scores of the most influential management journals are shown in Table 5.1.

Table 5.1 DCS scores of leading management journals

Journal Name	DCS Score	Rank
Journal of Consumer Research	29.16	1
Harvard Business Review	20.31	2
Journal of Marketing Research	20.18	3
Journal of Marketing	19.56	4
Academy of Management Review	19.29	5
Strategic Management Journal	19.17	6
Academy of Management Journal	10.95	7
California Management Review	10.07	8
Administrative Science Quarterly	9.75	9
Journal of Advertising Research	9.01	10

As discussed earlier, the purpose of the journal ranking procedure was to identify the leading management research journals, so that these journals could be included in the pilot study. The leading journal according to the DCS scores is the *Journal of Consumer Research*. This is a relatively specialised journal, concentrating upon a single aspect of management research. The highest ranked general management journal is Harvard *Business Review (HBR)*. This suggests that *HBR* has a strong influence on the immediate research area (in this case management). *HBR* was thus regarded as a suitable journal to include in the pilot study.

Selection of Articles for Pilot Study Having identified HBR as a leading management research journal, it was necessary to select which papers from HBR should form the 'seed publications' for the pilot study. In 1992 HBR published a book entitled '*Business Classics*'. This is a collection of the fifteen most influential papers published in the history of HBR (in the opinion of HBR's editorial board). By definition, this publication therefore contained the most influential papers published in the leading journal aimed at management researchers and practitioners. These fifteen papers were selected as seed publications for the pilot citation study.

It may have been beneficial at this stage to extend the sample to include articles published in journals other than *HBR*. However, such an extension was problematic for two reasons. The first of these was that *HBR* is the only one of the leading management journals which has been published throughout the period from 1956 onwards. The second problem was that no publication equivalent to *HBR's 'Business Classics'* could be located for journals such as *Administrative Science Quarterly* and the *Academy of Management Review*. The sample for the pilot study was thus based upon a single journal. Samples based on single journals may lead to a number of problems, as discussed earlier. However, given the exploratory nature of the pilot study, these problems were not regarded as critical to the overall project.

Results of Pilot Study

The pilot citation study was implemented based upon the fifteen articles in *HBR*'s '*Business Classics*'. Citations to these papers were collected from the *SSCI*. The number of citations received by these papers in the first ten years after their publication can be seen in Table 5.2. As shown in these results, a number of the papers in '*Business Classics*' received small numbers of citations. These numbers are, in many cases, too small to facilitate robust analysis.

Care must be taken in analysing the results of an empirical study based on such a small sample. However, the results of the pilot study suggested that the sampling frame employed at this stage may be inappropriate for the purposes of the research. The papers included in the pilot study were often relatively uninfluential, as reflected by the small numbers of citations that they received. Further investigations were thus undertaken to try to develop alternative methods of constructing samples of management literature. These methods had to produce samples which contained the most influential publications of management literature.

Table 5.2 Citations received by 'Business Classics' articles

Lead Author	Title	Year	Cites per year
Levitt T	Marketing Myopia	1975	2.8
Herzberg F	One More Time	1968	10.1
Katz R	Skills of an Effective Administrator	1974	3.5
Brouwer P	The Power to See Ourselves	1964	0.1
Rogers C	Barriers and Gateways to Communication	1952	0.8
Mayer D	What Makes a Good Salesman	1964	0.8
Drucker P	Managing for Business Effectiveness	1963	0.8
Nolan R	Computer Databases: The Future is Now	1973	2.7
Magee J	Decision Trees for Decision Making	1964	2.3
Livingstone J	Myth of the Well-Educated Manager	1971	3.2
Tannenbaum R	How to Choose a Leadership Pattern	1973	1.9
Fielden J	What Do You Mean I Can't Write	1964	0.2
Meyer H	Split Roles in Performance Appraisal	1965	10.1
Paul W	Job Enrichment Pays Off	1969	3.9
Blake R	Breakthrough in Organisational Development	1964	2.4

Problems Identified from Pilot Study

Detailed analysis of the pilot study revealed that many of the authors included in '*Business Classics*' had published work other than that in *HBR* which had been cited far more frequently. This may reflect the editorial policy of *HBR*. Leading management writers are often invited to write in *HBR*, offering a brief guide to their ideas. Future researchers may thus choose to cite the work in which the theories originally appeared (in much greater depth) rather than the *HBR* analysis.

Many of these highly cited source publications were found to be books. This reflects the importance of book publication in the social sciences (Bath University, 1980; Stahl *et al*, 1988). The approach to sampling therefore had to be modified, because *the importance of books in the dissemination of management research means that concentrating upon journals offers an incomplete picture of management literature.*

The sampling techniques suggested by previous researchers in their studies of scientific fields were thus found to be inappropriate for the study of management research. The lack of primacy of journals within social science disciplines compelled a modification of the sampling techniques employed within bibliometric studies of science. In particular a sampling frame was required which recognised the importance of *both* books and journals to the development of management research. A method therefore had to be developed which would identify the most influential works within management research, irrespective of their medium of publication.

Construction of Main Sample

The pilot study revealed that sampling techniques based solely upon journal publications may be inapplicable to the study of management literature. One aspect of the pilot study commanded particular attention. This was the manner in which highly cited published works could be located. As discussed earlier, it was discovered that the authors of papers in the pilot study had often published other works which were cited more frequently than those included in the pilot study. This serendipitous discovery resulted from the manner in which the main body of the *SSCI* is compiled. The *SSCI* is arranged alphabetically by cited author. The citations received by the works of a particular author in a given year are therefore located in a single section of the index, making it relatively simple to identify which work of a particular author has been cited most frequently. Hence, in locating highly cited publications, the critical process is the identification of which authors to examine.

The sampling method was therefore modified. The focus became the identification of *which management authors to include in the study*. If leading management authors could be identified, their most influential works could be isolated using the *SSCI*. By selecting the most influential works by leading management writers, whether journal articles or books, the sample should offer a more accurate depiction of leading management research literature.

In concentrating upon the academic author as the unit of analysis, this analysis builds upon the work of previous studies in similar fields. McCain (1984) implemented a bibliographic mapping of macroeconomics through the relationship between authors in that field; while Whittington (1992) used citation counts to study the influence of an individual author upon organisational theory. This approach has also been employed in the study of scientific disciplines. For example, Peters and van Raan's (1994) study of chemical engineering focused upon the output of leading researchers in that field.

Modified Approach to Sampling

In order to construct the new sample, a method was required which would identify leading management writers. The simplest, most effective way of achieving this was to refer to existing reviews of influential management theorists and management ideas. A number of writers have produced reviews of this type. The review selected in the first instance was '*Writers on Organizations*' by Derek Pugh and David Hickson. This review was selected for three reasons:

1. The review concentrates upon the contribution of particular authors, rather than individual papers or theories. This appeared to offer a relatively straightforward method of identifying leading management authors. Reviews concentrating upon management ideas, on the other hand, would only identify leading authors indirectly, through their association with particular management theories.

2. The *SSCI* is published in the USA, and concentrates mainly upon American journals. By employing a review written outside the USA (in the UK in this instance) it was hoped to counteract any potential bias within the citation index.

3. The selection of authors for inclusion in reviews is inevitably implemented retrospectively. As a result, reviews may concentrate upon authors who are influential at the point in time at which the review is published, at the expense of those authors whose influence was largely restricted to particular period in the past. They may also focus upon those authors whose work has remained influential over many years, rather than those authors whose influence was more transient. As outlined earlier, one of the main aims of the research was to study the possible existence of life cycles in the influence of management theories. Basing the sample upon a review written at a single point in time may underestimate the prevalence of life cycles by concentrating upon authors whose work has remained influential over many years.

Hence the most important reason for selecting '*Writers on Organizations*' as the initial basis for the sample for this project was that four editions of this review had been published (in 1964, 1971, 1983 and 1989). These four editions cover most of the period analysed in this book. The existence of these four editions reduced the problem of author selection being entirely retrospective. In each of the four editions of the review, the list of authors included in the review was modified. This occurred as the opinion of the reviewers changed regarding the influence of particular authors. The effect of this was to include in the sample those authors whose work may be more likely to be characterised by a life cycle pattern of influence (i.e. those authors whose work was no longer considered to be of central importance to management research when a particular edition of '*Writers on Organizations*' was published, having been defined as influential in an earlier edition).

Every author who appeared in at least one of the editions of '*Writers on Organizations*' was included in the sample. A number of authors from this list had to be excluded, since their work was published before 1956 (the beginning of the coverage of *SSCI*). A brief study of the citation patterns associated with the excluded authors was undertaken, in order to identify which of these authors could be regarded as being influential in the development of management theory. It was found that most the works published before 1956 received relatively few citations from 1956 onwards. This lack of citations may result from a relative lack of influence of a particular author's work upon the management research community. However, there may also cases where the published work was highly influential in the years following its publication, but this influence had receded by 1956.

There were four exceptions to the pattern of low citation rates to work published before 1956. These were the works published by Frederick Taylor, Max Weber, Chester Barnard, and the research emerging from the Hawthorne Studies (particularly that published by Roethlisberger and Dickson). These four authors (and research groups) may be regarded as being central to the development of management research. This is reflected in the continuing citation of their work many years after it was published. However, their work had to be excluded on methodological grounds. This must be acknowledged as a shortcoming in this study. It is a shortcoming which may apply to historical citation studies of many academic fields, particularly those without specialist published bibliographies.

Extension of Sample

The sample constructed from the four editions of '*Writers on Organizations*' was extended in two ways, as outlined below:

1. Many of the researchers discussed in '*Writers in Organizations*' have published work with co-authors. The work of each of these co-authors was included in the sample, with the intention of producing a more comprehensive sample of management authors. This two-stage approach to sampling is similar to that employed by Wallace (1986) in his study of scientific literature.

2. Problems may arise from basing the sample upon the editorial decisions of a single set of reviewers (i.e. those who compiled *'Writers on Organizations'*). The sample was therefore extended by incorporating other reviews of management literature. Two further reviews were included in the generation of the sample. The first of these (*'Classics of Organizational Theory'* (1979) by Jay Shafritz and P.H. Whitbeck) was selected because it concentrates upon the theoretical aspects of management research. The second review (*'Guide to the Management Gurus'* (1991) by Carol Kennedy) was chosen because its main concern is the impact of more populist writers upon management research and practice. These were identified by Stahl *et al* (1988) as two distinct aspects of management literature.

All authors appearing in these two reviews were included in the sample. Also included were all the co-authors who had published with these writers, thus replicating the sampling technique employed for the authors in *'Writers on Organizations'*. Unfortunately, only one edition of the two additional reviews exists. It was not therefore possible to overcome the problems of retrospective nature of these reviews. This limitation in the sampling frame must be noted.

Despite the slightly different focus of the three reviews, and the retrospective nature of the two reviews involved in the extension of the sample, the author lists included in each review shows a high degree of similarity. This suggests that there is broad agreement regarding the most influential authors in the development of management research. The final sample contained 81 distinct first authors.

Selection of Articles

Having identified the authors to be included in the study, the next issue that had to be addressed was which publications by these authors should be analysed. As discussed earlier, the purpose of the sampling procedure was to identify the most influential works of leading management authors. Ostensibly, the simplest approach to article selection would be to include all the source works listed in the *SSCI* for each selected author. This would, by definition, guarantee the inclusion of all influential work by those writers in the sample. However, such an approach may lead to a number of problems. The first is that it would involve the inclusion of publications which have had little influence upon management research. The lack of citations to these works may preclude meaningful analysis of their influence.

Inclusion of all works assigned to a particular author may also be problematic due to inaccurate referencing on the part of citing authors. Problems of incorrect citation are encountered within most citation studies (Franke *et al*, 1990). For example, during the implementation of this study, it was discovered that citing authors have assigned at least ten different second initials to James Thompson, who wrote '*Organizations in Action*', (the correct one being James D. Thompson). Other common errors involve: the misspelling of unusual surnames (such as Herzberg and Mintzberg); the allocation of publications to the incorrect lead author; and the assignation of incorrect publication years and journal volumes to cited works (Moed and Vriens, 1989). A single incorrect citation to an author's work is shown as a new source item in the citation index. Hence citations could be collected to a paper which has never been written.

A method was therefore required which would restrict the range of articles analysed for each author. The method employed involved two stages. The first stage was to include those publications defined in the reviews as suggested reading for each author. It was assumed that these works would offer a broad reflection of the most influential work published by a particular author. However, this method could not guarantee that all influential work by a particular author would be included in the sample.

A second stage was therefore added to the sampling procedure. The *SSCI* was studied in order to identify highly cited works which were not included in the reviews as suggested reading. 'Highly cited' was defined as an average of two citations per year over a period of five years at any point since the publication of the paper. This threshold was developed after preliminary analysis of the citation data. The threshold had the effect of removing incorrect citations from the analysis, and also publications which had little influence upon management research. All publications defined as highly cited were included in the sample.

Conclusion – How the Main Sample was Constructed

The procedure employed for the construction of a sample for the main empirical research involved two stages:

Stage 1 involved the identification of leading management authors. In order to identify such authors, three reviews of the development of management research were consulted. All authors appearing in one or more of these reviews were included in the sample, along with their co-authors.

Stage 2 was concerned with selecting which of the publications, written by the authors identified in Stage 1, should be included in the sample. All publications defined as 'highly cited' were included in the sample, as were the publications used as suggested reading by the reviews employed in Stage 1.

The final sample constructed using this approach contained 81 authors. The sample was restricted to the items published by these authors between 1956 (the first year covered by the *Social Science Citation Index*) and 1975. This period was chosen to ensure that sufficient data were available to support mathematical modelling of the citation patterns associated with each publication in the sample. *The sample contained 314 published works*. A list of these publications is shown in Appendix 1. This sample was considered to be large enough to facilitate meaningful analysis of the citation patterns associated with management research literature.

6 A Preliminary Analysis of Management Fashions

Introduction

From the discussion in Chapter 2, it emerged that fashions in management literature may be identified by the length of time over which they are influential. This is based upon the assumption that management literature which is subject to the pressures of fashion will have a shorter period of influence than literature which is free of such pressures. The purpose of this stage in the empirical analysis was therefore to identify those items of management literature which are characterised by a relatively short period of influence.

As discussed in Chapter 4, a number of mathematical models have been employed to determine the 'lifetime' of a particular piece of literature. Two of these models were regarded as particularly relevant to the study of management research literature. The first of these, the parabola, was selected for analysis because it has been identified by Gill and Whittle (1992) as representative of the pattern of influence of fashionable management ideas over time. This model was therefore employed for the preliminary empirical analysis, as outlined in this chapter. More detailed analysis was implemented using logistic curves. This analysis is detailed in Chapter 7.

Data Employed in Study of Life Cycles

A number of aspects of the sample employed in the preliminary analysis must be noted at this point. The first of these refers to the cases employed in the preliminary analysis. In order to limit the number of cases in the analysis, it was restricted to the 216 publications written by the authors covered by 'Writers on Organizations' between 1956 (the first year covered by the Social Science Citation Index) and 1975. Removing the authors in the other two reviews of management literature may raise problems regarding the validity of the preliminary analysis. However, the similarity of the author lists contained in all three reviews means that this problem should not be too damaging.

In order to generate meaningful models of citation patterns, there must be a reasonable amount of citation data available in each case. There is no method available to determine exactly what this amount of data should be. An arbitrary minimum figure of five years of data (in addition to the year of publication) was selected in the first instance. The number of citations received by the 216 cases in the preliminary study in the period 1956-80 was therefore collected from *Social Science Citation Index.*

A further aspect of the data employed in the preliminary analysis must be noted. This concerns the correction of citation data to account for changes in research fields. As discussed in Chapter 4, there is a continuing debate into whether citation data should be discounted to remove the influence of the growth in research fields, and also changes in referencing practices. A review of this debate led to the development of correction factor to be employed in the study of management research literature (see Chapter 4). However, this discounting factor was not employed at the outset of the preliminary analysis. This had the effect of revealing the influence of the discounting factor when it was introduced at a later stage in the analysis. Its pertinence to the current study could therefore be analysed.

Modelling Citation Patterns Using Parabolas

The use of parabolas to measure the longevity of the influence of published literature is based upon assertion that all published items have a 'life cycle' of influence associated with them. This applies to all articles, no matter how influential. The life cycles are simply of different lengths (the most influential articles may theoretically have life cycles of hundreds of years). Hence it can be argued that all citation patterns, even those which appear to be linear or exponential, are in reality simply part of a quadratic distribution.

Preliminary analysis was therefore undertaken into the accuracy of this assertion. A technique was developed for fitting parabolas to citation data. From these parabolas, the length of time over which an individual published item is influential could be calculated. The process through which this was achieved is explained below.

The equation for a quadratic curve is

$$y = ax^2 + bx + c$$

If we assume that no citations are received in the year of publication (i.e. $c = 0$) (see below for a discussion of this assumption)

Then $\qquad y = ax^2 + bx$

Therefore $\qquad ax^2 + bx = 0$ along the x axis

Hence $\qquad x(ax + b) = 0$

Hence $\qquad x = 0$
OR $\qquad\quad ax + b = 0$

At origin $x = 0$

At 2nd intercept $ax + b = 0$

Therefore at 2nd intercept $x = -b/a$

The value of this 2nd intercept therefore provides a prediction of the length of the life cycle for each article in the analysis.

Removal of the Constant Term

The equations outlined above rely upon the assumption that a published item will receive no citations in the first year after it appears. This assumption simplifies the calculations involved in fitting parabolas to the citation data. It also has practical underpinnings, since the presence of a constant may result in a negative first intercept. This is logically incongruous, since it suggests that an item was published before year 1 (the actual year of publication).

However, the removal of the constant term must be justified in both logical and empirical terms, since it has important implications for the measurement of the life cycles associated with particular published items. The logical justification for the assumption that a publication will not be cited in the first year after it is published is based upon the existence and influence of *publication lead times*. These refer to the time taken between the submission and publication of papers in academic journals. A number of factors may be involved in this time lag. There is a natural period of time associated with the publication process, due to requirements such as formatting and printing. However, the lead time is increased by the refereeing process, which is designed to guarantee the quality of the papers published by a particular journal. The refereeing process may involve the rewriting of submitted papers as a result of comments made by independent referees. This inevitably adds to the time which elapses between the original submission and eventual publication of a journal paper.

Publication lead times have an important influence upon measurements based on citations. They introduce a delay in the process through which researchers formally acknowledge the impact of previous research. A hypothetical example may be useful in highlighting this point.

Example A researcher reading a paper in a journal is influenced by its content, and decides to cite the earlier paper. The researcher then submits the citing work for publication in a journal. The mean publication lead time of this journal is one year. Thus, even if the citing author submits his/her work immediately after reading the earlier paper, on average the citing paper will not appear until one year later. Citations contained within any paper are classified by the year that the citing paper is published, not by the year it was originally submitted. In this example, therefore, the citation offered would be regarded as being to work which is one year old, though the acts of citation and submission had been virtually contemporaneous.

From the example above, it can be seen that papers published in a journal with a lead time of one year are most unlikely to cite papers which are less than one year old (unless the citations have been added at a later stage as a result of referees' comments). If a significant number of journals have a publication lead time of at least one year, this will dramatically reduce the number of citations received by any paper in the year that it is published. This represents the logical justification of the assumption that no citations would be received by items in the year in which they were published.

This assumption had also to be tested empirically. At first glance, the results of this empirical test were not encouraging. Out of the 216 cases contained in the sample, 93 had received citations in the year that they were published. This would appear to undermine the assumption upon which the calculation of parabolas was to be based. However, closer examination of the data suggested that this conclusion may be misguided. There are two reasons for this:

1. The number of citations received in the first year was negligible in the majority of cases.

2. Those citations that had been received were mainly to books, in the form of book reviews. These are included in the *SSCI*, but cannot be regarded as citations for the purposes of the current study.

The distortion of parabolas introduced by the assumption of no citations being received in the first year after publication should therefore be marginal in the majority of cases. Hence, it was possible to justify the method used to generate parabolas on the grounds of the simplicity of the calculations involved.

Fitting Parabolas to Citation Data

Having developed a method for calculating life cycles, parabolas were fitted to the citation patterns associated with all 216 cases in the sample. This was achieved using the *Statistical Package for the Social Sciences* (SPSS). The procedure employed was Curve Estimation. This procedure accepts as input the data being analysed by the user. The user is also required to specify the type of curve which is to be fitted to the data, and whether a constant term is to be included in the calculation. The curve estimation procedure then generates the closest fitting curve (of the type specified) to the data input.

Referring back to the equations outlined earlier, it can be seen that two values (a and b) are required in order to define a parabola. These values are returned by the curve estimation procedure (where they are labelled as b2 and b1). An example of the output of the curve estimation procedure for a single case is shown in Figure 6.1.

The output depicts the parabola fitted to the pattern of citations associated with '*New Patterns of Management*' by Rensis Likert, published in 1961 (VAR 171). From the graph, it can be seen that the parabola fitted to this data has a maximum turning point and a positive second intercept. This typifies the life cycle pattern suggested by Gill and Whittle (1992).

In order to calculate the length of the life cycle, the values for b1 and b2 were extracted, and the second intercept calculated. The calculations for this case are shown overleaf.

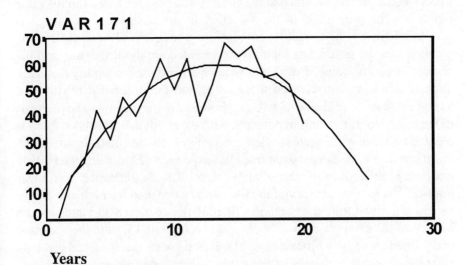

VAR171

Years

Figure 6.1 Parabola fitted to an individual case

Independent: Time

Dependent	Mth	Rsq	d.f.	F	Sig.	b1	b2
VAR171	QUA	.977	18	378.13	.000	8.8972	-.3314

Notes:
* Equation was estimated without the constant term; Rsq is redefined.
Dependent - published item whose citation pattern is being modelled
Mth - type of curve fitted (quadratic in this case)
Rsq - value of R^2
d.f. - degrees of freedom
Sig. - significance of F statistic

At the second intercept $x = -b/a$ (i.e. $x = -b1/b2$ using the SPSS notation)

$$b2 = -0.3314 \qquad b1 = 8.8972$$

Therefore $\qquad x = -8.8972 / -0.3314 = \underline{26.847 \text{ years}}$

In using this method, note must be taken of the R^2 and F values returned by SPSS when a parabola is fitted to the citation data for each case. The R^2 value represents the proportion of the variation in the observed figures that is accounted for by the model. It is therefore a measure of how closely the parabola fits the actual data input. Also provided are the F statistic, and the significance of its value. The significance represents the probability that there is no relationship between the fitted curve and the original data (the null hypothesis). A significance of $\leq .05$ (such as that in the example above) leads to the rejection of this null hypothesis, with the result that the curve fitted is regarded as being an accurate depiction of the citation data input. If the significance is $>.05$, the parabola fitted has to be regarded as being a relatively inaccurate reflection of the citation data. The significance has clear implications for the accuracy of the life cycles calculated for each case, since these are derived from the parabolas fitted to the citation data input. As can be seen in the example above, the R^2 value is high (0.977) and the accuracy of the fitted curve is significant ($p < .01$). This suggests that the fitted parabola offers an accurate depiction of the pattern of citations associated with this published item.

Parabolas with Minimum Points

The case above is characterised by a classic life cycle pattern of citation for an influential publication. There is an initial increase in the number of citations, followed by a period of citation at a relatively high rate. Finally, there appears to be a gradual decline in the number of citations offered to this published item. The parabola fitted to this citation pattern has a *maximum* point and a positive second intercept. This may therefore be regarded as the ideal case for the current research. Parabolas of this type were generated in 178 cases.

However, 38 cases were found to be inadmissible to the study of life cycles. This was due to the nature of the parabolas generated by the Curve Estimation procedure. These parabolas are characterised by a *minimum* point, as shown in Figure 6.2.

The graph in Figure 6.2 represents the parabola fitted to the pattern of citations received by '*Strategy and Structure*' by Alfred Chandler, published in 1962 (VAR 57). This parabola has a minimum point, and may be described as 'bowl' shaped. As can be seen in the calculations, when the life cycle is calculated for this case, the second intercept is negative, and therefore meaningless in the context of the current study.

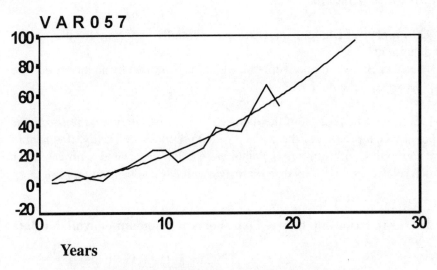

Years

Figure 6.2 Example of parabola with a minimum point

Independent: Time

*

Dependent	Mth	Rsq	d.f.	F	Sig.	b1	b2
VAR057	QUA	.964	17	225.76	.000	.6216	.1299

Notes:
*Equation was estimated without the constant term; Rsq is redefined.

At second intercept $x = -b1 / b2$

$b2 = 0.1299$ $b1 = 0.6216$

Therefore $x = -0.6216 / 0.1299 = \underline{-4.875 \text{ years}}$

Parabolas with minimum points may also result in positive second intercept. This occurs where the value of b2 is positive and the value of b1 is negative. Cases that are characterised by a parabola with a minimum point are inapplicable to the study of life cycles. The common feature of these parabolas is the positive value of b2 generated by the Curve Estimation procedure.

There are two possible reasons why a parabola with a minimum point may be fitted to the citation data:

1. The number of citations increases exponentially over time for the sample of data input.
2. There is a pattern of relatively stable citation, followed by an increase in the final year(s) of the data set.

A preliminary inspection of the data suggested that citation patterns of this type may be a product of the amount of data input. Specifically, it appeared that parabolas with minimum points were often associated with cases for which relatively few years data were available, as can be seen in Table 6.1.

Table 6.1 Relationship between parabolas and amount of available data

| | | Years of Data Available | | |
		< 10 Yrs	≥ 10 Yrs	TOTAL
Type of Turning Point	Maximum	46	132	178
	Minimum	23	15	38
	TOTAL	69	147	216

A chi-square test was run in order to determine whether there was a significant relationship between the amount of data included in the model, and the shape of the parabola generated. The models were divided into those based upon data from less than ten years, and those for which at least ten years of data were available. This point of segregation was selected after a preliminary inspection of the data, although it remains somewhat arbitrary. It was found that cases for which less than ten years of data were available were significantly more likely to result in the generation of a parabola with a minimum point ($\chi^2 = 17.32$; $p < 0.01$). A Yate's Correction was considered in order to modify the chi-square statistic, since the significance of chi-square tests may be overemphasised in 2x2 contingency tables, particularly when employing small samples. However, given the sample size, such a correction was unnecessary (Walpole, 1974). As a result of the chi-square test, the analysis was restricted to those cases for which at least 10 years of data were available. This reduced the size of the sample to 147 cases.

Smoothing the Citation Data

Having increased the minimum amount of data included in the modelling process, a further test had to be implemented to evaluate the stability of the parabolas generated. Particular attention was paid to the extent to which data from a single year could influence the value of the life cycle calculated. If the technique is robust, then a single piece of data should not affect too greatly the life cycle values calculated. This test involved a small sample of articles from the complete data set. Citation data were removed on a year-by-year basis, and the life cycles were then recalculated. When this test was carried out, the life cycle values were found to be unstable, with wide variations caused by the removal of data. An example of this instability is shown for a single case in Table 6.2. This case is a renowned article on job enrichment published in the 1968 *Harvard Business Review* by Frederick Herzberg (VAR 134).

The row highlighted in bold type reveals the effect of a single unusual data item. In this example, the receipt of 24 citations in a single year (almost double the number in any other year) increases the life cycle calculated by a factor of six. Clearly, instability of this type calls into question the robustness of the life cycles calculated. It thus appeared that a form of smoothing must be applied to the data in order to remove the instability caused by a single extreme data item.

Two approaches to this smoothing process were attempted. The first smoothing technique employed was *moving averages.* Centred moving averages were calculated with a span of 1. Hence the citation rate for a particular publication in a given year was calculated based upon the mean of the number of citations received in that year, the previous year and the following year. Life cycles were calculated on the basis of the new values generated.

There are three disadvantages associated with the employment of moving averages (Owen and Jones, 1990). The first two of these are the difficulty of selecting a suitable span for the calculations, and the loss of data for the first and last years in the sample. The most important disadvantage in terms of the current study is that the only data values which influence the moving average calculation are those within the span selected. The remainder of the data set has no influence upon the calculations, with the result that an overall trend in the data is more difficult to identify.

Table 6.2 Effect of removal of data upon life cycles calculated

YEARS OF DATA INCLUDED	FINAL YEAR INCLUDED	NO. OF CITATIONS IN FINAL YEAR	LIFE CYCLE CALCULATED
12	1980	7	15.77
11	1979	12	16.39
10	1978	13	15.96
9	1977	13	15.40
8	1976	9	15.37
7	1975	24	92.85
6	1974	12	11.12
5	1973	10	9.58
4	1972	12	11.16
3	1971	6	10.86

An alternative smoothing technique, *exponential smoothing*, was also employed in order to smooth the data. This process calculates an influence value for a given year based both upon the number of citations in the year being studied, and the citation rate in all previous years. The equation for exponential smoothing is shown below.

$$e_t = (\alpha * x_t) + (1 - \alpha)(e_{t-1})$$

where
e_t = value calculated by exponential smoothing for year being studied
α = smoothing coefficient
x_t = number of citations in year being studied
e_{t-1} = value in previous year (after smoothing)

As can be seen from the equation above, the weight given to the value in the current year depends on the value of alpha (α) included in the equation. Higher values of alpha will result in greater weight being accorded to individual data values. Lower values of alpha mean that greater weight is placed upon the overall trend, which is the product of earlier values. Three common values for alpha, 0.1, 0.25 and 0.5 were considered. In the first instance, an alpha value of 0.25 was employed. The Curve Estimation procedure was re-run with these smoothed values. The effect of this process on a single item can be seen in Table 5.3, which again represents the 1968 *Harvard Business Review* article by Frederick Herzberg (VAR 134). The row highlighted in bold type reveals the effect of the smoothing process. Smoothing the data results in the removal of the influence of a single extreme data item, such that the life cycles calculated are stabilised.

Table 6.3 Effect of exponential smoothing upon life cycles

YEARS OF DATA INCLUDED	NO. OF CITATIONS IN FINAL YEAR	ORIGINAL LIFE CYCLE	LIFE CYCLE (EXPO. SMOOTHED DATA $(\alpha = 0.25)$)
12	7	15.77	19.14
11	12	16.39	18.11
10	13	15.96	16.86
9	13	15.40	15.47
8	9	15.37	13.83
7	24	92.85	10.84
6	12	11.12	9.39
5	10	9.58	8.05
4	12	11.16	6.56
3	6	10.86	5.20

A further issue emerged from the smoothing process. It can be seen that the life cycle calculated increases as the amount of data is augmented. A Pearson Product Moment Correlation Coefficient was therefore calculated to examine the relationship between the amount of data included in the generation of models and the life cycles calculated. This was implemented for all cases for which a parabola with a maximum point had been generated. A positive correlation ($r = 0.4121$; $p < 0.01$) was discovered between these two factors. This suggests that care must be taken when comparing life cycles generated using different amounts of data.

Parabolas had therefore been generated based upon data smoothed using both moving averages and exponential smoothing. The shape of these parabolas was then tested, in order to analyse their applicability to the calculation of life cycles. The results of this analysis can be seen in Table 6.4.

The table reveals that the number of cases for which parabolas with minimum points (i.e. inapplicable cases) were generated actually increased when the data were smoothed using moving averages. When exponential smoothing was applied to the data, the number of inapplicable cases fell, suggesting that this technique may of greater use to the current study.

The ten cases for which exponentially smoothed data produced inapplicable parabolas were considered individually. These included a number of items which may be regarded as problem cases. Out of the ten cases, nine had also produced parabolas with minimum points when smoothed using moving averages; and seven cases were among those for which parabolas had been inapplicable based upon the original data. A smoothing coefficient of 0.1 was attempted with these cases, with the purpose of increasing the stability of the models generated. The result of this was that parabolas with maximum turning points were generated for each of these ten cases.

Table 6.4 Effect of smoothing upon shape of parabolas generated

		Original Data	Data Employed Moving Ave. (Span = 1)	Expo. Smoothed ($\alpha = 0.25$)
Type of				
Turning	Maximum	132	130	137
Point	Minimum	15	17	10
	TOTAL	147	147	147

However, there was a major disadvantage with the employment of such a low smoothing coefficient. The lack of weight placed upon individual data values meant that the life cycles generated for different cases were very similar. This reduced the potential analytical value of the models generated. Out of the approaches attempted, the one which offered the most useful results was thus to smooth the citation data using exponential smoothing with an alpha coefficient of 0.25.

Robustness of Models Generated

The analysis to this point tested the parabolas generated by the Curve Estimation procedure, and revealed that raw citation data may be too volatile for the development of accurate models. However, once smoothed, stable parabolas could be fitted in the majority of cases. A more stringent test of the applicability of parabolas had to be implemented at this stage. This concerned the *turning points* of the parabolas generated. This issue had far-reaching implications for the precision of the parabolas fitted, and therefore the accuracy of the life cycles calculated.

In order to define a parabola, it is necessary to possess knowledge of its turning point. If this point is unknown, it is impossible to define the parabola with any accuracy, with the result that the prediction of the second intercept cannot be regarded as robust. In fitting parabolas to the citation data, it is essential that the data should cover sufficient years to extend beyond this turning point.

The turning point of a parabola can be defined through differentiation:

Equation of parabola	$y = ax^2 + bx$ (assuming $c = 0$)
Therefore	$dy/dx = 2ax + b$
At turning point	$dy/dx = 0$
Therefore	$2ax + b = 0$
	$2ax = -b$
	$x = -b/2a$

The turning point can therefore be defined as $-b/2a$. Referring back to the original calculations regarding the fitting of parabolas, it can be seen that the x co-ordinate of the turning point is half that of the second intercept. This is a product of the symmetry of quadratic curves. Hence, if the life cycle calculated for a particular case is more than double the number of years of data included in the model, the turning point may be unknown.

The cases for which parabolas with maximum points were generated (using citation data which had been exponentially smoothed) were thus analysed further. This analysis revealed that the turning point may be unknown in twenty of these cases. The life cycles calculated in these cases could not therefore be regarded as accurate. When added to the ten cases for which parabolas with minimum points were generated, this meant that life cycles could not be accurately calculated for at least one fifth of the sample. This necessitated a modification of the data employed in the analysis.

Changes to the Data Employed in Fitting Parabolas

The lack of a definable turning point in the available data occurs mainly in cases where the citation pattern suggests a continuing rise in the influence of a published item. In these cases, the calculation of when the influence of an item will start to wane is based solely upon conjecture. Two possible causes of such a pattern of influence may be identified.

The first cause is a lack of data included in the modelling procedure. This means that the model is based upon citations from the years immediately after the publication of a particular item. The life cycle model suggests that these years are likely to be characterised by a pattern of increasing citation.

The problem of generating models from relatively few years of data was discussed earlier. This discussion led to an increase (from five to ten) in the minimum number of years of data which could form the basis of a model. As a result of this increase, the number of parabolas generated with minimum turning points was reduced. However, the increase in the amount of data included was found to be insufficient to address the problems associated with the lack of definitive knowledge of turning points.

The minimum amount of data from which a model could be generated was thus increased again, to twenty years. Such an increase was problematic, given that citation data for the preliminary empirical analysis had originally covered the period 1956-1980. As a result, the only cases for which twenty years of data were available were those published in the period 1956-1960. This was regarded as too narrow a sample to facilitate meaningful analysis. It was therefore necessary to collect additional citation data before continuing the empirical analysis. Citation data for those authors appearing in *'Writers on Organizations'* were thus collected for the period covering 1980-1995.

Discounting the Citation Data

The increase in the rate of citation over time may have an alternative explanation. As discussed in Chapter 4, one of the major problems associated with the measurement of citations over time is the increasing size of the published literature. It has been suggested that increases in the citation rate over time may be a function of the growth in the size of the published literature (Line and Sandison, 1974). In Chapter 4, a correction factor was developed in order to address this issue for the case of management research. This involved discounting the number of citations in a given year by the total number of citations contained in the *Social Science Citation Index*. The exponentially smoothed citation data employed earlier in the preliminary empirical analysis was therefore *discounted* to account for the growth in the literature over the period studied.

Having discounted the citation data, the Curve Estimation procedure was then implemented upon the resultant data set. Life cycles were again calculated for each case based upon the parabolas generated. As a result of the discounting process, citation patterns become more accessible to analysis using parabolas. A linear pattern of citations is transformed into a more parabolic form after the citation data has been discounted. This is because the main effect of the discounting process is to give greater weight to the citations offered in the early years after publication, at the expense of citations offered in later years.

When the parabolas based upon discounted data were analysed, it was found that the Curve Estimation procedure had generated parabolas with maximum turning points for *all* 216 cases in the sample. Hence, the shape of the parabolas was not problematic. Further analysis was undertaken regarding the number of cases in which the turning points could be defined (rather than predicted). It was found that out of 216 cases, only five had insufficient data to define the turning point of the parabola fitted to their pattern of citations. This was regarded as evidence to justify the employment of the correction factor when analysing citation data.

In the earlier analysis of life cycles calculated using exponentially smoothed data, a significant positive correlation ($r = 0.4121$; $p < 0.01$) was discovered between the amount of citation data included for each case, and the life cycles calculated. A similar test was implemented with the data which had been both smoothed and discounted. A strong positive correlation ($r = 0.7546$; $p < 0.01$) was again discovered between the amount of data included in the fitting of parabolas, and the life cycles calculated. This reinforces the need to employ the same amount of data across cases in order to make life cycles comparable.

Concluding Remarks

The preliminary empirical analysis studied one method for measuring the influence of management research literature over time. This method was based upon the parabolas generated by the Curve Estimation procedure in SPSS. A number of problems were identified with the use of parabolas for this purpose. These problems were mainly practical in nature. Hence, they do not necessarily invalidate the contention of Gill and Whittle (1992) regarding the validity of parabolas for mapping the influence of management ideas. Rather, they highlight some of the practical difficulties associated with empirical analysis of this type.

An alternative approach to the calculation of life cycles was therefore developed. There were two reasons for this. The first reason was based upon the problems encountered in the preliminary analysis, which arose chiefly as a result of the inherent sensitivity and instability of the parabolas generated by the Curve Estimation procedure. As a consequence of this instability, it was necessary to modify the original citation data in a number of ways in order to generate meaningful models of citation patterns over time. Various manipulations of the data were implemented, including smoothing and discounting. With this type of manipulation, there is always a danger that the meaning of the original data is distorted. A more robust model was therefore desirable, in order that fewer modifications would have to be made to the data.

The parabola was also regarded as insufficient for the purposes of this research since it reflects only one aspect of the influence of management literature. Parabolas facilitate analysis of the length of time over which a particular idea is influential. As discussed in Chapter 4, this measure may be used to identify management fashions. However, this measure in itself may be insufficient for the purposes of the current project. It is essential to discriminate between those management ideas which are highly influential for a short period, and those whose influence is short lived and negligible. The former represents a management fashion, while the latter is simply indicative of research which is of little influence. Similarly, a distinction must be made between highly cited items which have a long life cycle, and those items which are cited over a long period, but at a relatively low rate. The former may represent seminal management works, while the latter are of marginal, albeit continuing, interest to later researchers.

In order to achieve this delineation, it was necessary to include a measurement of the level of influence of a published item. This offers a guide as to the impact of a given idea upon the management research community.

The parabolas developed do not offer such a measure.

A more useful model would be one that incorporates both the life cycle and the level of influence of a published item. The *logistic model* may facilitate analysis of both of these aspects of the influence of management literature over time. This model also offers a more robust platform for data analysis, since it is based upon cumulative rather than simple citation data (as discussed in the following chapter).

The preliminary study raised three issues which had to be addressed by the main body of empirical analysis. These are outlined below.

1. *Stability of Models* - as discussed earlier, the main problem encountered in the preliminary analysis was the lack of stability associated with the models generated. This led to a number of modifications of the citation data. Emergent from this analysis was the necessity for the models generated for each case in the sample to be both stable and robust. This issue is addressed in depth in the following chapter.

2. *Amount of Data Included* - the issue of the amount of data to include in the generation of models proved to be problematic, leading to the employment of three different minimum data thresholds during the preliminary analysis. This highlights the problem of identifying a suitable time frame upon which to base analysis, since the competing requirements of stability of models and the size of the sample must be reconciled. One important point to emerge from the preliminary analysis was that stable models could not be generated on the basis of citation data from a small number of years.

A second issue had to be addressed concerning the amount of data included in the generation of models. As discussed earlier, it was discovered that there was a strong positive correlation between the amount of data upon which models were based, and the life cycles calculated from these models. Life cycles based upon different amounts of data cannot therefore be directly compared. The following chapter details the techniques employed to overcome this problem.

3. *Discounting of Citation Data* - in the early stages of the preliminary analysis, the citation data employed had not been corrected to account for the growth in the amount of published management literature. This was a conscious decision, since it facilitated analysis of the effect of the discounting factor once it was introduced. The analysis revealed that discounted citation data could be employed to greater effect in the modelling of the influence of

management literature than citation data which had not been corrected.

The results of this preliminary study were not included in the final empirical analysis. However, the significance of the preliminary work must be recognised, due to the issues it raises. These issues were to be of central importance to the main empirical analysis, as highlighted in the following chapter.

7 The Empirical Identification of Management Fashions

Introduction

As discussed in Chapter 4, various mathematical curves have been fitted to citation data by previous writers in order to measure the length of time over which a particular published item is influential. In the context of this study, these curves were regarded as a method through which management fashions may be identified. In the preliminary empirical analysis, the applicability of the parabola for this purpose was tested. The parabola was selected due to the assertion of Gill and Whittle (1992) that it offered an accurate depiction of the influence of management ideas over time. However, a number of problems were identified with the employment of parabolas for modelling citation patterns, as outlined in the concluding remarks of the previous chapter. Alternative modelling techniques therefore had to be considered. Particular attention was paid to the potential application of logistic curves.

The review in Chapter 4 revealed that logistic curves have been employed to depict the cumulative growth in the number of publications within a research field (Price, 1963), and also the number of citations within a field (Dequerioz and Lancaster, 1981). The application of logistic curves for this purpose is due, in part, to their empirical accuracy. A number of writers have suggested that they offer an accurate depiction of citation patterns over time (e.g. Egghe, 1993; Matricciani, 1994). Logistic curves are also of interest due to their apparent congruence with depictions of the growth of research fields. Crane (1972) employed logistic curves in order to depict disciplinary growth, and identified four distinct phases in this growth: isolated research; formal exploration; problem solving and elaboration; saturation.

The four stages of disciplinary growth may be linked directly with four periods of growth in the number of publications and citations (initial growth; rapid growth; slowing growth; saturation) within a research field. These periods of growth are reflected in the shape of the logistic curve shown in the graph overleaf. In turn, these four stages can be equated with the stages associated with the parabolic models of management fashions suggested by Gill and Whittle (1992). This highlights the common properties of the parabolic and logistic curves, since both offer similar depictions of the nature of influence over time. However, while parabolas concentrate upon simple values of influence for each year, logistic curves measure influence cumulatively. This has the effect of increasing the stability of logistic curves, since individual data items are considered in terms of the rest of the data set, rather than individually. Extreme values should not therefore influence the curves generated significantly.

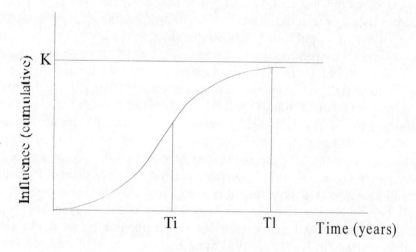

Figure 7.1 Shape of the logistic curve
Tl = Life Cycle
K = Upper Bound
Ti = Point of Inflection

Logistic curves were therefore employed in this analysis to map the cumulative influence of management literature over time. The purpose of this process was to identify those items of management literature which may be subject to pressures of fashion, through analysis of the patterns of influence and longevity associated with them.

Three important characteristics of the logistic curve are marked on Figure 7.1 above. The first of these is the *point of inflection* (Ti). Knowledge of the point of inflection is central to the generation of meaningful and accurate logistic models. This may be regarded as analogous to the necessity of being able to define the turning point of parabolas (see previous chapter). The issues concerned with the identification of inflection points are discussed in greater depth in the empirical work in this chapter. The second important characteristic of the logistic curve is the concept of the *upper bound* (or limiting value). This represents the hypothetical total influence of a given published item (K). The value of this upper bound is predicted rather than known. It is based upon both the level of influence suggested by the citation data, and also the rate of growth in this influence. The final aspect marked is the hypothetical *life cycle* (Tl). This represents the time taken for a particular published item to become relatively disregarded, with the result that its cumulative influence is saturated.

The values of the upper bound and the life cycle may be regarded as measures of the influence and longevity of individual items of published management literature. Analysis of the combination of these characteristics may facilitate the identification of management fashions. *Particular attention was paid to those published items characterised by a high level of influence over a relatively short period of time, since they may be subject to the pressures of fashion.*

Fitting Logistic Curves to Citation Data

Logistic curves were fitted to all 314 cases in the full data set. The citation data employed in this process were discounted by the growth in the number of citations included in the *Social Science Citation Index* in order to account for the increasing size of the published literature. The need for this discounting process was established as a result of the preliminary empirical analysis.

The first technique considered for fitting logistic curves was the Curve Estimation procedure in *SPSS*. This procedure offers a platform for modelling logistic curves. However, in order to generate logistic curves, the user must input the limiting value for the curve (i.e. the upper bound). However, in the context of this analysis, the upper bound was not regarded as a given value, but rather as a predicted value which had to be calculated. This precluded the use of the Curve Estimation procedure.

A method of fitting logistic curves manually thus had to be developed. The method selected was derived from the general form of the logistic curve. The general equation of the logistic curve is shown below.

$$P_t = k \quad \rightarrow \quad \frac{k}{1 + \exp[a - b_t]} \qquad (\text{as } t \rightarrow \infty)$$

where

P_t = cumulative influence at time t
k = upper bound (saturation point)
a,b = parameters of the model

As can be seen from this equation there are three unknown parameters (a, b, and k) in this equation. The values of these parameters must be calculated in order to define the logistic curve for a given set of citation data.

There are a number of ways in which the values of these parameters may be calculated. The method selected was the three point fit technique advocated by Leach (1981). In order to implement this technique, the cumulative influence in three equidistant years must be calculated. These values (defined as P_x, $P_{x+\delta}$, $P_x + 2\delta$) are entered as the data upon which the logistic curve is to be generated. The value of x determines the position of the first data item, while the value of delta (δ) denotes the number of years between the data items selected. In selecting these points, one important consideration must be taken into account. This is the *requirement that at least one point must lie before the point of inflection (i.e. point P_x) and one point must lie after the point of inflection (i.e. point $P_{x+2\delta}$*.

Substituting the three values into the equation above, three equations are generated, one for each point on the logistic curve. These equations are shown below

$$1. \qquad P_x \quad = \quad \frac{k}{1 + \exp[a - bx]}$$

$$2. \qquad P_{x+\delta} \quad = \quad \frac{k}{1 + \exp[a - b(x+\delta)]}$$

$$3. \qquad P_{x+2\delta} \quad = \quad \frac{k}{1 + \exp[a - b(x+2\delta)]}$$

We therefore have three equations, and three unknown parameters. The solution to these equations is

$$k = \frac{2(P_x\ P_{x+\delta}\ P_{x+2\delta}) - P^2{}_{x+\delta}(P_x + P_x + 2\delta)}{P_x\ P_{x+2\delta} - P^2{}_{x+\delta}}$$

$$b = \frac{1}{\delta}\ \log[\,P_{x+\delta}(k - P_x)\ /\ P_x\ (k - P_{x+\delta})]$$

$$a = \log[\,(k - P_x)/\ P_x\,]$$

The value of the parameter k represents the upper bound of the logistic curve. The discussion at the start of this chapter defined this upper bound as the predicted total cumulative influence of a particular case. It can therefore be established that *the value of the upper bound (k) may be regarded as a measure of the total influence of an individual published item.*

A measure also had to be developed regarding the longevity of published items. This was also derived from the logistic curve. The most obvious measure of longevity is the time taken to reach the upper bound (i.e. the point at which the influence has reached saturation). However, this point is theoretically infinite, thus invalidating this approach. It is also logically incongruent to define the point at which absolute saturation has been reached, since it is impossible to specify with any certainty a point beyond which no citations will be received by a particular published item. This lack of a perfectly definable life cycle is a product of the employment of a diachronous approach to the study of life cycles (see Chapter 4 for a more detailed discussion of this issue).

An alternative approach was therefore employed. Although a definitive life cycle cannot be established, it is possible to derive the time taken for the logistic curve to reach a given percentage of the upper bound. For example, the time taken to reach 90%, 95% or 99% of the total influence may be derived. These were regarded as suitable measures of the life cycle, since it is not logically possible to predict absolute longevity. The manner in which life cycles were calculated is shown below, using the example of the time taken to reach 99% of total influence:

$$P_t = \frac{k}{1 + \exp[a - bt]}$$

When 99% of cumulative influence has been reached, the value of $P_t = 0.99k$

Therefore $\quad\quad\quad 0.99k \quad\quad = \quad\quad \dfrac{k}{1 + \exp[a - bt_{99}]}$

Cancelling k from equation we get

$$1 + \exp[a - bt_{99}] \quad = \quad \dfrac{1}{0.99}$$

$$\exp[a - bt_{99}] \quad = \quad \dfrac{0.01}{0.99}$$

$$a - bt_{99} = \log(0.01 / 0.99)$$

$$bt_{99} - a = \log(0.99 / 0.01)$$

$$t_{99} \quad = \quad \dfrac{a + \log(0.99 / 0.01)}{b}$$

$$t_{99} \quad = \quad \dfrac{a + \log(99)}{b}$$

Following the same process, it may be inferred that the time taken to reach 90% of total influence is given by the equation.

$$t_{90} \quad = \quad \dfrac{a + \log(9)}{b}$$

and the time taken to reach 95% of total influence is

$$t_{95} \quad = \quad \dfrac{a + \log(19)}{b}$$

For the purposes of the current research, *the longevity of a particular published item was calculated on the basis of the time taken to reach 99% of its total influence.* This option was selected, rather than 90% or 95%, because it was regarded as offering the most 'accurate' reflection of the life cycle (clearly, accuracy is difficult to define, since the actual life cycle is theoretically infinite).

Selection of Data for Curve Fitting

The three point fit technique thus facilitated analysis of the total influence of a particular published item, and also the length of time over which it is influential. Measurement of these two variables may in turn make possible the identification of fashions in management literature. However, two issues had to be addressed before logistic curves could be fitted to the citation data. These issues concerned the processes through which the values in the three point fit technique are selected.

Selection of the First Data Item

The selection of data for the three point fit technique is based upon two factors - the position of the first data item (x), and the time periods between the three data items (δ). Hence, the first issue that had to be addressed was the selection of which data item should be employed as the first year in the model. As discussed earlier, the first point must lie before the point of inflection in order to generate accurate logistic models. This suggests that the first year chosen should be as early as possible. The first option considered was therefore to employ the year of publication as the first data value in the model. However, as discussed in the previous chapter, the number of citations received in the year of publication was negligible in many cases. This approach was thus unsuitable.

Logistic curves were therefore fitted using $x = 2$ (i.e. the first data value was the cumulative influence of an item two years after its publication). A number of problems were identified with taking the first data value from the second year after publication. The first problem is derived from the equation of the logistic curve. If the first point chosen is soon after the date of publication, there may have been no citations received up to this point. This will invalidate the calculations, since it will involve division by zero (since the value of P_X will be zero - see equations). This happened in 14 cases. An additional problem was introduced with regard to the predictive aspect of logistic curves. It has been established that the upper bound represents the theoretical total influence of a particular item. The value of this upper bound is influenced by two factors. The first of these is the cumulative influence, as measured by the final value in the model ($P_{x+2\delta}$). The second factor in the calculation of the upper bound is the slope of the curve after the final data value. Clearly, the steeper this curve, the higher the upper bound calculated.

The issue of the slope of the logistic curve is of particular interest here. Logistic curves are *symmetrical around their inflection points*. This means that the slope of the tails at each end of the curves is equivalent. If a very early year is chosen as the first value for the model, the number of citations received by this point will tend to be relatively low. Hence the slope of the first part of the curve will be low. As a result of this, the slope of the final section of the logistic curve will also be reduced in order to maintain the symmetry. The predicted value of the upper bound will thus be reduced, and may be little higher than the value of the final data item. This would suggest that the published item had no influence after the final year for which data was input, an assertion which cannot be supported logically.

It was hoped that the employment of a later year as the first data item would solve the problems associated with the test above. A second attempt at fitting logistic curves was thus undertaken, employing year five as the first data item (i.e. $x = 5$). It was found that this approach removed the problems associated with the employment of data values drawn from the period immediately after publication. Whereas 14 cases had no received citations by year two, only one case remained uncited by year five. This increased the number of cases for which logistic curves could be fitted. The problems associated with the slope of the tails in the logistic curves were also addressed. By selecting a later year as the first data value, the cumulative influence denoted by this data item increased in many cases. The effect of this was to increase the slope of the early part of the logistic curves fitted. The symmetry of the logistic curve thus led to an increase in the value of the upper bound. In many cases this appeared to offer a more realistic prediction of the total influence of a particular published item, since it suggested a pattern of continuing citation after the final data item.

As a result of this test, it appeared that the selection of the first data item had an important influence upon the fitting of logistic curves. If the year selected was too soon after the publication of a particular item, the resultant logistic curve may be distorted. The first data item should therefore not be selected from the period immediately after publication.

Amount of Data Employed in Modelling Procedure

The second issue that had to be addressed was the number of years upon which to base the logistic models. This issue had been problematic in the preliminary empirical analysis. In the previous chapter, a significant positive correlation ($r = 0.412$; $p < 0.001$) was discovered between the amount of data included in the modelling procedure, and the life cycles calculated. A similar test had to be carried out here, to establish whether this positive correlation was a characteristic of the parabola, or a problem inherent to modelling citation data using mathematical curves. This test had to establish the relationship between the amount of data included, and the values for both the life cycle and the upper bound.

The first test was therefore concerned with the question of whether the inclusion of different amounts of data across cases would have an impact upon the life cycles calculated. Changes in the amount of data included in the modelling procedure result from alterations in the value of delta employed. With reference to the equations employed to generate logistic curves, it can be seen that the value of delta is included in the calculation of the parameter defined as b. These equations reveal that as the value of delta increases, the value of b is reduced. The parameter b is involved in the equation used to calculate life cycles. If the value of b is reduced, the life cycle is augmented. Increasing the value of delta causes a decrease in the value of b, which in turn leads to the calculation of a longer life cycle. Hence, there is a direct relationship between the amount of data included in the modelling procedure, and the life cycles calculated.

The second test analysed the potential relationship between the amount of data included in the modelling procedure, and the predicted value of the upper bound. The equation employed to calculate the value of the upper bound does not involve the value of delta. This suggests that the amount of data is not directly related to the value of the upper bound. However, these two variables may be indirectly related. The value of the upper bound is dependent, in part, upon the final data value input ($P_{x+2\delta}$). This final data value reflects the cumulative influence of a published item after a given number of years. As this number of years is augmented, the value of the final data item will increase in most cases, as more citations are received by the published item. The value of the upper bound may therefore be influenced by the amount of data included in the modelling procedure, due to changes in the value of the final data item.

Practical Testing The relationship between the amount of data and the values returned for influence and longevity by the logistic model was analysed using actual citation data. The three data items included in the generation of logistic curves in each case were taken from five years after the date of publication (i.e. x=5), the final year for which data were available (i.e. 1995), and the year half way between these points. The values of delta employed in the test represent the time periods covered between these points. Cases were sorted by the amount of citation data available, which determined the value of delta employed in each case. The mean values for upper bound and the life cycle were calculated for each delta value employed, and can be seen in Table 7.1.

Table 7.1 Results of logistic curves sorted by values of delta employed

Delta Value	Years Included	No. of Cases	Upper Bound (Mean)	Life Cycle (Mean)
3	5, 8, 11	22	26.03	14.11
4	5, 9, 13	30	45.69	15.19
5	5, 10, 15	23	29.48	15.25
6	5, 11, 17	19	59.44	16.28
7	5, 12, 19	15	66.90	29.13
8	5, 13, 21	15	75.69	29.59
9	5, 14, 23	15	124.43	32.62
10	5, 15, 25	6	96.41	37.07

As can be seen from this table, the relationship between the amount of data employed and the mean of the upper bounds calculated appears to be generally positive. A Pearson Product Moment Correlation was calculated between the value of delta and the value of the upper bound. A significant correlation was discovered between these variables ($r = 0.343$; $p < .01$). With reference to the earlier discussion, it can be deduced that this relationship is the result of increases in the value of the final data item as more years are added to the model, rather than being the product of increases in the value of delta. A clearer relationship was discovered with reference to life cycles. It can be seen that as the value of delta increases, the value of the life cycles also increases. A Pearson Product Moment Correlation revealed that these variables are positively correlated ($r = 0.613$; $p < 0.001$). The strength of this correlation is greater than that discovered using parabolas ($r = 0.412$; $p < 0.001$).

Selection of Data Items

As a result of these tests, it emerged that it is not possible to compare the results of logistic models constructed from different amounts of data. There were two possible solutions to this problem. The first of these was to develop models based upon the maximum amount of data available in each case (i.e. all data from the date of publication until 1995). The resultant values could then be discounted by a given factor in order to make the values comparable. This approach has the advantage of utilising the totality of the available data. However, it may encounter problems with regard to the development of a universally applicable discounting factor. Such a factor is extremely difficult to define, since differences in publication dates result in a lack of uniformity in the amount of citation data available in each case. The number of cases published in each year is also relatively small, thus precluding the development of a robust discounting factor for each year separately.

The second approach considered was therefore to develop models based upon the same amount of data in each case. This guaranteed the comparability of the resultant models. In selecting the amount of data to be included, two competing requirements had to be reconciled. The first of these is the stability of the models generated. In the previous chapter, it was established that meaningful parabolic models were difficult to generate with small amounts of data. This was due to the lack of a calculable turning point. Given the requirement of knowing the point of inflection in the generation of logistic models, the same problem may apply here. The second consideration was the selection of a sample that was large enough to facilitate robust data analysis. The inclusion of large amounts of data, covering a significant period of time, will tend to result in stable models. However, increases in the amount of data required have a deleterious effect upon the sample size.

The minimum amount of citation data to be included for each publication emerged from the results of the preliminary empirical work. This analysis had employed three different thresholds for the minimum amount of data upon which models could be based (5, 10 and 20 years). The results of this analysis suggested that twenty years was sufficient to generate robust models (with an identifiable turning point) in the majority of cases. A minimum data threshold of twenty years was therefore employed in the generation of logistic curves.

Logistic curves were fitted to all 314 cases in the sample, using twenty years of data in each case. The year chosen as the first data item was year four, and the delta value selected was eight. The years included as data items in the model were therefore years four, twelve and twenty. (If year five had been selected as the first data item, the delta value would have to be reduced to seven. This would result in the generation of models based upon citation data from fewer years.) By employing the same amount of data in each case, the values returned for longevity and influence could be regarded as directly comparable.

The values returned for influence (the upper bound) and longevity (the life cycle) were recorded. At this stage, it was hoped that these values could be employed as the final measure of longevity and influence of individual published items.

Testing the Stability and Robustness of the Models Generated

Stability of Models

Before accepting the values for influence and longevity generated using the process outlined above, these values had to be tested in order to ascertain the extent to which they could be regarded as both stable and robust. The first test undertaken analysed the stability of the values generated. Individual cases were tested by removing data on a year by year basis. Logistic curves were then fitted each time the data set was modified. This mirrored the test implemented to analyse the stability of values calculated using parabolas. The test was implemented on the basis of the total available citation data for each case. This provided a more detailed depiction of the changes in the values generated as data were removed.

The results of the test carried out on an individual case can be seen in Table 7.2. This case is '*The Image*' by K.E. Boulding, published in 1956 (VAR 37). Two important points may be discerned with reference to the table above. In particular, attention must be paid to the values of the upper bound (k) and longevity (t99) returned as additional data is included in the modelling process. With little data included, the values are low. As data are added, the values become extremely unstable. There are two possible outcomes of this instability. It either precludes the possibility of fitting a logistic curve, or results in the generation of extremely high values for time and influence (figures highlighted in bold type). As the amount of data increases further, the values once again became stable.

This pattern of values can be explained with reference to the shape of logistic curves. The low values for longevity and influence associated with the inclusion of small amounts of data suggest that the point of inflection has not been reached by the year of the final data item. These values can be regarded as being extracted from the first area of the logistic curve, before the rate of growth increases. The very high values, and also the data for which no curve could be fitted, may be associated with the area surrounding the point of inflection. The curve is highly unstable at this point, and subject to rapid changes. After the point of inflection has been reached, the values again become predictable, at a higher level than before inflection. However, although predictable, the values are not constant. Rather they show a pattern of gradual increase, particularly with reference to the life cycle calculated. This reflects the positive relationship discovered earlier between the amount of data included and the values returned by the logistic model.

Table 7.2 Values for longevity and influence as data are removed

YEARS INCLUDED	DELTA VALUE	UPPER BOUND	LIFE CYCLE
4, 20, 36	16	93.63	53.72
4, 19, 34	15	90.14	51.65
4, 18, 32	14	88.04	51.17
4, 17, 30	13	88.76	49.75
4, 16, 28	12	87.31	44.56
4, 15, 26	11	86.91	46.24
4, 14, 24	10	92.54	48.13
4, 13, 22	9	152.39	65.94
4, 12, 20	8	*	*
4, 11, 18	7	892.08	95.75
4, 10, 16	6	1179072	180.68
4, 9, 14	5	*	*
4, 8, 12	4	*	*
4, 7, 10	3	*	*
4, 6, 8	2	27.54	19.54
4, 5, 6	1	25.99	16.79

* = Logistic Curve Could not be Fitted

Similar patterns of values to those in this table were also discovered in a number of other cases. This test therefore established the lack of stability in the values generated by logistic curves as data are removed from the analysis. It therefore reinforced the requirement of selecting a uniform amount of data across cases.

Robustness of Models

The test above also raised the issue of the robustness of the models generated. The wide variations in the values produced suggested that the models may not be sufficiently robust. Particular concern had to be accorded to the identification of the point of inflection in logistic curves. If the inflection point cannot be defined, the resultant values for longevity and influence may be too low or too unstable. A method therefore had to be developed to identify those cases for which the inflection point could not be defined. There were two groups of cases to be considered. The first group contained those cases for which the final data item lay in the area around the point of inflection. In these cases, the values returned tended to be very high; or the data items selected precluded the fitting of a logistic curve. These cases could be regarded as problematic, since the values associated with them could not be employed in the empirical analysis.

Also regarded as problematic were those cases which had not reached the area around inflection by the final data point, since the predicted values for the upper bound and longevity calculated in these cases may not reflect the 'actual' values for these variables. Specifically, the selection of three data points from the period before the area around the point of inflection may cause the predicted values for the upper bound and life cycle to be too low.

Identification of Problem Cases

The discussion above identifies two groups of cases which may encounter problems with regard to the data points employed in the generation of logistic curves. It was necessary to identify the cases within these groups. The major concern was those cases whose final data point was located around the point of inflection, since it was assumed that relatively few cases would not have reached the area around inflection before twenty years. In order for the latter situation to arise, the period of increasing growth in the influence of an individual published item must occur more than twenty years after publication. This was regarded as a pattern of influence which would be discovered infrequently (there were a small number of cases in which this pattern occurred, and these are discussed later in this chapter).

Attention was thus focused primarily upon those cases around the point of inflection. As discussed above, these cases were characterised by unusually high values for influence and longevity; or by the inability to generate a logistic curve to fit the data entered. This occurs due to the instability of logistic curves around the point of inflection. The clearest examples of this problem were therefore those cases for which a logistic curve could not be fitted. There were eight cases in this group. These cases were therefore defined as problematic, since the curves were around the point of inflection after twenty years.

In addition to these cases, it was also necessary to identify those cases whose final data point was positioned close to the point of inflection, resulting in values for longevity and influence that were inapplicable. The first concern was those cases for which an unexpectedly high upper bound was returned. Clearly, in identifying these cases, a definition was required of what is meant by 'unexpectedly high'. Such a definition was developed from analysis of the relationship between the upper bound (the predicted total influence) and the final data value input (the influence after twenty years). Large differences between these values were regarded as evidence that the last data item *may* be located around the point of inflection. The value of the upper bound in each case was therefore divided by the corresponding final data value. The cases were then sorted upon the result of this calculation.

The relationships between the upper bound and the final value varied widely across cases. At one end of the spectrum were cases where the upper bound was virtually equal to the final value input. This suggested that the influence of a published item has been saturated by the time of the final data value. The other end of the spectrum contained those cases for which the upper bound was significantly higher than the final value input. Referring back to the symmetry of the logistic curve, it can be inferred that any data value that is less than half of the value of the upper bound must lie before the point of inflection. The final data values in five of the cases were less than half of the value of the corresponding upper bound. Hence the point of inflection had not been reached in these five cases. They could therefore be defined as problematic in the current context. In addition to these cases, it was decided to also analyse the two cases for which the upper bound was more than 50% higher than the final data value. Although the final data value in these cases may lie after the point of inflection, the relatively high value for the upper bound necessitated more detailed analysis to confirm this.

The process described above identified cases for which the point of inflection may be unknown through the analysis of the value of the upper bound. It was also possible to implement this identification process on the basis the life cycles calculated. Referring back to the symmetry of the logistic curve, it is possible to deduce that the point of inflection lies at the mid-point of the total lifetime of a given published item. The final data value included in each of the cases represented the cumulative influence after twenty years. For this data value to lie after the point of inflection, therefore, the life cycle calculated could not extend beyond forty years. In cases where the life cycle extended beyond this limit, the point of inflection had to be defined as unknown. There were thirteen cases for which the life cycle calculated was greater than forty years. Among these cases were the seven which had been defined as problematic with regard to the upper bound. This suggested that the two methods for identifying cases in which the point of inflection had not been reached led to similar results.

Analysis of Problem Cases

As a result of the identification process above, twenty one cases were defined as problematic (thirteen due to the generation of inapplicable values, and eight as a result of the inability to fit a logistic curve to a given set of citation data). There were a number of ways in which these cases could be treated. The first (and simplest) approach would have been to discard these cases, and implement the analysis on the remaining cases. However, the removal of around 7% of the cases, simply because they did not fit the model, is not an ideal solution. An attempt was therefore made to devise a method through which the problem cases could be included in the analysis.

The twenty one problem cases were all characterised by the lack of a calculable point of inflection. In order to overcome this problem, the amount of data employed in the generation of models for these cases could be increased, in the hope that the final data item would then be after the point of inflection. The problem with such an approach is that resultant models would be incomparable with the rest of the data set, due to differences in the amount of data included in their generation.

One method of resolving this issue was to increase the amount of data employed in the generation of models for all cases. This would increase the stability of the models generated, and may therefore reduce the number of problematic cases. However, it would also reduce the number of cases which could be included in the analysis, due to a lack of available citation data. Given that no problems were encountered in the majority of cases, it seemed illogical to exclude these cases on the basis of a lack of data beyond twenty years, in order to resolve the instability discovered in a small number of cases.

An alternative approach therefore had to be implemented. This again involved increasing the amount of data employed in the generation of models, but only for those cases which had proved to be problematic. The values emerging from the resultant models were then to be modified (discounted) in order to account for the greater amount of data included in their generation. The discounted values could then be compared directly with those calculated for non-problem cases. This approach necessitated the development of a robust discounting factor with which to modify the results.

Development of a Discounting Factor

The first stage in developing a discounting factor was to calculate values for the upper bound and lifetime, based upon thirty years data, for those cases which had reached inflection after twenty years. These cases could be defined as 'stable'. There were 110 cases in this group. The selection of thirty years as the threshold for this test was based upon the requirements of generating stable models from a large enough sample (since models could only be generated for those cases with thirty years of available citation data).

The resultant values of the upper bound and life cycle, based upon citation data from thirty years, were then divided by the corresponding values for each case calculated using twenty years of data. This offered a guide to the increase in the values of the upper bound and life cycle associated with the employment of additional data in the generation of models.

Having compared the values for longevity and influence based upon twenty and thirty years of data, it was then necessary to derive a discounting factor from this relationship. Two methods were considered. These were both based upon the proportional increases in the values generated using thirty years data, in comparison with the values based upon data from twenty years. The first approach was to employ the mean of these increases as the discounting factor. However, this approach had to be rejected, since the pattern of increases did not conform to a normal distribution. As a result of this, the *median* of the proportional increases had to be employed as the discounting factor. The values of the mean and median for the increases in the upper bound and the longevity of influence can be seen in Table 7.4.

This table reveals that increasing the amount of data included in the models from 20 years to 30 years increases the values for the upper bound by 11%, and the life cycle by 30%. Values for influence and longevity calculated using 30 years of data must therefore be discounted by these amounts to make them comparable with models developed based upon 20 years of data.

Table 7.3 Development of a discounting factor

	Upper Bound (30 YEARS) / Upper Bound (20 YEARS)	Life Cycle (30 YEARS) / Life Cycle (20 YEARS)
MEDIAN	1.103	1.311
MEAN	1.167	1.301

Application of Discounting Factor

A discounting factor had therefore been developed. The next stage in the process was to generate logistic models for the problem cases using thirty years of data. By increasing the amount of data in this way, it was hoped that they would have reached the point of inflection by thirty years after their publication. The resultant values could then be modified using the discounting factor in order to make them comparable with the remainder of the cases in the study. In order to carry out this process, it was necessary for the problem cases to have at least thirty years of available citation data (i.e. they had to be published before 1966). Seven of the cases had less than this amount of data. Given that the point of inflection had not been established after twenty years in these cases, there was little option but to discard them, since the amount of additional data upon which to develop a stable model was negligible.

Logistic curves were fitted to the remaining fourteen problem cases using thirty years of data. The resultant value for longevity and influence can be seen in Table 7.4. The models generated had to be tested in order to establish whether the point of inflection had been reached in particular cases. This was achieved through analysis of the values returned for the upper bound and the life cycle. The analysis revealed that, in three cases, the point of inflection had not been reached after thirty years (i.e. the life cycle was longer than sixty years). These cases therefore had to be excluded from the study, since the values generated could not be regarded as robust. Closer examination revealed that in each of these cases the number of citations in the early years after publication was relatively high. However, the number of citations in later years failed to exhibit the expected pattern of growth. Instead the citation rate fell away rapidly. This suggests that the logistic curve may be unsuited to the modelling of citation patterns in these cases. Instead a negative exponential may be more applicable to the study of these cases.

Table 7.4 Logistic curves fitted to problem cases

Case No.	Upper Bound (30 Years Data)	Upper Bound / Final Data Value	Life Cycle (30 Years Data)	Discarded
371	10.09	1.42	94.05	Y
297	42.4	1.19	53.61	N
42	6.56	1.06	46.85	N
174	160.87	1.26	47.83	N
131	105.69	1.06	36.79	N
275	67.11	1.08	41.04	N
374	9.43	1.02	26.25	N
271	36.89	1.10	45.25	N
342	1.4	1.01	28.14	N
343	*	*	*	Y
290	18.38	1.27	78.28	Y
37	88.76	1.18	49.78	N
86	*	*	*	Y
85	8.81	1.25	298.16	Y

* = Logistic Curve could not be Fitted

There were also two cases for which logistic curves could not be fitted. These cases also had to be discarded. Both of these cases were characterised by extremely low citation rates (the number of citations they received in the first thirty years after publication were the lowest in the entire data set). It may therefore be concluded that these cases are unsuitable for analysis, since the citation patterns associated with them could be defined as 'noise'.

The remaining nine problem cases were thus defined as having reached inflection after thirty years. The values for influence and longevity generated with this data could therefore be regarded as robust and applicable to the current study. Having generated these values, they were then modified using the discounting factors defined earlier (i.e. the upper bounds were discounted by 1.103; and the life cycles by 1.311). This made them comparable with those cases for which values were calculated using twenty years of data.

Cases with Pre-Inflection Data Points

The nine cases in the table above were among those whose logistic curves had been around the point of inflection after twenty years. They were identified through the presence of high values for longevity and influence; or the failure to fit a logistic curve. As discussed earlier, it was also necessary to analyse those cases which had not reached the area around inflection after twenty years. These cases could be identified by unusually low values for influence and longevity. However, it is not possible to define a curve as being before point of inflection simply because it returns low values for the upper bound and life cycle. These low values may instead reflect the lack of influence of a published item. The identification of pre-inflection cases must therefore be implemented on the basis of low values *relative* to the corresponding values calculated with additional data. In the context of this study, a case which has not reached the area around inflection after twenty years, but is beyond inflection after thirty years will be characterised by a particular pattern of values for the upper bound and life cycle. The model at thirty years will have a calculable point of inflection, reflected in values for life cycle and upper bound that are significantly higher than those calculated using twenty years data.

There were two cases for which the upper bound and life cycle values calculated using thirty years of data were more than double the corresponding values using data from twenty years. This suggested that these cases had not reached inflection after twenty years. Hence, the values calculated for their influence and longevity may be inappropriate. These cases were therefore treated in the same way as those cases which had been defined as being around the point of inflection after twenty years. The values for influence and longevity in these two cases were thus calculated using thirty years of data, and modified by the relevant discounting factor.

The data set therefore consisted of values for influence and longevity calculated using two distinct methods. The first group (containing 292 cases) were those which had reached the point of inflection after twenty years. The values for these cases were calculated using twenty years of data (i.e. the values were those calculated in the original analysis, rather than those developed during the discounting procedure). The second group contained the 11 cases whose values were generated by the discounting process. Hence, these cases had not reached inflection after twenty years, but robust models could be constructed for them using data covering thirty years.

Testing the Validity of the Discounting Factor

As outlined above, the final data set contained values for longevity and influence calculated using two distinct methods. It was thus necessary to test whether the results of these methods could be directly compared. This comparability was dependent upon the influence of the discounting factor. A test was therefore implemented in order to analyse the effect of the discounting factor upon the position of the problem cases within the totality of the data set.

In order to implement this test, all of the cases included in the discounting process (i.e. the 107 'stable' cases, and the eleven problem cases) were ranked on the basis of the values calculated for influence and life cycle using thirty years of data. Rankings for these cases were then calculated based upon twenty years of data (using discounted data in problem cases, original data in those cases with calculable points of inflection). The rankings of the problem cases, based upon the upper bound generated under both of these conditions, were then extracted. These rankings can be seen in Table 7.5.

Table 7.5 Rankings of problem cases based upon value of upper bound

Case No.	Rank of Upper Bound (30 Years Data)	Rank of Upper Bound (20 Years 'Discounted')
297	57	59
174	21	20
131	29	29
342	116	116
37	34	32
42	108	107
275	43	42
374	102	101
271	63	67
349	113	113
425	48	48

The rankings of the problem cases after thirty years are based upon data for which the point of inflection has been reached. The ranking of the problem cases under these conditions may therefore be regarded as a depiction of their 'true' position relative to the remainder of the sample. If the discounting factor is to be regarded as applicable, the rankings of the discounted values for the problem cases at twenty years should be similar to those at thirty years. Otherwise, it must be concluded that the discounting factor distorts the position of the problem cases relative to the remainder of the sample. As revealed in the table above, the rankings of the problem cases at both twenty and thirty years are almost identical. This suggests that the discounted values for the upper bound represent a relatively accurate depiction of the influence of an individual case for which a robust model cannot be fitted using twenty years of data.

A similar process was undertaken with regard to the life cycles calculated for the problem cases. These were ranked, alongside the remainder of the data set, based upon twenty and thirty years of data. These rankings can be seen in Table 7.6.

Table 7.6 Rankings of problem cases based upon length of life cycle

Case No.	Rank of Life Cycle (30 Years Data)	Rank of Life Cycle (20 Years 'Discounted')
297	1	1
174	4	4
131	18	27
342	68	63
37	3	2
42	5	5
275	11	16
374	79	81
271	7	7
349	74	72
425	12	17

The comparative rankings revealed less similarity than had been discovered in the case of the upper bound (see previous table). This may be the result of the greater concentration among the values of the life cycles calculated (which range from 10.5 to 40.9), when compared with the values of the upper bound (which range from 0.8 to 466.8). This concentration means that small changes in the life cycle calculated for an individual case may lead to a marked alteration in the ranking accorded to it. However, there appeared to be sufficient similarity in the rankings at twenty and thirty years to suggest a relationship between the two.

A Spearman's Rank Correlation Test was implemented on the rankings of all cases at twenty and thirty years. When considering the values of the upper bound, an extremely high correlation was discovered ($r = 0.9915$; $p < .001$). The same test was also implemented on the rankings of cases based upon life cycles calculated. A lower correlation was discovered, although it was still highly significant ($r = 0.698$; $p < .001$).

These tests of the discounting factor revealed that it may be regarded as both robust and valid for the current study. The values for problem cases generated using the discounting process may be regarded as a reasonably accurate depiction of their longevity and influence. The discounting process thus led to the inclusion of eleven cases that would otherwise have been excluded from the analysis. Given the amount of analysis required to develop and test the discounting factor, this may seem to be a meagre result. However, the main benefit may be located in the development of the process itself, rather than its results in this individual context, since it offers a method for discounting which may be employed by later research.

The results of these tests also introduce an important corollary for the modelling of citation patterns using logistic curves. The significant correlations between the rankings based upon twenty and thirty years of data reveal that once the point of inflection has been reached, the values for influence and longevity become largely predictable. It is therefore unnecessary to obtain a complete set of citation data to predict the influence and longevity of the published literature, since it is possible to generate accurate models from partial data, on the proviso that the point of inflection is calculable. In the current project, robust logistic curves could be fitted in 96.5% of the cases in the sample.

A final data set had thus been developed, containing values for the life cycle and total influence of each case in the sample. The values for each case can be seen in Appendix 2. This data set formed the basis for the next stage in the empirical analysis.

Brief Discussion of Results

Before moving on to the next stage in the analysis, it may be useful to review briefly the results of the empirical research described in this chapter. The purpose of this review is to offer a brief guide to the general patterns of life cycles and influence generated by the analysis in this chapter. The review is by no means exhaustive. It simply provides an overall picture of the pattern of values discovered. More detailed analysis is provided in the following chapters.

In order to offer an overall depiction of the values for influence and longevity, the *Explore* facility in *SPSS* was employed. This produces summary statistics for a given variable. Figure 7.2 reveals summary statistics for the values of the upper bound generated using logistic curves. This variable is defined as K20 (i.e. the value of k calculated using 20 years of data).

Valid cases: 303.0   Missing cases: .0   Percent missing: .0
Mean 48.1085   Std Err   3.9852   Median 20.9351
Std Dev 69.37   Min .8092   Max   466.7581
Skewness 2.7140   S E Skew .1400
Kurtosis 8.1692   S E Kurt   .2792
95% CI for Mean (40.2662, 55.9508)

Figure 7.2 Summary statistics for variable K20

The mean value for the upper bound (k) was 48.1. This shows the average predicted total influence of the publications in the data set (i.e. the number of citations discounted by the increase in the number of items in the *Social Science Citation Index*). However, a number of other statistics suggest that the mean may be misleading in this context. The range of values is very high, the lowest predicted total influence being 0.8 (for an article by Derek Pugh published in *Organizational Dynamics* in 1973); and the highest being 466.8 (for '*Organizations*' by James March and Herbert Simon, published in 1958). The lack of consistency in the number of citations received by all cases in the sample is also reflected in the high value for the standard deviation.

The pattern of values for the upper bound was also found to be significantly positively skewed (t = 19.39; p<0.01). This skewness is reflected in the fact that the value of the median is less than half that of the mean. It may be inferred from this positive skew that there are a large number of cases in the sample which are cited relatively infrequently, and only a small number of highly cited items of management literature. As discussed in Chapter 5, the sample employed in this study concentrated upon the most influential authors within management research. The pattern of values discovered here thus suggests that most literature, even that published by leading authors, has relatively little influence upon the management research community. Only a small proportion of the literature may be defined as highly influential.

Summary statistics were also analysed for the values of the life cycles generated for each case in the sample. The results of this analysis are shown in Figure 7.3 (variable T99(20) representing the life cycles calculated using twenty years of data).

Valid cases: 303.0	Missing cases: .0	Percent missing: .0
Mean 21.9300	Std Err .3086	Median 21.0777
Std Dev 5.37	Min 10.5412	Max 40.8942
Skewness .7668	S E Skew .1400	
Kurtosis .6396	S E Kurt .2792	
95% CI for Mean (21.3227, 22.5373)		

Figure 7.3 Summary statistics for variable T99(20)

The mean value for T99 for all cases in the sample is 21.9. This value is calculated from the first data point in the model (year four in this context). Hence the average lifetime of the published items included in the sample is 25.9 years. As noted above, this finding cannot be generalised to all management literature, since the sample concentrates solely upon the work of leading authors in the field. The range of values reveals that the life cycles for the literature in the data set range from 14.5 years (a 1973 *Administrative Science Quarterly* article by John Child); to 44.9 years (for '*Productivity and Social Organization*' by A.K. Rice, published in 1958). This suggests that it is possible to observe distinct differences in the length of time over which published items are influential. However, the distinction is not as marked as that discovered with reference to the level of influence of individual items.

The pattern of values for the life cycles was found to be significantly positively skewed (t = 5.48; p <0.01). Hence, there may be a small number of items which are influential over a significantly longer period than the remainder of the sample. However, the degree of skewness is lower than that discovered in the analysis of the values of the upper bounds.

Concluding Remarks

A number of characteristics of the longevity and influence of published management literature emerge from the description of the data offered above. It reveals that the data regarding the level of influence is highly skewed, with only a small proportion of the cases in the sample being highly cited, such as those listed below:

> *Organization Man* by W.H. Whyte (1956)
> *Organizations* by J.G. March and H.A. Simon (1958)
> *A Behavioural Theory of the Firm* by R.M. Cyert and J.G. March (1963)
> *The Social Psychology of Organizations* by D.Katz and R.L. Kahn (1966)
> *Markets and Hierarchies* by O.E. Williamson (1975)

The life cycles generated are less variable. However, sufficient variation was discovered to suggest that distinctions may be made between cases on the basis of the length of time over which they are influential. As mentioned previously, particular attention was paid to those published items that were *highly influential*, but only for a relatively *short period*, since these items may be subject to the pressures of fashion. A number of such cases were identified, including:

> *Small is Beautiful* by E.F. Schumacher (1973)
> *Changing Organizations* by W.G. Bennis (1966)
> *Work and Motivation* by V.H. Vroom (1964)
> *The Human Organization* by R. Likert (1967)

This stage in the analysis has therefore generated measures of longevity and influence for individual published items. It has facilitated the identification of the most influential publications in the development of management research, and also those which are highly influential over a relatively short period.

A more formal analysis of the different patterns is offered in the second stage in the empirical analysis. The purpose of this second stage in the analysis is to study the factors that may affect the level of influence associated with published management literature, and also the length of time over which this literature is influential. This facilitates analysis of those factors that may lead to the influence of particular published items being fashionable in nature. The second stage in the empirical analysis is discussed in the following two chapters.

8 Identifying Factors Associated with Management Fashions

Introduction

The analysis implemented in the previous chapter offered a guide to the patterns of influence associated with published management research. It was purely *descriptive* in character, in that it produced a description of the patterns of influence discovered. However, it offered no *analytical* conclusions concerning the causes of the different patterns of influence associated with management literature. The purpose of the second stage of the empirical study is therefore to evaluate the effect of a number of factors upon the longevity and influence of published management literature.

Identification of Independent Variables

Various writers have attempted to analyse those factors which may influence citation patterns. As a result of these studies, a number of potential factors were identified. These are outlined below:

1. *Discipline of Author's Background*: a number of studies have analysed the effect of disciplinary background upon rates of citation (e.g. Garfield, 1979; Moed *et al*, 1985; Peters and van Raan, 1994). The results of these studies have revealed that there may exist differences in citation practices and rates across disciplines. The study by Folly *et al* (1981) revealed that the rate of obsolescence of literature is also influenced by the characteristics of a particular discipline.

It may appear that the issue of disciplinary background should not affect the current analysis, given that it focuses upon a single subject - management research. However, this assumption would be misguided. As discussed in Chapter 2, management research is informed by a number of reference disciplines, and management authors may often be identified as belonging to one of these individual academic traditions. For example, a management author may concentrate upon the economic aspects of organisation; the effect of organisational structures upon the operation of the organisation as a whole;

or the effect of work practices upon individual employees. These represent the broad concerns of the three main reference disciplines of management research (economics, sociology and psychology). Given the heterogeneous nature of management research, it might therefore be expected that the pattern of citations offered to a particular author would be influenced by the subject discipline of his/her background.

An independent variable thus had to be developed to address the issue of the academic background of management authors. Five subject categories were defined: psychology; sociology; economics; management; and interdisciplinary social science. The first three of these categories represent the three main reference disciplines of management research (ESRC, 1994). In addition to these categories, there is a group of authors whose work concentrates solely upon the nature of management itself. These authors tend to concentrate upon subjects such as corporate strategy and decision making. Such subjects are comparatively modern, and can be defined as a body of knowledge that is relatively self-sufficient, as opposed to being reliant upon reference disciplines for its theoretical foundation. The four categories outlined above mirror those employed by Glänzel (1996) in his analysis of management research. A further category was also constructed. This contained authors whose work could be identified as belonging to a variety of academic traditions, rather than being based upon an individual disciplinary background.

Having constructed the categories within which authors were to be classified, a method was required which would determine the category into which each author should be placed. The method employed referred to the journal publications of individual authors (the majority of the authors in the sample having published research in both book and journal form). The subject discipline of each of these journals was extracted using the journal lists in the *Social Science Citation Index*. It was discovered that the majority of authors who had published in journals concentrated their work in the journals of a single discipline. For example, the journal publications by Oliver Williamson are solely in economics; those by John Child appear in sociology journals; Edgar Schein publishes his work in organisational psychology journals; and Henry Mintzberg's work is published only in management journals. Other groups, such as that based at Aston University, publish across a range of disciplines, and so can be defined as multidisciplinary.

Where authors had not published any journal articles the classification was more difficult. The classification in these cases was based upon the pen portraits of the authors provided in the reviews from which the sample was drawn (see Chapter 5). These portraits offer a detailed description of the academic background and research interests of individual authors. It was possible to extract from these portraits a guide to the disciplinary background of individual authors. This approach was also employed to confirm the classifications made based upon the journal publications of individual authors. The classification emergent from this approach was found to support those developed based upon journal publications. There were no cases where the results of the two approaches were contradictory.

The methods employed did not produce a perfect classification of disciplinary background. However, this may be due to the nature of the variable. It is difficult to define authors as working purely within a single discipline, since it suggests that they are influenced by nothing outside their immediate research field. The process of classification is particularly problematic in interdisciplinary fields, such as management research. The variable constructed using the process described above may therefore be regarded as being as accurate as practical considerations allow.

2. *Nationality of Author*: the research communities of different countries vary in size and diversity. These characteristics may influence the rates of citation, as discovered by Lancaster *et al* (1986). Within the study of management, the American research community is particularly powerful. It is regarded as the progenitor of the majority of management ideas (Alvarez, 1993) and is the location for the editing and publishing of the leading management journals (as defined by the impact factors in the *Social Science Citation Index*). The dominance of the American research community means that other research communities must be regarded, to differing extents, as peripheral (Collin *et al*, 1996). A number of authors have studied the citation patterns associated with researchers from peripheral countries. These studies found that the citation rates of these authors tend to be lower than those authors from the central research community (Bekavec *et al*, 1994). Researchers from peripheral countries may also receive fewer citations where their research is published in languages other than English (Dieks and Chang, 1976). This may reinforce the dominance of the American research community.

Given the potential differences in citation patterns according to the nationality of the author, it was necessary to categorise the authors in the sample on this basis. In order to implement this categorisation, a method had to be developed to define the nationality of each author. To achieve this, the pen portraits associated with each author were consulted. These provided details of the academic background of each author in the sample. A decision had to be made at this point as to how to determine nationality. Nationality is commonly defined by place of birth. However, this definition may be inappropriate in this particular case. The place of birth of an author may be less important than the location in which s/he carries out research, since the location of employment of an academic may determine his/her access to potential publication media. It may also influence their access to the informal networks through which large parts of the research community operate (Crane, 1972). Hence, in terms of citation patterns, the place of employment of an individual author may be more important than place of birth, and nationality was defined on this basis. This replicated the definition of nationality employed by Glänzel (1996).

In the first attempts to categorise authors, they were grouped according to their individual nationalities. However, this led to a number of problems. Of particular concern was the issue of the number of cases within each group. The two largest groups contained American and British authors. The remaining categories, containing authors from countries such as Canada, France and Germany, only contained a small number of cases. This led to concerns that these groups may be too small to facilitate meaningful data analysis. A further problem was identified with the issue of migration. Where authors move between countries, it becomes difficult to define them within a single nationality.

The number of categories within this independent variable was therefore reduced. The first stage in this process was to combine the American and Canadian authors in a single category. This category was defined as North American authors. Problems were also encountered with reference to the categorisation of European authors. Originally, it was hoped that by defining separate categories for each nationality, it would be possible to analyse the effect of language differences upon citation rates. However, the small sample sizes precluded such analysis. All non-American authors were therefore included within a single category. Due to the nature of the sample, each of these authors was European. This may reflect a bias in the reviews of research upon which this study was based. The most notable absence from the sample is the influence of Japanese theorists, such as Kenichi Ohmae.

Two categories therefore remained - North American authors and European authors. This classification may appear to be crude and simplistic. However, it was necessary due to the concerns of sample size. It also helped to address the issue of migration. A number of authors have migrated between the USA and Canada, such as Henry Mintzberg. There are also European academics, such as E.F. Schumacher, whose academic background may be traced to more than one European country. However, there was little evidence discovered to suggest that there was large-scale migration between Europe and North America among the authors in the sample. (The only case where this occurred was that of Peter Drucker, an Austrian who emigrated to the United States. He was classed as North American for the purposes of this study, since he was based in the U.S. for most of his writing career.) The delineation of North American and European research may thus overcome many of the problems associated with migration. The categories also match those employed by Collin *et al* (1996) in their study of management journals.

3. *Publishing Media*: one factor which may influence the rate of citation is the medium through which a particular item is published. The majority of research into this issue has concentrated upon a single publication medium - academic journals (e.g. Doreian, 1988; Pichappan, 1993; Thomas, 1995). This is due to the dominance of academic journals within the scientific fields which represent the subject of many bibliometric analyses. There has been relatively little research into the relative citation rates associated with different publication media. As discussed earlier, management research is not disseminated solely through academic journals. Book publication also represents a major outlet for research findings. Publications were therefore classified according to publishing media. Two groups were defined - books and journals. Other publication media, such as technical reports and conference proceedings, are generally less influential in the dissemination of management research.

4. *Publishing History of Author*: a further factor which may influence citation rates is the publication history of academic authors (Moed *et al*, 1985). In studying this issue, two contradictory pressures must be acknowledged. The first of these is that the most prolific authors in any field may be those whose ideas are central to the development of the discipline. It might therefore be expected that the work of these authors would be highly cited. However, there is an opposite concern which must be addressed. One of the main concerns of the research community is that of 'salami' publishing. This occurs where researchers split their work into a number of small-scale publications, in order to increase their publication count. However, the content of each paper will be minimal, thus reducing the likelihood of each being cited by later researchers (Peters and van Raan, 1994).

In order to study the influence of the publishing history of authors, a variable was set up which measured the number of items published by each author in the sample. This measure was extracted from the number of published items accorded by the *Social Science Citation Index* to each author.

This method of counting publications meant that each item had to be cited at least once. However, as discussed in Chapter 5, problems were identified with this approach, due to the influence of erroneous citations. The 'highly cited' threshold (2 citations per year) was thus employed. The output of each author was therefore measured by how many highly cited articles they published. In order to make this measurement comparable across cases, only those publications from the first twenty years of each author's publishing career were included.

Construction of Independent Variables

From the discussion of the potential influences upon the longevity and influence of management literature, four independent variables were constructed, as outlined below:

1. *Nationality of Author* (variable name: *newcoun*) - this variable was categorical. The two categories constructed were North American authors and European authors.

2. *Academic Discipline of Author* (variable name: *authdisc*) - this variable was categorical. Five categories were constructed. Three of these represented the reference disciplines of management research (economics, sociology and psychology). The remaining two categories contained those authors whose work concentrated purely upon management; and those authors or groups with an interdisciplinary background.

3. *Publishing Media* (variable name: *pubmedia*) - this variable was categorical, and contained two classes. Published items were classified into books and journals.

4. *Publishing History of Author* (variable name: *numart*) - this variable contained ratio level data. It measured the number of 'highly cited' articles published by the author in the first twenty years of his/her publishing career.

Three out of the four independent variables were categorical. In order to include these variables in the regression equation, *dummy variables* had to be constructed. Dummy variables measure individually the influence upon the dependent variable of each class within categorical variables. Dummy variables were set up for the three categorical independent variables, as outlined in Table 8.1.

Table 8.1 List of independent variables

VARIABLE NAME	DUMMY VARIABLES
NEWCOUN	isameric, iseuro
PUBMEDIA	isabook, isajourn
AUTHDISC	ispsych, issocio, isecon, ismanag, ismiscss

As can be seen, one dummy variable is constructed for each class in the categorical variables. For purposes of clarity, dummy variables will henceforth be denoted by italics, while the original independent variables will be referred to using capital letters.

Definition of Dependent Variables

Two dependent variables were defined, the first being the *level of influence* of published items, and the second representing the *life cycles* associated with these items. In order to simplify the regression analysis, models were developed for these two variables in isolation. However, a note must be made of the relationship between the two factors. A Pearson Product Moment Correlation was implemented, and a significant positive relationship was discovered between the longevity and level of influence of published items ($r = 0.238$; $p < 0.01$). This finding suggests that further analysis of this relationship may be required. A two dimensional, multivariate approach is required to implement such analysis, which is discussed in greater depth in the following chapter.

Analysis of Dependent Variables

There are various assumptions which form the foundation of regression analysis. Two of the most important of these assumptions are associated with the characteristics of the dependent variable. These assumptions are:

1. The dependent variable has *no outliers* - if the dependent variable includes a number of extreme values (or outliers) the regression model generated may be distorted. This occurs because individual extreme data values can have an inordinately large influence upon the model.

2. The dependent variable should ideally be *normally distributed* - if the values of the dependent variable do not conform to a normal distribution, this may result in excessively large error terms for certain cases. This has the effect of reducing the reliability of the model. The requirement of a normally distributed dependent variable is not as essential as the removal of outliers from the model. However, it is advantageous to have a normally distributed dependent variable for regression analysis.

It was therefore necessary to study the dependent variables in greater depth, in order to determine whether they violated either of these assumptions.

Analysis of the Literature Influence Variable

The first regression model to be developed analysed the relationship between the independent variables outlined earlier, and the level of influence associated with individual published items. The dependent variable was thus the level of influence measured using the logistic modelling technique. As discussed at the end of the previous chapter, this variable was defined as *K20* (referring to the value of the upper bound in the logistic model (K) calculated using twenty years of data). The characteristics of this variable were analysed to establish whether it violated either of the assumptions outlined above (i.e. the pattern of values should approximate to normal distribution; and there should be no outliers).

The analysis at the end of the previous chapter revealed that the distribution of values for variable K20 is positively skewed ($t = 19.39$; $p <0.01$). There is a large concentration of cases with low values for the level of influence. This suggests that most of the cases in the sample are relatively uninfluential. However, there also exist a small number of cases which are highly influential. This results in a positively skewed distribution, with a small number of outliers at high values of K20. The pattern of values calls into question the normality of the distribution.

A *Kolmogorov - Smirnov* test was implemented in order to test whether K20 could be defined as being normally distributed. The null hypothesis of this test is that there is no significant difference between the pattern of values for a given variable, and the pattern suggested by the normal distribution. The significance value thus represents the probability of a given set of values occurring, given the assumption that they form part of a normal distribution. The results of this test ($K-S = 0.2468$; $p < 0.01$) led to the null hypothesis having to be rejected, with the result that the assumption of normality could not be supported. A boxplot was also produced in order to establish whether any outliers could be identified within the distribution of values for K20. This boxplot revealed a number of outliers.

Transformation of Literature Influence Variable   In the case of variable K20, the requirements of lack of outliers and the normal distribution of the dependent variable had not been satisfied. The data could not therefore be employed in its original form as the basis of a regression model. Instead the data had to be transformed before it could be included in the regression analysis. One of the most common methods of transforming data is to take the *natural log* of each value. The natural log of the value of K20 for each case in the sample was thus calculated. These values formed the basis of a new variable (*LOGK20*).

The characteristics of the variable LOGK20 were analysed in order to test whether this variable satisfied the requirements of regression analysis. It was established that the transformation of the data removed the significant skewness of the distribution ($t = 0.91$; $p > 0.05$). A Kolmogorov-Smirnov test was carried out to confirm the normality of the resultant distribution of values. The results of this test ($K\text{-}S = 0.0413$; $p > 0.2$) revealed that the probability of this pattern of values occurring, given the assumption that they form part of a normal distribution, was greater than 0.2. The null hypothesis (that the data followed a normal distribution) therefore could not be rejected. A boxplot was also produced in order to identify any outliers in the transformed data. This boxplot confirmed that the transformation of the data resulted in the removal of outliers from the distribution.

Hence, the values for LOGK20 satisfied the assumptions of regression analysis regarding the lack of outliers and the conformation to a normal distribution. This variable could therefore be included as a dependent variable in the regression analysis.

Analysis of Life Cycle Variable

The second dependent variable was analysed in order to establish whether it violated either of the assumptions of regression analysis outlined earlier. This dependent variable represented the predicted time taken to reach 99% of the total influence of a published item; this prediction being based upon data from the first twenty years after publication. The variable was defined as *T99(20)*. The characteristics of this variable are shown in the analysis at the end of the previous chapter. This analysis revealed that the distribution of values for T99(20) is significantly positively skewed ($t = 5.48$; $p < 0.01$). In order to test the effect of this skewness upon the normality of the distribution, a Kolmogorov-Smirnov test was carried out. This test revealed that the assumption of a normal distribution of values could not be supported (K-S = 0.0836; p<0.01). The lack of normality may result from the presence of outliers in the data set; with the result that long 'tails' may be identified in the distribution of values. In order to test for the presence of outliers, a boxplot was produced. As in the case of variable K20 the boxplot revealed that there were a number of cases which may be defined as outliers. These were located at both ends of the set of values for the life cycle variable. The existence of these outliers violates one of the assumptions of regression analysis.

Transformation of Life Cycle Variable Given the problems encountered with the presence of outliers and the lack of normality in the data, it was necessary to transform the data. This was achieved by taking the natural log of each value. The resultant values formed a new variable, which was defined as LOGT99. The distribution of values for the transformed data was not significantly skewed (t=0.32; p>0.05). A boxplot confirmed that transforming the data had also solved the problem of outliers. Having addressed the issue of outliers, it was then necessary to study whether the transformed values conformed to a normal distribution. A Kolmogorov- Smirnov test was carried out, and the results revealed that the values for LOGT99 could be regarded as being normally distributed (K-S = 0.0373; p>0.2).

The problems associated with outliers and lack of normality encountered in the analysis of the original data thus appeared to be addressed using transformed data for the variables measuring both the influence and longevity of management literature. These data could therefore be included in the regression model developed to study these aspects of management literature.

Approaches to Regression Analysis

Having defined the independent and dependent variables to be included in the analysis, it was necessary to select a method of relating these variables. The technique employed was *multiple regression analysis*. This method generates forecasts of the value of the dependent variable based upon the values of various independent variables.

There are a number of approaches that can be employed in the implementation of regression analysis. The difference between these approaches emerges from the manner in which independent variables are entered into the regression equation. A brief description of each method is offered below:

1. *Enter method* - this involves the inclusion of all independent variables in the regression equation, irrespective of the significance of their contribution to the overall model. The main problem with this approach is that the inclusion of non-significant independent variables may increase the complexity of the model, without increasing its predictive power. As a result, meaningful analysis of the model becomes problematic.

2. *Forward Selection* - this approach starts with no independent variables in the model. The independent variable with the greatest influence is then included in the equation, provided it is above the significance threshold. The significance levels of the remaining independent variables are then recalculated. These levels reflect the influence upon the model of each independent variable, after the influence of the included variable has been incorporated. This process is then repeated until all significant variables have been included in the regression model. The advantage with this method is that it excludes non-significant variables from the model. However, there is a problem with this approach with regard to the significance of variables once they have been included in the regression model. As discussed above, the significance of independent variables will alter as the combination of variables in the model changes. Hence, a variable that is included due to its significance may become non-significant as additional variables are included in the model. This may be caused by correlation between the independent variables. As a result, the final regression model may contain non-significant independent variables.

3. *Backward Selection* - this approach represents the converse of the forward selection technique. All variables are included in the regression model at the outset. The significance of each independent variable is then calculated, and the least significant variable removed from the model. The significance of the remaining variables is then calculated, on the basis that the influence of the excluded variable has been removed. This process is repeated until all non-significant variables have been removed from the model. The purpose of backward selection is to include only significant variables in the regression model. However, the problem faced by backward selection is the opposite to that encountered when using the forward selection approach. As variables are removed from the model, the significance of those variables already excluded may change. The final regression model may thus exclude variables that are

significant.

4. *Stepwise Regression* - in order to overcome the problems associated with the employment of forward and backward selection techniques, a method combining these approaches may be employed. This can be defined as the stepwise approach. As in forward selection, no independent variables are included in the model at the outset. Variables are then entered into the model using the same criteria as employed in forward selection. The difference between the stepwise technique and forward selection may be located in the treatment of variables that have been included in the model. In forward selection, once a variable has been included in the model, it cannot be removed. However, in stepwise regression, variables which become non-significant as variables are added, are excluded from the model (although in *SPSS* the significance threshold for removal of cases is slightly different from the criteria employed for their inclusion). This reflects the method used in backward selection. As a result of this combination of approaches, the stepwise technique guarantees that all significant independent variables are included in the model, and all non-significant variables are excluded. The stepwise technique also ensures that the regression model accounts for any correlation between independent variables.

The advantages associated with the stepwise approach cause it to be the most commonly used method of implementing regression analysis (Bryman and Cramer, 1990). This technique was thus employed in the regression analysis.

As mentioned at the start of this chapter, separate regression models were developed for influence and longevity, in order to simplify the analysis involved. The following sections outline this analysis. The first section discusses the development of a regression model for the influence of management literature. The second section will then outline the construction of a regression model for the longevity of management literature.

Analysis of the Influence of Management Literature

Before regression analysis was undertaken, preliminary analysis was implemented into the nature of the relationship between LOGK20 and the categorical independent variables. As discussed earlier, the manner in which the independent variables were operationalised resulted in the development of three categorical variables, and one ratio level variable. A one-way ANOVA test was implemented to analyse the hypothesis that the level of influence (LOGK20) differed across classes for each categorical independent variable.

The null hypothesis for the ANOVA test is that there is no variation in the means for different categories of an independent variable. The F value for all three independent variables revealed that the probability of there being no variation was less than 0.001. The null hypothesis therefore had to be rejected, and the alternative hypothesis (i.e. that there were differences between the means associated with different categories of the independent variables) was accepted. This finding led to the assumption that the regression analysis would discover significant coefficients based upon the categories of nationality, publishing media and academic discipline.

Development of the Regression Model

Stepwise multiple regression analysis was implemented in order to test the influence of the various independent variables upon the value of LOGK20. Five variables were included in the final model. With reference to the discussion of the stepwise method, it can be discerned that these variables were included in the regression model because they had a significant influence upon the accuracy of the model. The final regression equation was

$$\text{LOGK20} = 1.621 + 0.027_{\text{NUMART}} + 0.985_{\text{ISABOOK}}$$

$$+ 0.754_{\text{ISAMERIC}} + 0.879_{\text{ISECON}} + 0.459_{\text{ISMISCSS}}$$

The coefficients associated with each of the variables in the equation are defined as the partial regression coefficients. The equation above can be interpreted in the following way. The constant term is 1.62. This means that the 'baseline' forecast equals this value. Since the regression equation forecasts the natural log of the influence of a published item, it is necessary to take the antilog of this value to calculate the baseline influence. The antilog of the constant is 5.06. This denotes the baseline influence of a published item (in addition to the effect of the number of published items by a particular author). This level of influence is predicted for an item which is not contained within any of the categories included in the regression equation. Hence the item cannot be a book or American authored; it must also not be written by an economist or an interdisciplinary author. By a process of deduction, therefore, the baseline influence is associated with a journal article written by a European psychologist, sociologist or management author. Any change in these characteristics will result in an increase in the level of influence predicted. For example an American economics book would be forecast to have an influence measure of

$$1.621 + 0.985 \text{ (ISABOOK)} + 0.753 \text{ (ISAMERIC)} + 0.878 \text{ (ISECON)} = 4.237$$

given that the value of the three dummy variables in this equation would be 1. Taking the antilog of this forecast, the predicted influence of an American economics book can be calculated as 69.2, in addition to the coefficient based upon the number of published items from a particular author. The final regression model included dummy variables from each of the categorical independent variables. This supports the finding of the ANOVA test that all three variables are significantly related to the level of influence of individual published items. The number of items published by individual authors (NUMART) was also included in the regression model, and was found to be positively related to the level of influence of published items.

The *coefficient of determination* (R^2) is a measure of the goodness of fit of the regression model. In this case, the value of R^2 was 0.226. This reveals that 22.6% of the variation in the level of influence of published items may be accounted for by the variables included in the regression equation. The remainder of the variation is caused by factors not included in the model. In order to test the significance of the fitted model, an F statistic is calculated. This compares the variation accounted for by the regression equation, and that part of the variation that is not accounted for by the model (the residual). The F statistic tests the null hypothesis that there is no linear relationship between the independent variables included in the regression model and the data associated with the dependent variable (i.e. it tests the assumption that $R^2 = 0$). In this case, the F statistic was significant at the 0.01 level. This means that the null hypothesis must be rejected, and the hypothesis accepted that there exists a linear relationship between the dependent and independent variables. The model may therefore be regarded as a relatively accurate tool for forecasting the level of influence of published management literature.

Analysis of Residuals

There are a number of requirements that must be satisfied concerning the regression model generated. These requirements may be addressed through analysis of the *residuals* emergent from the modelling procedure. Residuals represent the error terms generated when the regression model is applied to each case in the original data. There are three specific requirements that must be satisfied:

1. *Equality of Variance* - this refers to the requirement that the error term must have equal variance across different values of the dependent and independent variables. With regard to the dependent variable, for example, a lack of such equality would suggest that as the level of influence of published items changes, the accuracy of the model is affected. In order to test the equality of variance assumption, a Pearson Product Moment Correlation Coefficient was calculated between the values of LOGK20 and the residuals generated by the model. The correlation between these variables was not significant ($r = 0.093$; $p = 0.104$), suggesting that the equality of variance assumption had not been violated.

A second test must also be implemented to test whether the error terms differ for different values of the independent variables. If such a pattern is discovered, it may suggest that the accuracy of the model differs across values of the independent variables. For the categorical variables (PUBMEDIA, NEWCOUN, AUTHDISC) a one-way ANOVA test was implemented. This tests whether the values of the residuals vary for different categories of the independent variables, or whether there are any systematic errors across one or more variables.

The ANOVA revealed that there is no significant relationship between the independent variables and the value of the residuals, since all the significance values were greater than 0.05. However, it should be noted that the relationship between the variable AUTHDISC and the residuals was almost significant ($p = 0.07$). This suggests that the accuracy of the model may vary across different disciplines, but not to an extent which can be defined as significant. The ANOVA also revealed no significant interaction between the independent variables.

The relationship between the residuals and the remaining independent variable (NUMART) was also analysed. This independent variable contained ratio level data. The relationship between NUMART and the residuals was analysed using a Pearson Product Moment Correlation. This revealed a significant correlation between these variables ($r = -0.148$; $p < 0.05$). Hence, there may be problems regarding the validity of the inclusion of NUMART in the model. These problems are discussed in greater depth later in this chapter.

2. *Normality* - the second assumption that must be adhered to is that the residuals follow a normal distribution. If the residuals are not normally

distributed, this may show that the model contains outliers, which may distort the values of the parameters. A P-P plot was therefore produced, showing the pattern of standardised residuals. The values of the residual adhered to the normal line very closely, thus supporting the finding that the residuals are normally distributed. This was confirmed by the results of a Kolmogorov-Smirnov test (K-S = 0.0335; p > 0.2).

3. *Outliers* - if individual cases are not accurately depicted by the regression model, the error terms (residuals) associated with these cases will be relatively large. This may reduce the overall accuracy of the model. Outliers could also distort the values of the partial regression coefficients. In order to identify any outliers, a boxplot was produced. This revealed that there are no outliers in terms of residuals.

Testing the Robustness of the Regression Model

The analysis discussed above established that the regression model generated did not violate any of the assumptions underlying regression analysis. The next stage in the analysis was to study the robustness of the model. This was achieved using the *jackknife technique*, which is described in Miller (1974). This technique has been used previously in bibliometric analysis to test the stability of multiple regression models (Peters and Van Raan, 1994). The jackknife technique tests the stability of the overall regression model by comparing it with the results of regression models generated using a sample from the total data set. If the model is stable, it should not be affected significantly by the removal of sub-sets of the data.

In order to achieve this, a number of samples of data from the total data set must be drawn. The most common method employed is to split the data set into ten groups, each containing 10% of the overall data set. Each of these groups is removed from the data set in turn, and a regression model generated using the remaining cases. Ten regression models are thus generated, each based upon 90% of the total data set.

In the current case, there were 303 cases in the overall data set. Ten groups of data were defined, seven containing thirty cases, and three containing thirty-one cases. In constructing these samples, it was important that any systematic elements should be avoided. This meant that there should be no characteristics individual to one or more of the groups. Hence it was not possible to define samples by the order of cases in the original data set (i.e. group 1 being cases 1-30; group 2 as cases 31-60 etc), since the cases are ordered alphabetically by author. An alternative approach was therefore employed. Consecutive cases were placed in successive samples, with the result that each sample contained every tenth case (i.e. the first sample contained cases 1, 11, 21, 31 ... 301; the second sample contained cases 2, 12, 22, 32 ... 302 etc.). This approach generated an ordered sample. Although this sampling technique was not entirely random, there was no reason to presume that there would be any significant differences between the samples caused purely by the sampling technique employed. This sampling technique thus satisfied the purpose of ensuring the construction of unbiased samples.

As outlined earlier, jackknifing is based upon the exclusion of cases from the analysis, and the generation of models based upon the remaining data. For this test, therefore, each group of data defined was excluded in turn. A regression model was then developed based upon the remaining data. Ten regression analyses were thus carried out, each on the basis of either 272 or 273 cases from the original data set (90% of original data set).

There are two main points of interest in the analysis of these jackknife models. The first of these is the comparison of the variables included in the various regression models. As discussed earlier, the model constructed from the overall data set included five independent variables (NUMART, *isameric, isabook, isecon, ismiscss*) along with the constant term. If the original regression model is to be regarded as robust, these variables should remain significant as cases are removed in the jackknifing process. Variables found to be non-significant in the original model should also remain thus as cases are removed. Differences in the variables included may be regarded as evidence that there are a number of individual cases which have an inordinately large influence upon the regression model; or that there are one or more variables which are only just statistically significant or insignificant. This may suggest that the overall model is unstable.

The second point of interest concerns the values of the partial regression coefficients. It was necessary to measure the coefficients associated with the models generated during the jackknifing process. If the original regression model is to be regarded as stable, the coefficients associated with these models should not differ significantly from those in the original regression model. If the values of the coefficients vary significantly, this may reflect a lack of stability in the nature of the influence of individual independent variables.

Table 8.2 Summary of results of jackknifing (LOGK20)

Cases Excluded	Num art	Is Americ	Is abook	Is Econ	Is Miscss	B Values Outside C.I.
	Variables Included in Regression Equation					
NONE	YES	YES	YES	YES	YES	NONE
1,11,..301	NO	YES	YES	YES	YES	NONE
2,12,..302	YES	YES	YES	YES	YES	NONE
3,13,..303	NO	YES	YES	YES	YES	NONE
4,14,..294	NO	YES	YES	YES	YES	NONE
5,15,..295	NO	YES	YES	YES	NO	CONSTANT
6,16,..296	YES	YES	YES	YES	YES	NONE
7,17,..297	YES	YES	YES	YES	YES	NONE
8,18,..298	NO	YES	YES	YES	YES	NONE
9,19,..299	NO	YES	YES	YES	YES	NONE
10,20.300	NO	YES	YES	YES	YES	NONE

A summary of the results of the jackknifing process is provided in Table 8.2. The central part of the table reveals the degree of stability in the *significance* of different independent variables. The right hand column facilitates analysis of the stability of the *nature* of the influence of individual independent variables.

Referring to the central section of this table, it may be discerned that the variables *isabook*, *isameric* and *isecon* appear in each of the models generated using sub-sets of the original data set. This suggests that the relationship between each of these variables and the dependent variable may be regarded as both significant and robust. The variable *ismiscss* is included in nine out of the ten models generated using the jackknife technique. In the tenth model the value of this coefficient is non-significant, but only marginally ($t = 1.73$; $p = 0.085$). This result suggests that the analysis of the significance of this variable must be approached with caution. However, there is relatively strong evidence to show that it is significantly related to the dependent variable.

The table also reveals that the regression model generated for the overall data set may contain one variable whose significance cannot be defined as being stable. The variable NUMART (the number of articles published by each author) was included in the original regression model. However, when successive subsets containing 90% of the overall data set were employed, this variable became non-significant in seven out of the ten models generated. This pattern may be expected, given that, in the original regression model, NUMART is only marginally above the significance threshold for inclusion in the model ($p = 0.0466$). Hence, although NUMART must be included in the regression model, since it was found to be significant, its influence should not be overstated.

The second issue that had to be addressed concerned the stability of the values of the partial regression coefficients. These can be tested with reference to the original regression equation (see below).

$$LOGK20 = 1.621 + 0.027_{NUMART} + 0.985_{ISABOOK} + 0.754_{ISAMERIC}$$
$$(0.2205) \quad (0.0136) \quad (0.1340) \quad (0.1477)$$

$$+ 0.879_{ISECON} + 0.459_{ISMISCSS}$$
$$(0.2726) \quad (0.1641)$$

The values on the top line of this equation represent the partial regression coefficients of each variable. These coefficients together form the original regression equation. A further term has been added in brackets below each coefficient. This represents the standard error of each coefficient. From these standard errors, it is possible to develop 95% confidence intervals for each coefficient. These confidence intervals are defined as two standard errors each side of the value of the coefficient (assuming independence between the independent variables).

Having defined 95% confidence intervals for each coefficient, the next stage was to establish whether the values of the coefficients generated in the jackknifing procedure were contained within these intervals. The results of this analysis can be seen in the right hand column of the table above. As can be seen, the coefficients generated using the jackknife technique were contained within the 95% confidence interval in each case. The only model in which further analysis was necessary was the fifth one, where the value of the constant lay outside the confidence interval. However, this can be explained by the absence of the variable *ismiscss* from the equation, which had the effect of inflating the value of the constant term.

The results of this jackknifing analysis thus appeared to show that the coefficients associated with *isabook, isameric* and *isecon* (and to a lesser extent *ismiscss*) were both stable and robust.

Conclusions Regarding Level of Influence

From the analysis above, it was possible to draw the following conclusions:

1. The medium through which research is published has a significant effect upon the level of influence associated with management literature. It was possible to determine that, in management research, books are significantly more influential than journal articles.

2. There is a significant difference in the influence level based upon the nationality of the author. The work of North American authors is significantly more influential than that published by authors from Europe.

3. The results concerning disciplinary background were less clear. This may be the result of the larger number of categories contained in this variable. However, it is possible to draw a number of conclusions. Authors writing about economic aspects of management are the most influential, followed by those authors whose work covers a number of aspects of the study of management. There was no significant difference between the influence of work of authors with a background in sociology, psychology or management.

4. There is a positive relationship between the number of items published by authors, and the influence of these items. This suggests that there are a number of seminal management authors who publish widely in the field. It also suggests that 'salami publishing' may not have a significant impact upon the publication of management research. However, this finding must be approached with care, due to the lack of stability discovered in the influence of this variable.

Regression Analysis of Life Cycles

Analysis of the level of influence of management literature had therefore been completed. Attention was therefore moved to the influence of the independent variables (outlined earlier) upon the *longevity* of individual published items. The techniques involved in this process were the same as those employed in the regression analysis implemented to study the level of influence of individual published items. In the discussion below, therefore, these techniques are described more briefly.

Having established that the dependent variable (LOGT99) did not contravene any of the assumptions upon which regression analysis is based (see earlier discussion), it was possible to implement analysis of the relationship between the independent and dependent variables. Before regression analysis was undertaken, a one-way ANOVA test was carried out to offer a preliminary indication of the relationship between the categorical independent variables and the dependent variable.

With regard to two of the independent variables (PUBMEDIA and NEWCOUN), the null hypothesis - that there is no difference in the values of the dependent variable across different categories of the independent variables - could not be rejected. It must therefore be assumed that there is no relationship between the nationality of the author and the length of time over which his/her work is influential. A similar conclusion may be reached with reference to the medium of publication - there is insufficient evidence to suggest that the medium through which research is published affects the longevity of its influence. With regard to the discipline of the author, however, a significant relationship ($p < 0.05$) was discovered. This suggests that the subject discipline of the author may influence the longevity of the work s/he publishes.

The results of the ANOVA test had important implications for the implementation of the regression analysis. They indicated that significant differences could not be identified between different categories of publishing media and nationality. It was thus expected that these variables would be non-significant in the regression analysis. This may be regarded as a justification for excluding these variables from the analysis. However, the inclusion of the additional (non-categorical) independent variable may influence the significance of these categorical variables. All three categorical variables were thus included in the regression analysis, along with the sole ratio-level variable (NUMART).

Development of the Regression Model

Stepwise multiple regression analysis was undertaken in order to test the influence of the various independent variables upon the longevity of individual published items. In the first model, two outliers were discovered. The transformation of the data using natural logs had therefore removed many of the outliers, but had not eradicated the problem entirely. In order to implement regression analysis, these outliers had to be excluded, since their presence may have distorted the model. Having removed the outliers, the regression analysis was re-run. The resultant model can be seen below.

$$LOGT99 = 3.0914 - 0.0927_{ISPSYCH}$$

This equation reveals that only one of the variables entered in the analysis has a significant influence upon the longevity of published items. This is the variable *ispsych*. The model thus suggests that the life cycle of the majority of cases may be predicted simply by the constant term. This constant term produces a value of LOGT99 of 3.0914. Taking the antilog of this value produces a value of 22.01 years. Adding the four years between the date of publication and the first data item included in the logistic modelling procedure (see Chapter 7), this reveals a that the life cycle of the majority of the sample can be predicted as 26 years. The predicted lifetime must be modified, however, where a published item is written by an author with a background in the psychological aspects of management research. The calculation of the life cycle in these cases is 3.0914 - 0.0927 = 2.9987. The antilog of this value is 20.06. Added to the four years between publication and the first data item, this produces a predicted lifetime of published management psychology items of 24.06 years.

The final regression model includes dummy variables from only one of the original independent variables. This suggests that the other three independent variables (nationality of author, publishing media, and publication history of the author) are not significantly related to the longevity of individual published items. None of these variables were close to being significant, since they were well below the 5% significance threshold. This confirms the finding of the ANOVA model, which suggested that there is no relationship between the publication media and the longevity of a published item; or between nationality of author and longevity.

The resultant model thus appears to offer little power in the analysis of the longevity of management literature. This is reflected in the value for the coefficient of determination (R^2=0.033). This reveals that only 3.3% of the variation in the longevity of influence of published items may be accounted for by the variables included in the regression equation. The remaining 96.7% of the variation is caused by other factors. This suggests that the independent variables included do not have significant predictive power in this example. An F test was carried out to test the significance of the fitted model. The F statistic calculated was significant at the 1% level. This means that the null hypothesis must be rejected, and the hypothesis accepted that there exists a linear relationship between the dependent variable and the independent variable included in the equation. However, although a linear relationship exists between the predicted and actual values, the predictive power of the model should not be overstated.

Analysis of Residuals

Having developed a model of the relationship between the longevity of management literature and various independent variables, it was necessary to test the residuals associated with this model. This analysis was implemented in order to ascertain whether the model violated any of the assumptions which form the basis of regression analysis.

1. *Equality of Variance* - in order to test the assumption of equal variance across different values of the dependent variable, a Pearson Product Moment Correlation was implemented. This revealed no significant correlation ($r = 0.009$; $p = 0.875$) between the values of LOGT99 and the residuals generated by the model, thus suggesting that the assumption of equality of variance has not been violated.

A test was also required in order to analyse the pattern of residuals across different values of the independent variables. This entailed analysis of both categorical independent variables (i.e. PUBMEDIA, AUTHDISC AND NEWCOUN) and the single ratio level independent variable (NUMART). However, given that NUMART was not included in the final regression model, it was not necessary to carry out the latter analysis. A one-way ANOVA test was implemented to examine whether the error terms differed across different classes of the categorical independent variables. This revealed that there is no significant relationship between any of the independent variables and the value of the residuals, since all the significance values are greater than 0.05.

However, the ANOVA test revealed that there is an interaction between the independent variables AUTHDISC and PUBMEDIA that is significant at the 5% level. One of the assumptions of regression analysis is that there is no significant interaction between independent variables. Further analysis was therefore required to address this problem, as discussed later in this chapter.

2. *Normality* - the second assumption that must be adhered to is that the residuals follow a normal distribution. In order to test the normality of this distribution, a Kolmogorov-Smirnov test was carried out. This revealed that the null hypothesis (that the residuals form part of a normally distribution) could not be rejected (K-S = 0.0499; $p = 0.067$). However, the non-significance of the test statistic is marginal, thus suggesting that the

assumption of normality must be approached with care. A P-P plot of the standardised residuals was also generated. This revealed some discrepancy around the centre of the data set, which may explain the marginal nature of the non-significance of the test statistic.

3. *Outliers* - in order to identify whether any of the residuals could be defined as outliers, a boxplot was produced. This plot suggested that there are four residuals which may be defined as outliers. These are located at both ends of the range of residual values. The presence of outliers may result from the uniformity of the predicted values generated by the regression model. This uniformity means that the regression model may not depict accurately those cases with unusually long, or unusually short, life cycles.

Testing the Robustness of the Regression Model

It was necessary to analyse the stability of the regression model generated. This was achieved using the jackknifing technique outlined earlier. As discussed previously, jackknifing is based upon the exclusion of a given percentage cases from the data set, and the generation of regression models based upon the remaining data. Ten regression analyses were implemented, each based upon either 272 or 273 cases from the original data set (90% of original data set). A summary of the results is provided in Table 8.3.

As discussed earlier, the jackknifing process raises two issues of concern. The first of these is the variables included in the regression equation. In this example, there is only a single variable included in the overall regression model, along with the constant term. It was thus necessary to analyse whether this variable remained significant when the jackknife technique was applied, and also if any other variables were added to the regression model. The middle column in the table reveals that the variable *ispsych* is included in each model. This suggests that this variable has a significant influence upon the longevity of management literature. No other variables were included in the models generated from the reduced data sets, thus confirming the non-significance of these variables.

It was also necessary to examine the stability of the partial regression coefficient associated with *ispsych*. As before, 95% confidence intervals for the coefficient were defined, based upon the original regression model. The coefficients generated during the jackknifing process were then analysed to establish whether they were contained within these intervals. As can be seen in the right hand column of the table above, the partial regression coefficients generated for the variable *ispsych* were contained within the 95% confidence intervals in each model. This suggests that the nature of the influence of *ispsych* is relatively stable.

Table 8.3   Summary of results of jackknifing (LOGT99)

Cases Excluded from Analysis	Variables in Regression Model	Variables with B Values Outside 95% C.I.
1, 11, 21 .. 301	ISPSYCH	NONE
2, 12, 22 .. 302	ISPSYCH	NONE
3, 13, 23 .. 303	ISPSYCH	NONE
4, 14, 24 .. 294	ISPSYCH	NONE
5, 15, 25 .. 295	ISPSYCH	NONE
6, 16, 26 .. 296	ISPSYCH	NONE
7, 17, 27 .. 297	ISPSYCH	NONE
8, 18, 28 .. 298	ISPSYCH	NONE
9, 19, 29 .. 299	ISPSYCH	NONE
10, 20, 30 .. 300	ISPSYCH	NONE

The results of the jackknifing process appeared to show that the regression model generated using the total data set could be regarded as robust. However, two problems may be identified in employing this model. The first of these is that the model offers a simplistic depiction of the longevity of management literature. The only conclusion that may be reached from the analysis is that psychology items have a significantly shorter lifetime than those items covering other aspects of management. Analysis of the residual terms also revealed that the model may violate some of the assumptions of regression analysis. Further examination of this issue was therefore necessary. In particular, analysis was required into the interaction discovered between the independent variables.

Regression Analysis of Life Cycles Using Combined Independent Variables

As outlined above, a problem was identified in the regression model of longevity due to the interaction between categorical independent variables. It was necessary to remove this interaction, since it violates one of the assumptions underlying regression analysis. To achieve this, new independent variables were constructed which combined those independent variables whose interaction was significant. In the original regression model, the variables AUTHDISC and PUBMEDIA were significantly related. A new variable was therefore constructed, based upon all combinations of the levels within these two independent variables. This new variable was entitled PUBDIS, and contained ten categories (*psybook, psyjourn; socbook, socjourn; econbook, econjour; mgtbook, mgtjourn; miscbook, miscjour*). As can be seen these categories encapsulated all combinations of the discipline of the author, and the media through which research is published.

The interactions between other pairings of the three categorical variables in the original model were non-significant. However, the interaction between NEWCOUN and AUTHDISC was only marginally non-significant. A combined variable was therefore constructed from these two independent variables. The new variable was entitled COUNDIS, and had ten categories, representing all combinations of the nationality and discipline of the author of a particular published item (*ampsyc, othpsyc; amsocio, othsocio; amecon, othecon; ammgt, othmgt; ammisc, othmisc*).

A regression analysis was implemented, incorporating the combined independent variables (PUBDIS and COUNDIS) along with the variables included in the original regression model (AUTHDISC, PUBMEDIA, NEWCOUN and NUMART). The regression was implemented using the stepwise method. The first model generated revealed the presence of two outliers. These outliers were removed, and the regression procedure re-run. The equation of the model generated by the regression analysis is shown below

$$LOGT99 = 3.067 + 0.0912_{AMMISC} + 0.2024_{OTHPSYC} - 0.1492_{PSYJOURN}$$

This equation reveals some interesting information when analysed in conjunction with the regression model for longevity produced with simple, rather than combined, independent variables. That model revealed that the only significant influence upon the longevity of published management literature was the disciplinary background of the author. In particular, the work of authors with a background in psychology appeared to have a shorter lifetime than the remainder of management research. The model generated using combined variables offers a more complex perspective on this relationship. The equation above reveals that psychologists from outside North America (*othpsyc*) produce research with a significantly greater longevity than the average. However, the positive effect of this upon the longevity of psychological articles in general is offset by the significantly below average longevity of psychology journals. This suggests that the overall lack of longevity of psychological items may be traced to the relative short life cycles associated with psychology journal articles.

One further variable was included in the regression model. This was the variable *ammisc* (North American authors with an interdisciplinary background). The presence of this variable suggests that American authors with an interdisciplinary background publish items whose longevity is significantly greater than average. In isolation, this should theoretically produce a difference in the longevity of work written by American and European authors. However, the influence of this variable is offset by the positive coefficient associated with non-American psychology authors (*othpsyc*). The contradictory influences of these two variables results in a lack of significant difference between the longevity of American and non-American management research.

The inclusion of the combined independent variables thus facilitates more complex analysis of the relationship between the longevity of published management research, and the various independent variables. The regression model generated using combined variables was tested for goodness of fit. It was found that the coefficient of determination was 0.085, thus suggesting that 8.5% of the variation in the longevity of the published items could be accounted for by the regression model. This compares favourably with the 3.3% of variation accounted for by the original regression model. The F statistic was also found to be significant (F = 9.259; p <0.001). This suggests that the model generated using combined independent variables may offer a more powerful tool in the prediction of the longevity of management literature. However, before accepting the results of the model, its validity and robustness had to be analysed.

Analysis of Residuals

The residuals associated with the model were tested in order to establish whether any of the assumptions underlying regression analysis had been violated. The results of these tests can be seen below.

1. *Equality of Variance* - the correlation between the values of LOGT99 and the residuals was calculated, in order to test the equality of variance assumption. This revealed no significant relationship between these variables ($r = 0.078$; $p = 0.173$) suggesting that the variance is equal across different predicted values of the dependent variable.

An ANOVA test was also carried out to examine whether the residuals vary significantly for different values of the independent variables included in the regression model (COUNDIS and PUBDIS). It was not possible to carry out an ANOVA simultaneously on both variables since they are, by definition, interrelated. Two separate analyses were therefore implemented. No significant relationship was discovered between either variable and the values of the residual terms.

2. *Normality* - a Kolmogorov-Smirnov test revealed that the null hypothesis that there was no difference between the pattern of residuals and a normal distribution had to be rejected (K-S $= 0.0538$; $p = 0.035$). This lack of normality was supported by a P-P plot of residuals, which revealed that the residuals do not follow the normal line particularly closely. These results suggest that this regression model violates the assumption of normality.

3. *Outliers* - the presence of outliers among the residuals was depicted using a boxplot. This revealed that there are five cases whose residuals could be defined as outliers, thus suggesting that the assumption of lack of outliers among the residuals could not be supported in this instance.

The analysis of residuals thus revealed that the regression model of longevity generated using combined variables may violate some of the assumptions underlying regression analysis. The residuals are not normally distributed, and a number of outliers may be identified. As a result, the model may not be valid.

Testing the Robustness of the Regression Model

The validity of the regression model based upon combined independent variables was therefore questionable. This may have implications for the robustness of the model, which was tested using the jackknifing procedure. A brief summary of the results can be seen in Table 8.4. There are two points to note from this table. The first is that there is little consistency in the variables included in the regression equations developed during the jackknifing process.

Table 8.4   Summary of results of jackknifing (LOGT99 - combined variables)

Cases Excluded	Am misc	Oth psyc	Psy jour	Additional Variables	B Values Outside C.I.
	Variables Included in Regression Model				
1, 11 .. 301	Yes	No	Yes	Othecon Socjourn	Constant
2, 12 .. 302	Yes	No	Yes	----	----
3, 13 .. 303	No	Yes	Yes	Othmisc Miscbook Isabook	Psyjour Constant
4, 14 .. 294	Yes	Yes	Yes	----	----
5, 15 .. 295	No	Yes	Yes	Isabook	Psyjour Constant
6, 16 .. 296	No	No	Yes	----	Constant
7, 17 .. 297	Yes	Yes	Yes	Econjour	----
8, 18 .. 298	Yes	Yes	Yes	----	----
9, 19 .. 299	Yes	Yes	Yes	----	----
10, 20 .. 300	Yes	Yes	Yes	----	----

Only four out of the ten models contain exactly the same independent variables as the original regression model. Particular problems were encountered with regard to the relative lack of significance of *ammisc* and *othpsyc* across the models generated. Another problem was identified with regard to the variables not included in the original regression model. A number of these became significant when the jackknife technique was employed. The variables which became significant varied across the models generated. This may result from the fact the combined variables split the data set into a large number of groups, with relatively few cases in each category. The exclusion of an individual case from a particular group may therefore have a marked effect upon the partial regression coefficient of that group. This will result in changes in the significance of the coefficient, which may alter its position relative to the significance threshold. Hence, the inclusion of variables in the regression model becomes unstable.

Changes in the nature of the influence of individual categories may also be manifested in significant alterations in the value of the partial regression coefficients for these groups. To study this issue, 95% confidence intervals were constructed for the partial regression coefficients in the original model. As can be seen in the right hand column of the table, the partial regression coefficient of the variable *psyjour* lies outside the 95% confidence intervals in two of the models generated. It may therefore be concluded that, although this variable was the only one that was included in each of the models generated, it cannot be regarded as stable.

Conclusions Regarding Longevity

The results of the jackknifing process revealed that the three variables included in the original regression model developed using combined independent variables could not be defined as robust. Two of the variables (*ammisc* and *othpsyc*) became non-significant as the data set was reduced, while the value of the partial regression coefficient of *psyjour* became unstable when the jackknife technique was applied.

It may therefore be concluded that the employment of combined independent variables led to the generation of a regression model which offered a more complex depiction of the relationship between the input characteristics and the longevity of published management research. However, a number of problems were identified with the model, concerning its validity and robustness. These were mainly due to the employment of small sample sizes. The model must therefore be regarded as exploratory rather than definitive, and its contribution should be analysed with reference to this qualification.

Two models of longevity had therefore been developed. The first of these was based upon the independent variables defined originally. This model appeared to be robust. However, it failed to offer analysis of any complexity regarding the relationship between the input characteristics of management research and its longevity. The only conclusion which could be drawn was that items covering organisational psychology have a significantly shorter lifetime than the remainder of management literature. An alternative model was therefore constructed. This was based upon combined independent variables. The resultant model offered a less simplistic analysis of the influences upon the longevity of management research. However, this model was found to lack both robustness and stability, and so could only be employed in an exploratory fashion.

Concluding Remarks

The regression analysis described in this chapter identified the factors which may affect the longevity and level of influence of published management research. This analysis proved to be more successful with regard to the issue of influence levels. The results regarding the longevity of this influence were more ambiguous.

Further analysis was therefore required into the factors which may affect the longevity of management literature. This analysis is outlined in the following chapter. The chapter will also offer more detailed analysis of the relationship between the level of influence of management literature, and its longevity.

9 Case Studies of Management Fashions

Introduction

As discussed in the previous chapter, the influence and longevity of management literature are related. This is reflected in the positive correlation ($r = 0.238$; $p < 0.001$) between these dependent variables. It was therefore necessary to combine these elements within a single analysis. Particular attention was paid to the longevity of management research publications. The regression analysis had revealed that the input characteristics of research publications provide a relatively powerful tool for the prediction of their level of influence. However, the predictive power of the input characteristics with regard to longevity was less evident. This suggests that other factors may have a greater influence upon the longevity of management research.

Approaches to Cluster Analysis

The first stage of this detailed empirical analysis was to combine within a single analysis the influence and longevity of published items. A two-dimensional approach was therefore required. The technique selected was cluster analysis, which groups cases together into clusters, on the basis of their similarity with reference to certain characteristics (Everitt, 1980). For the purposes of this analysis, publications were grouped according to their longevity and level of influence. The purpose of this analysis was to discover whether groups of published items could be identified based upon the similarity of their influence and longevity. In implementing cluster analysis, two issues must be addressed:

1. *Measurement of Similarity*: in cluster analysis, cases are mapped onto a space containing as many dimensions as there are explanatory variables. In this example, a two-dimensional plot was generated, since there were two such variables (influence and longevity). Having mapped the points, it is then possible to measure the distance between them. This distance is regarded as

a measure of the degree of similarity between cases. A number of methods are available for measuring this distance. The most commonly employed measure is the *Squared Euclidean Distance*. This measure was employed in the current analysis.

A problem was encountered in the employment of Squared Euclidean Distance, due to the nature of the data included in the cluster analysis. The data employed for this analysis were the original data (rather than the transformed values employed in the regression analysis). This produced a more 'natural' depiction of the data. However, it also resulted in a distortion of the analysis, due to the different orders of magnitude associated with the data pertaining to influence and longevity. The values of the former extended to around five hundred, while the highest value for longevity was around forty. Squared Euclidean Distance is based upon absolute, rather than relative, differences between cases. In the current analysis, therefore, a difference of ten units in the level of influence between two cases has the same effect upon the distance between them as a difference of ten years in their life cycles. Given the greater dispersion of the data associated with level of influence, this had the effect of grouping clusters chiefly on the basis of their level of influence, since greater arithmetic differences were identified in the data associated with this variable. With longevity mapped on the x-axis, and influence on the y-axis, the clusters developed were simply horizontal bands containing cases with similar levels of influence.

It was therefore necessary to standardise the values for influence and longevity. Standardisation removes the effect of differences in the orders of magnitude of the data associated with the two variables. The values for each factor were scaled between 0 and 1, with the result that the data on influence and longevity were directly comparable. The original pattern of data for each factor was retained, so that no detail regarding the relationship between cases was sacrificed. The standardised data could thus be included in the cluster analysis.

2. *Criteria for Clustering Cases* - in hierarchical cluster analysis, all cases are considered as separate clusters at the outset. Hence the number of clusters equates to the number of cases. Cases are then grouped together to form larger clusters on the basis of their similarity. In turn, these clusters are joined together as a result of their relative similarity. This process is iterative, and continues until no further clustering is possible, due to the lack of similarity among the remaining clusters. The important information emergent from this process is which cases are grouped together, and the level of similarity

between them. The three most commonly used methods for clustering cases are:

1. Single Member Linkage - this includes cases in a given cluster on the basis of their similarity (distance) to the nearest case already included in the cluster. Clusters are also joined on the basis of the similarity of their closest points. This approach to clustering tends to result in long, chain-like clusters, since cases are included with reference to a single point. The main problem with this approach is that it may produce clusters which appear to be illogical, with cases with little similarity included in the same cluster.
2. Furthest Member Linkage - this approach includes cases in a given cluster on the basis of their similarity to the furthest case already included in the cluster. Clusters are also joined on the basis of the similarity of their most distant points. This approach tends to result in small, tightly grouped clusters, since it is based upon reducing the level of dissimilarity within each cluster. The main problem with this approach is that it often produces a large number of clusters, particularly at the first level of clustering. This may reduce the analytical power of the resultant analysis.
3. Between Groups Linkage - this approach includes cases in a particular cluster on the basis of their similarity to the cluster in its entirety. It is thus based upon a measure of the distance between a case and all the cases contained in a given cluster. Clusters are combined based upon the distance between all the cases in both clusters. Between Groups Linkage may be regarded as a combination of the two approaches outlined above, and so overcomes the problems associated with each of them. This approach was therefore appropriate to this study.

Cluster analysis was implemented based upon the level of influence and longevity of management research publications. The measure of similarity employed was Squared Euclidean Distance, and clustering was based upon Between Groups Linkage.

Results of the Cluster Analysis

The results of the cluster analysis can be seen in the chart in Appendix 3. (The clustering is depicted in a simplified form in order to aid presentation. There is no relationship between the size of each bubble and the number of cases in the corresponding cluster.)

A number of interesting results emerge from this chart. The first of these is that the majority of cases in the sample are contained within two large clusters (defined as Clusters A and B). Cluster A contains cases which are relatively uninfluential, and have a short life cycle; while Cluster B contains clusters which are again relatively uninfluential, but whose life cycle is longer, without being among those with the longest life cycles.

The presence of these two large clusters requires further discussion, particularly with reference to the nature of the sample. At first glance, it may appear that the cases in these clusters have little influence upon the management research community. Given the number of cases in these clusters, the conclusion could be reached that the majority of management research is relatively uninfluential. However, such a conclusion would be misguided, due to the nature of the sampling frame employed in this research. The sample constructed is not representative of management research in its entirety. Rather, its purpose is the identification of the most influential management writers of recent decades. This must be recognised when analysing the cases contained in the two large clusters. They are not necessarily uninfluential in comparison to the totality of management research. However, they are relatively uninfluential when compared with the remainder of the work of leading management authors. The conclusion must therefore be reached that the majority of the research published by leading management authors does not have a far-reaching influence upon the management research community.

Forty two cases (out of the sample of 303) were not contained within these two large clusters. The cases outside the main clusters are characterised by significantly high influence and/or long life cycle. The pattern of influence associated with these cases can therefore be defined as exceptional in some way. These cases were divided into three clusters, with a single case forming a cluster on its own. This case was *'Organizations'* by James March and Herbert Simon (1958), which was highly influential over a long period of time. Its level of influence was so high that it could not be clustered with any other cases.

The important point to note with regard to the clustering resultant from the analysis above is the basis upon which it was achieved. There were two characteristics which informed the clustering process - the level of influence and longevity of published items. However, referring to Appendix 3, it can be seen that the clusters were mainly formed on the basis of the level of influence of individual cases. The main difference between the main clusters and the forty one cases outside them was that the cases outside the main clusters (with the exception of the three cases in Cluster 3) were significantly more influential than those cases in the main clusters. The life cycles of the cases in Clusters 1 and 2 were not significantly different to those publications contained in the main clusters. *The thirty eight publications in Clusters 1 and 2 were therefore be considered to have had a profound influence upon the management research community at some time. A list of these publications is provided in Table 9.1. These publications were selected for more detailed analysis.*

The publications in Cluster 3 are characterised by the longest life cycles in the entire data set. However, they have received relatively few citations, suggesting that their longevity may result from small increases in the number of citations in the final years included in the logistic modelling procedure. This was confirmed with reference to the original citation data for these cases. The three publications in this cluster were not therefore selected for further analysis.

Characteristics of Seminal Management Publications

The input characteristics of the publications in Clusters 1 and 2 were analysed. A clear pattern emerged with reference to publishing media and nationality of author. Out of the 38 cases, 36 were published in book form, and 34 were written by North American authors. None of the cases were journal publications written by European authors. Given that there were large numbers of journal articles and European publications within the data set, this supports the finding of the regression analysis that nationality of author and medium of publication were significantly related to the influence of published items. The pattern with regard to the academic background of the authors was less clear, as there was a spread of disciplines for the items outside the main clusters.

The 38 seminal management publications were split into two distinct groups by the cluster analysis. This delineation was based chiefly upon the longevity of these items. Cluster 1 contained those publications that had relatively short life cycles. These publications are therefore highly influential, but their influence is relatively short lived. Using the definition of fashions suggested by Kroeber (1919) Cluster 1 may be regarded as containing seminal management works which are subject to pressures of fashion.

Publications in Cluster 2 were characterised by longer life cycles. These publications are therfore highly influential over a long period of time and, as such, may be regarded as central to the development of management research over a long period of time. They are considered to be relatively free of fashionable pressures. Further analysis was therefore undertaken into the characteristics associated with these two categories of management publications. Such analysis may reveal reasons why some management publications are more susceptible than other to fashionable pressures.

Table 9.1 List of highly influential management publications

Cluster	Lead Author	Title	Year
1	Argyris C.	Integrating Individuals	1964
1	Etzioni A.	The Active Society	1968
1	Fiedler F.	A Theory of Leadership Effectiveness	1967
1	Etzioni A.	Modern Organizations	1964
1	Schumacher E.	Small is Beautiful	1973
1	Bennis W.	Changing Organizations	1966
1	Crozier M.	The Bureaucratic Phenomenon	1963
1	Woodward J.	Industrial Organization	1965
1	Likert R.	The Human Organization	1967
1	Lawrence P.	Organization and Environment	1967
1	Blau P.	Exchange and Power in Social Life	1964
1	Vroom V.	Work and Motivation	1964
1	Braverman H.	Labor and Monopoly Capital	1974
1	Gouldner A.	The Coming Crisis in Western Sociology	1970
1	Kahn R.	Organizational Stress	1964
1	Etzioni A.	Comparative Analysis of Complex Organizations	1961
1	Maslow A.	Towards a Psychology of Being	1962
1	Galbraith J.K.	The New Industrial State	1967
1	McClelland D.	The Achieving Society	1961
1	Whyte W.	Organization Man	1956
1	Thompson J.	Organizations in Action	1967
1	Katz D.	The Social Psychology of Organizations	1966
1	Cyert R.	A Behavioral Theory of the Firm	1963
1	Williamson O.	Markets and Hierarchies	1975
1	Blau P.	The American Occupational Structure	1967
1	Likert R.	New Patterns of Management	1961
1	Blau P.	Formal Organizations	1962
1	McGregor D.	The Human Side of Enterprise	1960
2	Herzberg F.	The Motivation to Work	1959
2	Simon H.	Administrative Behavior	1957
2	Galbraith J.K.	The Affluent Society	1958
2	Simon H.	Models of Man	1957
2	Argyris C.	Personality and Organization	1957
2	Burns T.	The Management of Innovation	1961
2	Chandler A.	Strategy and Structure	1962
2	Selznick P.	Leadership and Administration	1957
2	Gouldner A.	American Sociological Review 25: 161-178	1960
2	Lindblom C.	Public Administration Review 19: 79-88	1959

Subject Discipline and the Longevity of Management Literature

An extended evaluation of the groupings resulting from the cluster analysis raised an interesting issue with regard to the subject discipline of the authors in specific clusters. In particular the clustering of items written by authors with a background in sociology and psychology appeared to be significant. As discussed in Chapter 2, psychology and sociology are regarded as two of the major influences upon organisational research. Authors from these disciplines were responsible for 27 of the 38 cases (i.e. 71%) selected for further analysis (59% of the publications in the total data set were written by sociologists and psychologists). Sixteen of these items were written by sociologists, eleven by psychologists. This supports the central role accorded to these disciplines in the development of management theory.

Further analysis revealed that out of the twenty eight cases in Cluster 1, twenty three were written by authors with a background in either psychology or sociology (13 from sociology, 10 from psychology). Hence all but two of the sociology publications defined as seminal, and all but one of the seminal psychology publications, were contained within Cluster 1. This cluster represents management research which is highly influential, but whose influence is relatively short-lived, and is therefore regarded as being subject to pressures of fashion. Further analysis was thus necessary to examine possible causes of the fashionable nature of some of the work written by authors with a background in sociology and psychology.

Particular emphasis was placed upon the study of psychology authors. There were two reasons for this. The first reason was that detailed analysis of the clustering revealed that psychology publications in Cluster 1 tended to have shorter life cycles than the sociology publications in that cluster.

The second reason for concentrating upon psychology items was based upon the regression analysis described in Chapter 7. In this analysis, it was revealed that the life cycles associated with psychology items were significantly shorter than those written by authors from other disciplines. As discussed in the previous chapter, one of the main problems encountered with the regression analysis was its overall lack of predictive power with regard to the longevity of published items. By implementing more detailed analysis of the significant finding regarding psychology items, it may be possible to offer an insight into the factors which influence the longevity of published items.

Analysis of Psychological Theories of Management

As outlined above, eleven published items outside the main clusters were written by authors with a background in psychology. These items were written by nine distinct authors. Each of these items was a book, and they were all written by North American authors. Hence the input factors for each case were identical. However, when the longevity of these cases was analysed, it was found that this differed markedly across cases. The lifetime of these items ranged from 19.43 years to 35.72 years. A more detailed analysis of the life cycles associated with these psychology publications was therefore required. The purpose of this analysis was to identify any factors which may cause the lack of consistency, in terms of life cycles, of cases with the same input characteristics.

One interesting point which emerged from this analysis concerned the relationship between the date of publication and the length of life cycle associated with each item. It was found that the items with the longest life cycles were those which were published earliest. The life cycles of items published at a later date declined at a roughly constant rate. This pattern therefore seemed to suggest that there was an underlying factor in the life cycles of these items, associated with the time at which they were published.

The life cycles calculated for the psychology items were such that the point in time when these items would be disregarded seemed to be similar in each case. One possible explanation for this is that an overall pattern exists regarding the general influence of psychological approaches to organisational issues. Such a pattern would be manifested in similar levels of influence for individual published items at given points in time. In order to test the validity of this explanation, a measure of the similarity between the patterns of influence of individual psychology items was required.

If the pattern of influence of each psychology item is similar, this will be evident in the similarity of the peaks of influence of these publications. Further analysis was therefore undertaken in order to identify the peaks of interest associated with the eleven psychology publications.

Defining Peaks of Influence

A method was required which would identify the year in which the influence of a published item was at its peak. In developing this method two problems had to be addressed:

1. *Lack of Stability in Citation Rates* - the simplest definition of the peak of influence of a published item is the year in which the rate of citation is at its highest. However, a problem may be encountered with this definition, as a result of the lack of stability in citation rates. As outlined in the preliminary empirical analysis (see Chapter 6), the number of citations received by a published item can vary greatly between years. It is therefore necessary to discern the underlying trend in citations, in order to remove the effect of the erratic nature of the data.

In order to identify the underlying trend in the rate of citations, the data was smoothed. As discussed in Chapter 6, two methods of smoothing are available - moving averages and exponential smoothing. The latter had been employed in the preliminary empirical analysis, since analysis was required of the trends within the data set in its entirety. For the purposes of the current analysis, however, a smoothing technique was required which only referred to the data around the peaks in citation rates. The data was therefore smoothed using centred moving averages. These moving averages were calculated with a span of three years (i.e. the averages were calculated from the year being studied, the previous year and the following year). In this way, the peak of interest in individual publications was defined on the basis of three years of citation data, rather than data from a single year. This reduced the effect of any unusually large individual data items.

2. *Presence of Local Maxima* - there exists no method of identifying the definitive peak of influence of a particular published item, since this peak may lie beyond the available data. This is one of the main problems associated with the employment of diachronous techniques in the study of obsolescence, as discussed in Chapter 4. In the current example, there is no way of measuring the influence of the cases in the sample beyond the present day. The peak of influence of one or more of these cases may in fact be located some time in the next century or beyond. Hence the peak identified from available data may be a local, rather than overall, maximum. The only way to address the problem of local maxima is to employ the greatest amount of citation data available. The data employed in identifying the peaks of interest in published items thus covered the period from the date of their publication until the most recent data available (i.e. 1994). It was hoped that by employing the maximum amount of available citation data (at least 25 years in each case), the peak would be correctly identified.

Moving averages were calculated for the period between the date of publication and the most recent year of citation data available. This produced values for the moving average in all years except the year of publication and the final data year, since the smoothing technique precludes the generation of a value for the initial and final periods. The highest average value for each case was then identified, and defined as the peak of influence of a published item. Table 9.2 shows the years which represented the peak of interest identified for each of the psychology items.

As can be seen in this table, the peak of interest in each of these items covered a relatively short period, between 1974 and 1978. This finding supports the hypothesis that there exists an overall pattern of influence of psychological approaches to organisational issues. It was necessary to analyse why such a period factor should exist. A number of possible explanations may be postulated for the similarity identified in the peaks of influence associated with these cases. For the purposes of this project, the most interesting of these possibilities is that these items were influential in the same years because they were fashionable at that time. In order to study the accuracy of this explanation it was necessary to study the published items in greater depth.

Table 9.2 Peaks of interest in the work of leading psychology authors

AUTHOR	PUBLICATION	PUB	PEAK
C. Argyris	Personality and Organization	1957	1977
C. Argyris	Integrating Individuals	1964	1976
A. Maslow	Towards a Psychology of Being	1962	1978
D. McGregor	The Human Side of Enterprise	1960	1975
D. McClelland	The Achieving Society	1961	1976
V. Vroom	A Theory of Leadership Effectiveness	1964	1977
R. Likert	New Patterns of Management	1961	1975
R. Likert	The Human Organization	1967	1975
F. Fiedler	A Theory of Leadership Effectiveness	1967	1977
F. Herzberg	The Motivation to Work	1959	1974
W. Bennis	Changing Organizations	1966	1974

The analysis of the items published by authors with a background in psychology involved two stages. The first stage was to implement case studies of the work of these theorists, to highlight possible relationships between the content of research publications, and the longevity of their influence. These case studies place particular emphasis upon the relationship between the work of different theorists, with specific reference to their similarity. The second stage in the analysis studied the extent to which the apparent similarity in the citation patterns associated with these published items results from the similarity of their content. Other potential factors that may affect the patterns of influence discovered are also discussed.

Case Studies of Early Psychological Theorists

Psychological approaches to organisational research started to emerge on a significant scale during the 1950s. These theories must be placed in the context of the nature of organisational research at this time. The dominant theory in organisational research throughout the early part of this century was scientific management, originated by F.W. Taylor (1911). In extremely simplistic terms, scientific management was based upon the assumption that workers simply laboured for money. Tasks were therefore designed for maximum efficiency, with no reference to the psychological or social needs of employees. This often resulted in the proliferation of repetitive, unskilled jobs. Taylor's work, and the validity of its assumptions, had been challenged during the 1930s by the human relations theories of Elton Mayo (1933). Mayo emphasised the social aspects of the work environment. He pointed to the need for association between workers, and advocated the construction of work teams to increase motivation among employees.

Despite the challenge of the human relations school, Taylor's theories were still dominant in many organisations in the 1950s (Rose, 1988). In response to Taylor's work, a number of theorists emerged who emphasised the psychological aspects of work. They can therefore be contrasted with earlier human relations theorists, who concentrated upon the social characteristics of work organisation. Psychological theorists paid particular attention to the design of jobs, and the relationship between the psychological well-being of individuals and their motivation. The work of these psychological theorists is outlined below.

The forerunner of psychological approaches to management was *Abraham Maslow*. His book '*Motivation and Personality*' (1954) represents one of the earliest attempts to formalise the nature of the relationship between the work undertaken by employees and their psychological well-being. The rationale of this study was the assumption that workers who are satisfied with their work will be more productive than those who are not. Maslow postulated that individuals possess a 'hierarchy of needs'. The most basic of these needs are those for food and shelter (defined as physiological needs). Once these needs have been satisfied, individuals aim to satisfy their need for love and respect. Finally if these needs are satisfied, individuals will seek self-actualisation, through which they fulfil their potential and feel a sense of self-worth. Through self-actualisation, they become satisfied with their role within social and organisational settings. The needs outlined here are dependent upon the previous level, so that if an individual cannot satisfy their needs at one level s/he cannot achieve higher level satisfactions. This may lead to frustration, resulting in pathological behaviour.

In organisational terms, this pathological behaviour may be manifested in wilful lack of concern for organisational goals among employees. If the nature of their work precludes the satisfaction of their needs, workers will become frustrated and so demotivated. This may result in less productivity and lower quality work from employees. Maslow thus argued that it was in the interests of organisations to ensure the psychological well-being of their employees. He contended that job satisfaction, which is dependent the ability of employees to achieve self-actualisation through their work, would result in a more committed and productive workforce.

The book '*Motivation and Personality*' was not included in the sample for the current study, since its publication date is earlier than the point at which the coverage of the citation indexes begins (i.e. before 1956). However, a later work by Maslow ('*Towards a Psychology of Being*', published in 1961) was also found to be highly influential. This book represents an extension of Maslow's work into the postulation of a general theory for psychological well being. It provides an overall statement of the ideas and beliefs of his humanist psychology. As such, its influence may be regarded as offering a reliable guide to the influence of Maslow's ideas upon the academic community. The peak of influence of this book was 1978.

One of the earliest theorists influenced by the ideas of Maslow was *Chris Argyris*. In his book '*Personality and Organisations*', published in 1957, he studied the nature of personal development and self-actualisation. Particular attention was paid to the manner in which the design of jobs affected the extent to which employees achieved self-actualisation. Argyris pointed to a fundamental paradox faced by many employees in the expectations made of them inside and outside the workplace. As individuals in society they are expected to progress from infantile dependence as a child, into mature independence as an adult. They are therefore expected to accept responsibility for their own behaviour, and to make decisions for themselves. However, the design of organisations precludes the extension of these expectations to the workplace. Employees are treated as irresponsible and dependent once they enter the workplace. The jobs they hold often offer little independence or responsibility. Employees thus become frustrated by the lack of potential to exercise their own discretion; which may in turn be manifested in apathy among employees, lower productivity, and higher rates of absenteeism.

Argyris built on these ideas in a number of books, including '*Integrating Individuals*', which was published in 1964. This represented an extension of his earlier studies, and also studied how organisations could be changed to foster greater involvement on the part of employees. This interest in organisational change mechanisms later led Argyris (in partnership with Donald Schon) to study the role of learning in the transformation of organisations. However, the work on organisational learning is not included in the current study, since it was published after the sampling frame constructed. The peak of influence of '*Integrating Individuals*' was in 1976, while the peak of citations to '*Personality and Organisations*' was in 1977. This suggests that the peak of interest in the early research undertaken by Argyris could be clearly defined as being in the mid 1970s, a similar peak to the work of Maslow. This may reflect the similarity of their work on self-actualisation.

A similar study to that of Argyris was implemented by *Douglas McGregor*. In his most influential book, '*The Human Side of Enterprise*', published in 1960, McGregor studied the assumptions about human nature which form the basis of the design of jobs within organisations. McGregor argued that there are two alternative assumptions about human nature. He defined these as Theory X and Theory Y. Theory X is based upon the assumption that fundamental human nature determines that human beings dislike work. They must therefore be coerced and directed in the workplace, since they will not work effectively unless they are forced in some way. McGregor argued that this assumption formed the traditional basis of the design of organisational structures and individual jobs. Direct parallels may be thus drawn between this analysis and that offered by Argyris.

The second theory, Theory Y, offers an alternative view of the relationship between individuals and work. This theory assumes that individuals appreciate physical and mental effort, and will be self-motivated in their approach to work, provided that their work is designed to be challenging and stimulating. They will also seek responsibility and become involved in decision making processes. McGregor argued that the assumptions about workers accepted by senior managers will affect the managerial style and design of jobs within any organisation. He contended that only by accepting Theory Y can organisations prosper in the long term. In this respect, McGregor's work may be compared directly with that of Argyris. Both authors point to the need for autonomy to be granted to employees in order for them to contribute fully to the success of the organisation. This congruence is reflected in the similarity of the peak of interest in the work of these authors. The citation peak for '*The Human Side of Enterprise*' was in 1975, just before the peak of interest in the work of Argyris.

The theories outlined above offer an analysis of the overall effect of different management styles upon employee satisfaction and motivation. In this analysis, little attention is paid to differences between individual employees. It therefore suggests that the effect of different management practices will be the same on all employees. However, a number of theorists have highlighted the need for analysis at the level of the individual employee. One of the most influential of these theorists was *Victor Vroom*. He studied the effect of participation in decision making upon worker motivation and attitudes, and found its influence to be generally positive. However, the size of the effect upon motivation was not uniform. Rather, it was mediated by the personality characteristics of individual employees, thus necessitating the study of these individual characteristics. This led Vroom to develop 'expectancy theory', which states that the increase in motivation experienced by an individual employee in response to a particular change will be the product of two factors. The first of these is the value (or valency) placed upon the outcome of the change by the individual. Increased motivation will only occur where an employee places great value upon the outcome of a particular stimulus. The second factor is expectancy. An individual will only be motivated in response to a stimulus if the outcome is perceived as attainable. Hence goals which are perceived as being unattainable and/or of little value will only have a marginal effect upon the motivation of an individual employee. The peak of interest in the work of Vroom occurred in 1977.

David McClelland also implemented analysis of individual motivations. He defined four motives for human activity. These were achievement, power, affiliation and avoidance. Of particular interest to McClelland was the nature of the motivation of individuals to achieve (hence the name of his most famous work '*The Achievement Motive*'). In organisational terms, this motivation would result in greater productivity among employees. He found that the need to achieve was particularly prevalent among managers, and could be regarded as an explanation of their relative seniority within an organisation. However, McClelland did not regard the various motivations as purely innate. He suggested that the motivation to achieve emerges from environmental influences. This has two important implications. The first of these is that individuals may be trained in order to increase their achievement motivation. The second is that employees will respond to the nature of the work in which they are involved. McClelland found that the need to achieve was positively associated with work which offered responsibility, innovation, moderate task difficulty and high levels of feedback. Hence jobs which offer these characteristics may result in a workforce with a greater interest in achievement, which is assumed to increase their productivity and job satisfaction. The peak of influence of McClelland's work was in 1976. This is close to the peak of interest in the work of Vroom, whose theories addressed similar issues.

The main focus of the research implemented by McClelland was the nature of employee motivation. This work may be regarded as similar to that undertaken by Maslow, Argyris and Vroom. A number of writers extended this work by introducing the influence of management styles upon employees motivation. In *'New Patterns of Management'* (1961) and *'The Human Organisation'* (1967), *Rensis Likert* studied different approaches to management, and their influence upon the productivity of employees. His early work was based upon the observation of supervisors. He identified two approaches to the supervision of workers. The first approach is 'job centred', and places primary importance upon the completion of the tasks undertaken. Less attention is paid to the effect of the work upon individual employees involved in the tasks. Likert defined the alternative approach as 'employee centred'. This focuses chiefly upon the employees involved in a particular task. Supervisors are concerned with designing jobs in order to maximise the satisfaction of employees. In this way, it is believed that the workers will be more productive. Likert found that employee centred supervisors were more successful, both in terms of output and employee satisfaction.

Likert extended his study to the overall management of organisations, and defined four types of management - exploitative authoritarian, benevolent authoritarian, consultative and participative. These represent an ordered sequence, with the involvement of employees, and concern for their well-being, following an increasing pattern. Likert argued that participative management would produce the greatest employee commitment and productivity in the long term. He also contended that the type of management employed would influence organisational structure, which would in turn determine future management styles. It is therefore necessary for organisations to accept participative management styles, and to design organisational structures accordingly.

An analysis of management styles was also implemented by *Frederick Fiedler* in his book *'A Theory of Leadership Effectiveness'*, published in 1967. Fiedler concentrated specifically upon the subject of leadership, particularly with reference to work groups. Strong comparisons may be made between the work of Fiedler and that of Likert. Fiedler identified two types of leaders - relationship motivated and task motivated. These types can be associated directly with Likert's depiction of employee-centred and job-centred supervisors. However, while Likert advocated the employment of a participative, employee centred approach to management in all circumstances, Fiedler's conclusions are less definite. He argues that the style of leadership employed should depend upon the nature of the situation faced by managers. This represents a contingency approach to management, in which management styles are contingent upon external pressures. Fiedler found that task motivated leaders are most successful in very favourable and unfavourable situations, while employee centred approaches are best suited to conditions characterised by neither of these extremes. The style of management employed must therefore be flexible, in order to respond to the changing conditions faced by organisations. The peak of interest in the work of Fiedler was in 1977. This is slightly later than the peak associated with Likert. The citation rate to both of Likert's books was at its highest in 1975.

Case Study of the Organization Development Movement

The theories outlined above all share a common theme. This is the positive impact that concern for the nature of the work undertaken by employees has upon organisations. Such concern is not advocated for purely altruistic reasons. It is also regarded within these theories as desirable in commercial terms, since it will result in higher motivation among the workforce. In turn this higher motivation will lead to higher productivity, lower absenteeism and lower labour turnover.

These theories were instrumental in the evolution of the *Organization Development (OD)* movement. This was the name given to the work of a number of theorists during the 1960s. The OD movement advocated active intervention in organisations by external consultants using behavioural science techniques, which are based upon the psychological approaches outlined above. This intervention was designed to transform organisations to increase their efficiency and the satisfaction of their employees (hence the name of the book by *Warren Bennis*, one of its main proponents – '*Changing Organizations*', published in 1966). Bennis highlighted the lack of understanding of organisational processes on the part of managers, and the necessity of educating them so that they could become involved in the programs through which their organisations would be changed.

The OD movement may be regarded as the practical implementation of the psychological theories outlined above. Whereas the early theorists studying psychological approaches to management concentrated upon the depiction of the nature of employee motivation, the OD movement prescribed specific solutions to organisational problems. It offered a number of different techniques, including managerial grids and T (training) groups. Essentially, it was a movement which believed that organisational change was both attainable and desirable. It argued that through the employment of OD techniques, organisations would become both more efficient and more harmonious.

One early psychological theorist who later advocated specific intervention in organisations was *Frederick Herzberg*. In his book '*The Motivation to Work*' (1959, with B. Mausner and B. Snyderman), Herzberg studied the psychological effects of the nature of work upon employees. His main finding was that the causes of job satisfaction are different to those factors that cause dissatisfaction among workers. The factors that cause dissatisfaction are all related to the need for workers to avoid physical and social deprivation. These include supervision, pay and working conditions. Herzberg defined these as hygiene factors. The factors leading to job satisfaction relate to the need for individuals to realise their potential, and are defined as motivating factors. These include responsibility, advancement and achievement. Herzberg's findings may be compared with those of Maslow, since the hygiene factors are similar to Maslow's physiological and social needs; and the motivating factors are comparable with Maslow's depiction of the need for self-actualisation. Perhaps the most interesting finding of Herzberg's research is the nature of the relationship between satisfaction and dissatisfaction. Since the factors that lead to each of these conditions are distinct from each other, the two conditions cannot be regarded as opposites. Rather, the opposite of job satisfaction is lack of job satisfaction; and the opposite of dissatisfaction with work is an absence of such dissatisfaction.

Herzberg's findings led him to develop a specific theory of how the motivation of employees could be enhanced. From the discussion above it is clear that changing the hygiene factors will not increase motivation. Instead, the motivating factors must be altered in order to increase the motivation of employees. In order to achieve this, work must be redesigned using 'job enrichment' principles. Job enrichment advocates the design of jobs which enhance the opportunity for employees to experience psychological development. In order to facilitate such development, jobs must offer increased autonomy, responsibility, learning and recognition. This is not the same as job enlargement (increasing the number of tasks undertaken by an individual) or job rotation (switching workers periodically between tasks). Both of these approaches simply extend the number of mundane, undemanding tasks undertaken by employees, and will not increase their motivation in the long term. Only by offering employees work that is both challenging and relatively autonomous will their motivation be increased. The peak of interest in the work of both Bennis and Herzberg occurred in 1974. This was the earliest peak discovered among the psychological theorists located outside the main clusters as a result of the cluster analysis. Further analysis of this finding is offered in the following section.

Relating Psychological Theories to their Citation Patterns

From the discussion above, it can be established that the peak of interest in each of the works described was located between 1974 and 1978. Given the length of time over which these items were published (10 years), this was a finding which required further analysis. In particular, attention had to be paid to the potential causes of the similarity of the peak of interest across these cases.

Rose (1988) argues that there was an increase in the interest in psychological theories in the late 1960s and early 1970s. This represented part of the wider concern with the nature of capitalist, industrial organisations, and the position of individual workers within these organisations. The radical political movements of the 1960s had questioned the logic of capitalism, and had opened debate upon the role of political, social and economic institutions. In sociological terms, this led to the questioning of the ability of traditional theories to cope with these radical ideas (Gouldner, 1970). In terms of organisational theory, the main effect was to challenge the dominant position of scientific management techniques within the management of organisations. In particular, there were increasing calls for the dehumanising influence of scientific management to be contested.

One of the main outcomes of the search for alternatives to scientific management was the increased interest in psychological theories. Their emphasis upon psychological well-being was in accord with the wider social concerns at this time. In particular, the ideas of Organisation Development (OD) theorists became popular at this time (Gill and Whittle, 1992). This is reflected in the increasing number of citations received by these theorists in the mid-1970s. The peak of interest in the OD theories of Bennis and Herzberg occurred in 1974 (N.B. the time lags resulting from the publication process must be taken into account. A citation peak in 1974 may therefore reflect a peak of interest in the period 1971-1973). Further analysis of other OD publications revealed a similar pattern. The peak of influence of Blake and Mouton's '*Managerial Grid*' (1964) occurred in 1973; and the *Harvard Business Review* articles on job enrichment written by Herzberg (1968) and Paul *et al* (1969) were at their most influential in 1975. These findings suggest that the peak of influence of the OD movement occurred in the early part of the 1970s. This result is in accord with that of Gill and Whittle (1992).

As outlined earlier, OD theories may be regarded as a development upon the work of early psychological authors. It was therefore necessary to explain the pattern of influence of these early theorists. Before the OD movement became influential, interest in the work of early psychological theorists was relatively stable, and the rate of citation to this work was roughly constant during the 1960s. The increased popularity of OD theories in the early 1970s then led to a growth in the influence of the theories which had informed the development of the OD movement. The peak of influence of these early theories occurred in the period between 1975 and 1977, which is later than that identified for the OD theories. A possible hypothesis for this difference between the peaks of influence is offered below.

Researchers in the early 1970s studying OD theories would have largely employed the work of writers such as Bennis, Herzberg and Blake and Mouton as the starting point for their research. They would have therefore cited publications written by these authors. This is reflected in the increase in citations to these authors at this time. Some researchers may then have extended their work in order to study the academic roots of the OD movement. This would have led them to study the psychological theories of writers such as Maslow, Likert and McGregor, thus increasing the rate at which the work of these authors was cited. The later citation peak associated with the work of these early theorists may thus result from theorists wishing to develop greater understanding of the foundations of the OD movement.

This hypothesis suggests that the lack of longevity associated with psychological theories may be traced to the fashionable nature of these approaches during the early 1970s. This contention is supported by Gill and Whittle (1992), who depicted OD as a management fashion, and also by Hackman (1975) who questioned the long term influence of job enrichment.

The analysis above may lead to the conclusion that the influence of particular theories is purely a product of their relationship with wider social and political conditions. However, such a conclusion would be overly simplistic. There are a number of other factors which may affect the pattern of influence associated with organisational theories. The first of these is the similarity of the theories developed within a given discipline. The effect of the fashionable nature of OD theories upon other psychological approaches to organisational research may have been particularly strong due to the similarity of their concerns. Although psychological authors postulate a number of different theories, they share a common theme. This is the idea that one of the main concerns of managers should be to motivate the employees under their supervision. In order to achieve this, managers must be aware of the psychological needs of employees, and design their work accordingly. Only by designing work with reference to the psychological well-being of employees can managers develop a satisfied, motivated and productive workforce.

It is the similarity in these approaches that may explain the correspondence between the peaks of interest in them. Due to this similarity, once the interest in OD and job enrichment waned, this had a direct effect upon the influence of the earlier psychological studies. Hence, the number of citations received by both the OD theorists and the early psychological authors declined at a similar rate after the peak of interest had occurred during the 1970s.

The correspondence in the peaks of interest in the work of these authors may be partially explained with reference to the literature of epidemiology (Bailey, 1975). As discussed in Chapter 2, epidemiology (the study of contagious diseases) has been applied previously to the study of management fashions. Abrahamson (1991) identified two factors, drawn from the study of epidemiology, which may lead to the diffusion of management fashions. The first of these (heterophily) is of particular relevance here. Abrahamson (1991) contended that management fashions would diffuse most rapidly where the concerns of managers are similar. This similarity of concerns may lead managers to seek similar solutions to their problems, causing the diffusion of a particular group of management techniques. The current research offers support for this contention, as the similarity in the ideas of psychological authors appears to contribute to the correspondence in the peaks of interest in their work.

The next issue which had to be addressed was why such a decline in the influence of particular theories should occur. One possible explanation for the relative decrease in the influence of psychological theories may be located in the nature of their content. O'Reilly (1991) highlights the tendency of psychological approaches to organisational issues to concentrate upon narrow theories of behaviour, specifically designed to be applied in practical situations. This practical emphasis has important implications for the longevity of psychological approaches to management. Researchers in this area (such as Herzberg and Likert) often develop theories based upon empirical research of behaviour within certain organisations. The resultant theories are then postulated to be generalisable to all organisations. Later researchers can then study the validity of this generalisation, by analysing the application of the theories in different organisations. This may lead to confirmation of the earlier findings. However, it may produce findings which contradict earlier research. Such findings may cast doubt upon the original theory, and its applicability to organisations in general. If sufficient contradictory results are reported, this may lead to the original theory being relatively disregarded.

This argument thus suggests that psychological approaches to management may lack longevity because they are open to falsification. There are a number of examples where falsification of this type has occurred. For example, McGregor's Theory X and Theory Y were studied in practical situations by both McClelland (1969) and Maslow (1970), and found to be insufficiently flexible in their depiction of attitudes to work. Similarly, Drucker (1974) argued that Maslow's hierarchy of needs would be inapplicable in the long term, since needs, once satisfied, would be accepted as the norm by workers, and would no longer represent motivating factors. Fiedler and Vroom also reported contradictory findings with respect to the positive benefits of training managers to change their leadership styles. The theoretical foundation of OD was also questioned by Hulin and Smith (1967).

The issue of falsification has been the subject of debate over many years, concerning the philosophy of science and social science. Popper (1959) contended that one of the main distinguishing features of scientific research is its susceptibility to falsification by later research. Building on Popper's work, Price (1963) postulated the existence of hard science, soft science and non-science. The position of a discipline within this continuum is dependent upon the extent to which ideas may be falsified, and the degree to which there exists a unifying paradigm for research (cf. Kuhn, 1970). Heisey (1988) defined social science disciplines such as archaeology and economics as soft sciences, since they are characterised by falsification of theories and unifying paradigms *to some extent*. These characteristics are not as prevalent as they are in hard sciences (such as mathematics and physics). However, they may be identified to a greater degree than in non-science subjects, such as history and literature studies. In comparison with the disciplines outlined above, psychology may be defined as a soft science, since it is largely based upon the generation of research which is repeatable, and therefore open to falsification (O'Reilly, 1991).

Psychological approaches are not only susceptible to empirical falsification. They may also be subject to problems associated with their application in practical situations. OD techniques are based upon the assumption that organisations can be changed through intervention by external consultants. However, such change may be problematic, since many organisations are highly complex. The changes suggested may also face opposition from members of the organisations involved. As a result of these problems, the changes advocated may fail to deliver the improvements promised originally. For example, Hackman (1975) argues that problems of implementation were instrumental in the lack of long term influence of job enrichment.

The hypothesis developed here is that the psychological approaches to organisational issues included in this project tended to lack longevity for a number of reasons. These are summarised below:

1. The prevailing *social and political ideas* of the late 1960s and early 1970s led to the popularisation of theories which emphasised the psychological well-being of the individual. As a result of this, the OD movement became fashionable in the early and mid 1970s.

2. As OD theories were tested in practical situations, they often failed to accomplish the objectives that they proposed. This was due to both a lack of theoretical foundation (Gill and Whittle, 1992) and problems in implementation (Hackman, 1975). The nature of OD theories meant that they were susceptible to *falsification* by the work of later researchers.

3. The *similarity* between the concerns of the psychological theorists was such that the falsification of parts of their research had a direct impact upon the influence of all of the authors in this area.

In conclusion, the fashionable nature of the influence of psychological approaches to organisational issues may have resulted initially from the pressures of social and political ideas. The impact of this pressure was later exacerbated by the similarity of the theories of the various researchers working in this area; and the susceptibility of their theories to empirical falsification.

Analysis of Sociological Theories of Management

From the discussion above, it appears that psychological approaches to management were subject to the pressures of fashion, particularly during the 1970s. This finding supports the results of the regression analysis, which highlighted the lack of longevity of psychological theories in comparison to other approaches to management. In order to analyse the validity of the conclusions regarding psychological theories, it was necessary to compare the pattern of influence associated with theories from a different discipline. This would facilitate analysis of the similarities and differences between the patterns of influence of the two disciplines.

The psychological theorists discussed earlier concentrated upon the human aspect of the management of organisations. This has often been defined as organisational behaviour (OB), which is chiefly informed by two academic disciplines - psychology and sociology (Staw, 1984). These disciplines influence two distinct aspects of organisational behaviour. The first of these is defined by O'Reilly (1991) as micro-OB. This is concerned with the attitudes and behaviour of individuals (and groups of individuals) within organisations, and is based mainly upon psychological approaches to behaviour. The psychological theorists discussed above may be regarded as contributors to the development of micro-OB. The second area is macro-OB, which is mainly concerned with how the behaviour of individuals is related to the structure of the organisation, and the position of the organisation within the wider environment. Macro-OB draws mainly upon sociological theories. It therefore appeared logical to employ those management theories underpinned by sociology as a comparison with the psychological theories outlined earlier.

There were sixteen publications written by sociologists outside the two main clusters (see Table 9.3). These were written by 11 different authors. Out of these sixteen, fourteen were written by American authors, and fifteen were published in book form. None of these cases was a journal article written by a European author. This again supports the finding of the regression analysis that books were more influential than journal articles, and that American authors were more influential than their European counterparts. Less definitive patterns were identified with reference to the longevity of these items. Most of these items were characterised by similar input characteristics, since they were books written by American authors with a background in sociology. However, there was a wide variation in the longevity of these items. The life cycles associated with these items ranged from 22.1 years to 36.31 years.

Table 9.3 Peaks of interest in the work of leading sociology authors

AUTHOR	PUBLICATION	PUB	PEAK
Burns T. and Stalker G.	The Management of Innovation	1961	1985
Selznick P.	Leadership and Administration	1957	1993
Gouldner A.	American Sociological Review 25: 161	1960	1976
Gouldner A.	Coming Crisis in Western Sociology	1970	1978
Whyte W. H.	Organization Man	1956	1960
Thompson J.	Organizations in Action	1967	1985
Blau P. and Scott W.	Formal Organizations	1962	1974
Blau P.	Exchange and Power in Social Life	1964	1978
Blau P. and Duncan O.	American Occupational Structure	1967	1977
Lawrence P. And Lorsch J.	Organization and Environment	1967	1979
Braverman H.	Labor and Monopoly Capital	1974	1987
Etzioni A.	A Comparative Analysis of Complex Organizations	1961	1975
Etzioni A.	Modern Organizations	1964	1975
Etzioni A.	The Active Society	1968	1975
Crozier M.	The Bureaucratic Phenomenon	1963	1980
Woodward J.	Industrial Organization	1965	1981

The lack of consistency regarding longevity of published items with similar input characteristics had therefore been established in both sociology and psychology. The next stage in the analysis was the evaluation of the extent to which sociology publications were subject to the same fashionable pressures after publication as those identified in the analysis of psychological theories. The techniques employed in the study of psychological theories were therefore applied to sociology publications. The first stage in this process was to define the peak of interest in each of the sixteen sociology publications. Centred moving averages, with a span of three years, were calculated for the citation rate of each case, using all citation data since the date of publication.

The peak of interest in each of these items was defined as the highest number of citations, after the data had been smoothed using moving averages. This mirrors the technique employed in the analysis of publications by authors with a psychology background. The peak for each item was identified, as shown in Table 9.3. This table reveals that the peak of interest in these cases is spread over a large number of years, between 1960 and 1993. This finding can be contrasted with that in psychology, where the peak of interest lies within a five year period between 1974 and 1978. Hence, it could be argued that a peak of interest in sociological theories is more difficult to identify. In turn, this may suggest that, taken as a whole, the sociological theories included in this analysis are less susceptible to the influence of fashion than those items covering psychological aspects of organisational research. In order to test the validity of this proposition, it was necessary to study the sociological theories in greater depth.

Case Studies of Sociology Authors

The relationship between the work of Frederick Taylor and the ideas developed by psychological theorists was discussed earlier. Taylor was not the only influential organisational theorist in the early part of this century. Another writer of great significance was Max Weber. The main concern of Weber's study of organisations was the nature of large, formal organisations. Weber (1930) defined these as bureaucracies. Weber studied the operation of these bureaucracies, particularly in terms of the relationship between formal structures and individual employees. His major interests were the nature of power and authority within bureaucracies; and how bureaucracies developed and continued to operate. The work of Weber may be regarded as the forerunner of macro-OB theories. It influenced a number of researchers, as outlined below.

One of the early studies of the application of Weber's theories of bureaucracy was carried out by *Alvin Gouldner*. He extended the work of Weber by studying the effect of challenges to the legitimacy of bureaucratic rules, an area which Weber had not analysed. As a result of his study, Gouldner identified three types of bureaucracy - mock, representative and punishment centred, which were characterised by different applications of bureaucratic rules. The type of bureaucracy evident in an organisation will influence its operation, and style of management. It will also affect the power relations within the organisation. Gouldner identified two major sources of power - knowledge and position. Emergent from these two bases for power, Gouldner argues, are two types of workers within bureaucracies. These are defined as 'cosmopolitans' and 'locals'. Cosmopolitans are dedicated to their particular skill, and their power is based upon their expertise. They are primarily concerned with their trade, and their loyalty to particular organisations is minimal. Locals, on the other hand, are workers whose primary loyalty is to the organisation in which they are employed. Their main power comes from familiarity with the operation of their organisation, and from their position within it. Gouldner's analysis may therefore be regarded as a development of Weber's work. Weber concentrated upon the operation of formal rules within organisations. Gouldner extended this to include analysis of the reaction of employees to bureaucratic rules, and their resultant orientation to the organisation in which they are employed. The peak of interest in Gouldner's work occurred in 1976.

The loyalty of employees was also analysed by *W.H. Whyte*. In his book, '*The Organization Man*', published in 1956, Whyte studied the development of middle class of 'organisation men' whose lives are centred upon the organisation in which they work. In this sense they are regarded as 'belonging' to that organisation. These workers find their meaning in a social ethic based upon the feeling of togetherness and security engendered through belonging to a specific organisation. The organisations in turn encourage their employees to accept the prevailing organisational practices, and not to question existing norms and values. As a result, employees are encouraged to display conformance rather than initiative, which in turn leads to the promotion of mediocrity rather than excellence. This work was at its most influential in 1960, soon after it was published.

The issue of the reasons why individuals conform to organisational values was examined in more general terms by *Amitai Etzioni*. This formed part of his wider concern with societal issues, particularly social control mechanisms. Etzioni identified two reasons why employees conform. The first of these is bureaucratic, and suggests that people conform because of the regulations that they face. The second reason is motivational, in that employees conform with organisational values because they believe them to be desirable. Etzioni also argued that the extent to which motivational compliance would be encountered depended upon the nature of the association between employees and their organisation. He identified three types of involvement - alienative, calculative (instrumental) and moral - with the level of association with organisational norms increasing across these three categories. The nature of the relationship between employees and their organisation and its goals has clear implications for the nature of the control systems employed by an organisation. Etzioni identified three methods of control - coercive, remunerative and identitive. These three methods of control may be associated directly with the three orientations to the organisation held by employees. Etzioni was also concerned with the issue of organisational goal setting. He argued that it is often difficult to define any single organisational goal to which all members would subscribe. This is because of the various groupings present within organisations, each of which may have its own commitments and goals. Three of Etzioni's books lay outside the main clusters. The peak of interest in each of these books occurred in 1975.

The extent to which different groups in organisations achieve their goals is dependent upon the power they hold within the organisation. As outlined earlier, both Gouldner and Weber locate the source of power in the knowledge of individuals, and the position they hold in the organisations. Neither author, however, defines in great depth how this power is exercised. This was the main concern of *Michel Crozier* in his book, *'The Bureaucratic Phenomenon'*, which was published in 1963. In this book, Crozier observes the characteristics of power relations, and concludes that they may be analysed as an amalgamation of elaborate power games undertaken by organisational actors. These games exist as a result of the uncertainty that pervades organisations. As Etzioni argues, organisations are characterised by a multitude of goals, and there is uncertainty and ambiguity as to the overall goal of each department or the organisation as a whole. Organisational actors thus compete in order to impose their objectives on other groups within the organisation. In times of rapid organisational change, which occurs infrequently, increased opportunities exist for individuals and groups to redefine organisational goals. At this point, bureaucratic leaders emerge who direct this redefinition process. Crozier's work was at its most influential in 1980.

The peaks of interest in the work of the four authors outlined above occurred across a large number of years. Referring back to the discussion of psychological theories, the similarity of theories was one factor that was believed to cause similarities in the patterns of influence associated with them. Hence the lack of similarity in the peaks of interest in the work of these four writers may result from the different aspects of bureaucracies that they analysed.

Analysis of the concept of leadership within large organisations was relatively scarce in early studies of bureaucracy. One writer who addressed this issue was *Philip Selznick* in his book *'Leadership in Administration'* published in 1957. In this book, Selznick delineated leadership and administrative efficiency. He regarded the latter as being concerned solely with organisational processes, with little reference to the justification for the processes. Leadership, on the other hand, sets the context within which the processes are designed, by defining organisational goals. As a result, leadership is 'beyond efficiency'. Selznick regarded leadership as a creative process, since it has to determine the future development of the organisation. It involves the creation of institutional myths which promote the values and identity of the organisation, both to its employees, and to the wider society. The peak of interest in Selznick's work occurred in 1993 (or possibly has still not occurred), thirty seven years after it was published. Possible reasons for this are discussed in later in this chapter.

Selznick offers a depiction of charismatic leaders who transform the success of their organisation almost single-handedly. *Peter Blau* suggests an alternative conception of the nature of leadership in his book *'Exchange of Power in Social Organisations'* (1964). He argues that the process of leadership is inextricably tied to the power relations within an organisation. Leadership derives from an exchange process in which the leader offers benefits to his/her subordinates, in return for their continued support within the organisation. This is a political view of the process of leadership, and may be regarded as similar to that developed by Crozier in his depiction of organisational processes and politics. The citation peak to this book was in 1978.

Blau's theory of leadership forms part of a wider concern with the nature of formal organisations. He argues that large organisations are characterised by high levels of differentiation between departments, and a more complex division of labour. In order to control the operation of these organisations, formal bureaucratic structures must be introduced to co-ordinate the different activities undertaken. This inevitably causes problems of communication and integration between departments, particularly where their objectives are in conflict with each other. In this way, Blau's analysis of formal organisations may be regarded as similar to that offered by Etzioni and Crozier.

However, Blau's analysis extends beyond the processes involved in the operation of large scale formal organisations, to the question of why particular organisational structures emerge. He argues that structures are largely the product of organisational size. In turn, the size of organisations is a product of the economic system in which they operate. Large organisations, in general, emerge from smaller organisations. This occurs where organisations produce a surplus, in terms of profit, which then encourages the organisation to grow in order to exploit this surplus. Blau thus regarded large scale organisation as an inevitable result of the economic system, and highlighted the problems associated with operating at this scale, as outlined above. Two of Blau's books on the nature of formal organisations were outside the main clusters. The peaks of interest in these books occurred in 1974 and 1977.

The relationship between organisational structure and environmental conditions, highlighted by Blau in his analysis of organisational size, has been studied by a number of writers. *James Thompson*, in his book '*Organizations in Action*' (1967), highlighted the uncertain nature of the environment faced by organisations. This uncertainty results mainly from changes in the markets in which an organisation competes. Thompson depicts organisations as attempting to act rationally within an environment which is neither rational nor certain. In order to achieve this, it is necessary for organisations to insulate their critical components (defined by Thompson as the technical core) from this external uncertainty using 'boundary spanning units'. These units, which include public relations sections and stock control departments, operate in such a way that the central production department is not affected by external changes. However, the uncertainty of the environment still affects the organisation through its attempts to set objectives. Thompson offers a similar analysis to that of Crozier, in which he argues that the uncertainty of objectives leads to a struggle for the power to control organisational objectives. His work was at its most influential in 1985.

The relationship between organisational structure and the external environment was also analysed by *Paul Lawrence* and *Jay Lorsch*, in their book '*Organization and Environment*', published in 1967. They studied the question of why humans build organisations, and argue that it is the result of the complexity of the environment that they face. This complexity means that it is not possible for individuals to act alone. Organisations are therefore constructed which match the complexity of the environment. The design of organisations tends to reflect external pressures, with distinct departments set up to deal with specific issues. However, as organisations become more complex, and the level of differentiation between departments increases, the problems of co-ordination increase. This may lead to conflict between departments due to incompatible goals (as defined by Thompson, Etzioni and Crozier); and introduces the need for integration between departments in order to accommodate the different objectives present within an organisation, using integrative devices such as liaison officers. Lawrence and Lorsch argue that successful organisations will be those which can match their levels of integration and differentiation to the complexity of the external environment. The work of Lawrence of Lorsch was at its most influential in 1979.

Lawrence and Lorsch, Blau and Thompson all concentrated their analysis upon the relationship between environmental conditions and organisational structure. Their particular emphasis was upon economic and market conditions. The peak of influence of their work was relatively similar, covering the late 1970s and early 1980s. However, the level of similarity in these peaks was lower than that associated with psychological theories.

An alternative determinant of organisational structure was suggested by *Burns and Stalker*. They argued that the major determinant of organisational form is the technology employed by an organisation. This in turn is influenced by technological advances made outside the particular organisation. Burns and Stalker identified two organisational responses to technological change. The nature of the response results from the characteristics of the organisation. The first type of organisation is mechanistic, and is based upon clearly defined rules and hierarchies. This type of organisation is suited to stability, and so fails to exploit fully new technologies. The second type of organisation is organic, which is characterised by flexibility and the lack of formal hierarchies. This type of organisation is receptive to change. Burns and Stalker argued that technological change should encourage organisations to adapt and develop an organic structure. However, this often fails to occur, due to opposition on the part of organisational actors (as discussed by Crozier). This led Burns and Stalker to contend that organisations are not simply a formal structure. They are also an informal political system constructed from individuals, who may have commitments other than those fostered by the organisation. Overall, the organisation is therefore depicted as a socio-technical system, influenced both by technical change and informal responses. The peak of interest in this work occurred in 1984.

This systems view of organisations was also advocated by *Joan Woodward*. She argued that technology is the major determinant of organisational form, and defined three types of technology - small batch, large batch and process. These are characterised by increasing need for predictability, and therefore require increasingly close supervision and control structures. Woodward also studied the nature of these control structures, in terms of whether they were based upon personal or impersonal control, and whether the controls were fragmented (set by departments) or unitary (set by the organisation). This led to the development of a four-fold (2x2) typology of control. Woodward argued that the type of control employed should reflect the structure of the organisation, which in turn depends upon the technology it employs. Thus the social system of control is a reflection of the technical system employed. The influence of Woodward's work was at its greatest in 1982, similar to the peak of interest in the work of Burns and Stalker.

The approaches to organisational analysis outlined above study the operation of industrial organisations in a largely non-critical manner. Their chief objective is to generate greater understanding of organisations. There have also been theorists who have offered a more critical analysis of the operation of industrial organisations. In 1970, Alvin Gouldner wrote '*The Coming Crisis in Western Sociology*', the peak of interest in which occurred in 1978. In this book, Gouldner highlighted the inability of traditional sociological theories to explain the radical political and social movements of the 1960s, including the civil rights movements, anti-war groups and student protest groups. These groups were regarded as part of a general protest against existing social and political institutions.

This protest also manifested itself with regard to organisational theories. As discussed earlier, one effect was the popularisation in the early 1970s of theories which promoted the psychological well-being of individual workers. Another influential idea which emerged at this time was labour process theory, the main proponent of which was *Harry Braverman* in his book '*Labor and Monopoly Capital*', published in 1974. This presented a neo-Marxist analysis of organisations in which workers were depicted as being exploited by their employers, who appropriate the surplus profit created by their labour. Employers are seen as regarding employees as a commodity, which can be treated in the same way as the other (non-human) factors of production. The view of organisations presented is not therefore neutral, as had been the case with earlier theorists. Rather it presents an overtly political view of both organisations and the capitalist system in general. In this way, it may be regarded as being in concordance with the prevailing political and social ideas. The influence of this work was at its height in 1987.

Relating Sociological Theories to their Citation Patterns

From the discussion above, it may be discerned that the peaks of interest in publications written by authors with a background in sociology covered a relatively long period. This may be contrasted with the findings with regard to authors with a background in psychology. The peak of interest in the work of these writers was found to be located within a relatively short time period. It was therefore appropriate to analyse possible reasons for this difference.

The similarity in the peaks of interest in psychological approaches to organisations was regarded as evidence that they may be subject to pressures of fashion. It was postulated that the initial fashionable pressures emerged from prevailing social and cultural ideas. The impact of these pressures was then exacerbated by the similarity and susceptibility to falsification of the findings of psychological theorists. These factors were analysed with regard to the sociological theorists discussed above.

The first issue that had to be addressed was the extent to which sociological theories were subject to the pressures of fashion. The lack of similarity in the peaks of interest in these theories may suggest that such pressures are largely absent. However, this conclusion may be inaccurate. Analysis of the work of individual authors, and of theorists within similar schools of thought, provided evidence that fashion may have an influence upon sociological theories of organisation. For example, the peak of interest in each of the three books published by Etzioni in the sample occurred in 1975, thus suggesting that his ideas were fashionable at this time. This may be explained with reference to his concern with the issue of social order and why individuals conform to organisational rules. Such conformance was being widely questioned at this time by authors such as Gouldner and Braverman.

A further example was analysed regarding the systems theories of Burns and Stalker and Woodward. The work of these theorists was at its most influential in the early part of the 1980s. Further analysis of systems theorists, in particular Katz and Kahn (1966) revealed a similar pattern of influence. The peak of interest in their work occurred in 1980. This suggests that systems theory was fashionable at this time. As mentioned in the discussion of psychology authors, the fashionable nature of certain theories may lead researchers to study the background to these theories. Such a pattern may be identified with regard to systems theory. The early work of Kenneth Boulding (1956) studied the nature of systems, both physical and social. This work was largely disregarded after its publication, until the early part of the 1980s. It was then cited at a much higher rate for a relatively short period of time, before being disregarded again. This pattern suggests that the work of Boulding became influential as a result of the fashionable nature of systems theory. The patterns of citations associated with systems theory may therefore be regarded as similar to those discovered in the analysis of psychological approaches to organisations.

The discussion of systems theory and the work of Etzioni suggest that fashionable pressures may be identified in the pattern of influence associated with particular sociological theories of organisation. It was necessary to examine why these pressures do not result in similar peaks of influence for the sociological theorists in the sample. The first point that should be noted is that the sociology authors do not share a common objective in the same way as psychology authors. Their interests cover organisational politics, technology, economic conditions, decision making and control, along with a number of other subjects. This variety of interests makes it more difficult to define sociology authors as a single grouping with similar interests. For example, the fashionable nature of Etzioni's work in the mid-1970s did not necessarily result in an increase in the influence of the work of the other sociologists in the sample. Hence there was not a concentration of peaks of interest in sociological theories around this time. This may be due to the lack of similarity between the work of Etzioni and the totality of sociological research. Where the interests of sociologists are similar, this is reflected in a pattern of relative consistency between their peaks of influence. Such a pattern was discovered among systems theorists.

The lack of a definitive issue of concern among sociologists may be contrasted with the content of psychological analyses of organisations. These analyses were chiefly concerned with a single issue - the relationship between psychological well-being and employee motivation and job performance. In the discussion of psychological theories, their similarity was defined as a factor which would exacerbate the impact of the pressures of fashion. This would be manifested in the similarity in the peak of interest in the work of the various theorists. The relative lack of similarity in the concerns of the sociology writers may thus explain the disparity in terms of the peak of interest in their work. This finding offers further support for Abrahamson's (1991) contention, based upon epidemiological theories, that similarity of concerns is directly related to the diffusion of management fashions.

The breadth of subject matter covered by the sociology authors also increases the extent to which parts of their work may be re-interpreted by later theorists. Various writers have argued that management theories are recycled on a regular basis by later researchers (Carson and Carson, 1992; Thompson and Davidson, 1994). As a result, elements of existing theories may be rediscovered at a later date, although presented in such a way as to appear entirely original. For example, Selznick's depiction of the charismatic leader was employed by a number of writers in the 1980s, notably Peters and Waterman in their highly influential book '*In Search of Excellence*' (1982). Selznick's work was therefore 'rediscovered' and continued to be cited throughout the 1980s. As can be seen in Table 9.3, the peak of citations to Selznick's work was in 1993, suggesting that his theory of leadership remains influential.

The extent to which management theories can be recycled is not only influenced by the breadth of the subject matter that they cover. It may also result from the epistemological basis of these theories. As discussed earlier, psychological approaches are generally based upon the development of generalisable theories of behaviour within organisations. These theories are designed specifically for application in practical situations. Theories derived from a sociological perspective, on the other hand, are mainly based upon the observation of particular organisations (O'Reilly, 1991). These theories are often not specifically designed for direct application to practical situations, but rather offer an analysis of the manner in which organisations operate. As a result, they are often less prescriptive than psychologically-based theories.

The main outcome of this difference in emphasis is that sociological theories are generally not open to empirical falsification (cf. Popper, 1959). For example, it is possible to test the validity of psychological theories of employee behaviour, such as those suggested by McGregor and Herzberg, through replication of their studies in different organisations. Where theories can be falsified, their influence may be reduced in the long term. This was defined in the discussion of psychological theories as one of the factors which led to the lack of longevity of the Organisation Development movement in the 1970s. However, such replication is more problematic in sociology, since the contexts in which sociological studies are undertaken are largely non-repeatable, particularly the wider environmental conditions in which organisations operate. It is therefore not possible to replicate exactly the studies across organisations, reducing the likelihood of sociological theories being falsified. This will have a positive influence on the potential for these theories to be reinterpreted at a later date, since they have not been refuted definitively.

The lack of potential for falsification of sociological theories is enhanced by the nature of their conclusions. The psychological theorists included in the sample often defined distinct types of behaviour which would emerge when particular organisational changes were implemented. A number of sociological authors (among them Lawrence and Lorsch, Woodward, Etzioni, Blau and Burns and Stalker) offer more complex conclusions, based upon the 'contingency theory' of organisations. This theory states that the structure of an organisation, and the actions of its members, are contingent upon the nature of the environment in which the organisation operates. It also (more importantly in this context) contends that the optimal structure and operation of an organisation is dependent upon its own characteristics, and its position relative to the wider environment. The logical outcome of this approach is that no two organisations are alike, and they must be analysed individually. This has the positive effect of taking into account the characteristics of particular organisations. However, it also means that findings cannot be generalised. The results found in one organisation are not falsified if they are contradicted by findings from another organisation (or from the same organisation at a later date), since their characteristics and relationship with the wider environment will be different. Hence, conclusions based around contingency theory are inherently more difficult to test.

Referring back to the continuum of hard science, soft science and non-science suggested by Price (1963), sociology may therefore be regarded as a non-science. Its theories are generally more descriptive than those developed by psychological theorists. As such, it may have greater similarities to humanities disciplines, which are defined as non-sciences. Given that non-science disciplines are characterised by relatively slow literature obsolescence (Heisey, 1988), the *relative* lack of fashions in sociological theories of management (in comparison to psychological approaches) may be partially explained by their epistemological basis.

The discussion of sociological approaches to organisational theories suggests that these theories are subject to the pressures of fashion in the same way as psychology. However, the factors which magnify the impact of these pressures (i.e. similarity of theories and susceptibility to falsification) appear to be largely absent from the work of sociology authors. This may explain the lack of similarity in the peaks of interest in their work.

Concluding Remarks

The analysis undertaken in this chapter concentrated upon the longevity of management research publications. A number of factors were identified which may affect this longevity. It was postulated that the initial popularisation of theories occurs because of their compatibility with prevailing social and political ideas. They may therefore be defined as being influential as a result of the fashionable nature of their theoretical content and resultant conclusions. The example offered to highlight this hypothesis was the Organisation Development movement, which was fashionable in the early part of the 1970s. The resultant impact of these fashionable pressures on related theories was hypothesised to be mediated by the similarity and susceptibility to falsification of these theories.

In the concluding chapter of this book, the results of the cluster analysis are combined with those of the regression analysis. The former concentrates upon the factors that affect the longevity of management literature; while the latter focuses upon the level of influence of this literature. From the combination of these factors, it is possible to develop a theory of fashions in management literature, which can be compared with previous analyses of management fashions.

10 Towards a Theory of Management Fashion

Introduction

This book has offered an empirical analysis of the issue of fashions in management research. It has drawn upon a variety of disciplines, in order to develop an appropriate theoretical and empirical foundation. The theoretical framework for the analysis emerged largely from analysis of previous research in two distinct areas. The first of these was the literature concerned with the study of *management fashions*. This literature concentrates largely upon the employment of fashionable techniques by practising managers. As such, its focus is slightly different to that of this project, which attempts to analyse fashions within management literature. Such literature is largely a reflection of the ideas of the management research community, rather than the interests of practising managers (although there should theoretically be a link between the two groups).

In order to reflect the focus of this project upon the research community, it was necessary for the theoretical framework to be informed by a second research discipline. *Bibliometric analysis* is concerned with the evaluation of the development of research fields, based upon the study of the literature through which research is disseminated. The branch of bibliometrics employed in this study was citation analysis. This involves studying the development and structure of research fields on the basis of the citations received by publications within these fields.

By combining existing research concerned with both management fashions and citation analysis, it was possible to develop a method through which fashions in management research could be identified. This method was based upon the patterns of citations received by management literature published over recent decades. Particular attention was paid to the number of citations received by management research publications, and the length of time over which they are cited. Existing research into literature obsolescence was thus consulted in detail to provide a basis for the analysis of citation patterns over time.

One of the major problems faced by this study was the generation of an appropriate sample of management literature. Most bibliometric studies are based upon scientific, rather than social scientific, disciplines. An important aspect of scientific disciplines is the primacy of academic journals among the media through which research is disseminated (Cronin, 1984). Basing the first sample upon sampling techniques employed in the study of scientific disciplines thus meant that only journal publications were included. This sample was found to be inappropriate, due to the importance of books in the dissemination of management research. An alternative sample had to be constructed, based upon the most influential work of leading management authors. The resultant sample contained the most influential publications in the development of management research, irrespective of the medium through which they were published.

Having developed a method for identifying management fashions, and constructed a sample of literature for analysis, it was possible to implement the empirical analysis. A number of techniques were involved in the empirical analysis undertaken, including mathematical modelling of quadratic and logistic curves; multiple regression analysis; and cluster analysis. As mentioned in Chapter 1, this book offers the first large scale *empirical* analysis of fashions in management literature. Hence, although the techniques employed in the empirical analysis are well established, their application in this context is relatively unusual. Particular attention thus had to be paid to the appropriateness of the techniques employed in the empirical analysis, and the validity of the results emergent from the analysis. At each stage in the empirical analysis, the results were therefore tested for stability and robustness. Where necessary, modifications were made to the techniques employed in order to overcome the problems encountered. As a result, the findings of the empirical analysis may be regarded as both valid and robust.

Discussion of Findings

A number of interesting results emerged from the empirical analysis. These have been discussed in some detail throughout the book, as the empirical work has developed. It is now possible to combine the findings of the various stages in the empirical analysis, in order to provide an evaluation of the factors which impel the dissemination of fashions via the management literature; and the impact these fashions have upon the development of management research. The results of this analysis may then be compared with existing models of management fashions.

First Stage of the Empirical Analysis

The first stage in the empirical analysis studied citation patterns associated with the research published by leading management authors. These citation patterns were modelled mathematically using logistic curves. This stage in the research revealed that it was possible to distinguish between management publications on the basis of the level of influence associated with them, and the length of time this influence covered. The combination of these characteristics was defined in Chapter 2 as a method which could be used to identify management fashions. This was based upon the assumption that fashions may be identified on the basis of the impact that they have (Kroeber, 1919; Gill and Whittle, 1992).

The results of the first stage in the empirical research offered a guide to the pattern of influence associated with management publications. These results are of interest in themselves, since they provide an empirically validated evaluation of the influence of particular theorists upon the development of management research. They may also be compared with previous analyses of the impact of management fashions. Gill and Whittle (1992) postulated that fashionable management techniques would be characterised by a life cycle pattern of influence. This project confirms that such life cycles may be associated with many items of management literature. However, the length of these life cycles appears to differ from that suggested by Gill and Whittle, who contended that management fashions have a life cycle of around forty years (a contention based upon conjecture rather than empirical research). This project reveals that the life cycle of many items of management literature is in fact shorter than that suggested by Gill and Whittle. The life cycles calculated in this project had a mean of around twenty five years. As such this finding is in closer agreement with the study by Castorina and Wood (1988), who depicted management fashions as being more short-lived than Gill and Whittle hypothesised.

The first stage in the empirical analysis also revealed that there is a great deal of variation in the levels of influence associated with individual items of management literature. The majority of publications in the sample had been cited relatively infrequently; only a small number of publications received a large number of citations. This result is of particular interest given the nature of the sample constructed for this project. The sample is not representative of the totality of management literature. Rather, it focuses upon *leading* management authors, with the purpose of including their most influential management publications within the sample. The disparity in the level of influence associated with cases in the sample thus highlights the fact that the majority of management publications, even those written by leading authors in the field, have relatively little influence upon the development of management research. Only a very small number of 'classic' management publications may thus be regarded as being central to the development of research in this area.

Second Stage of the Empirical Analysis

The second stage in the empirical analysis involved a study of the factors which may affect the longevity and influence of management publications. These factors could be split into two categories. The first category contained the input characteristics of research publications, including: publishing medium; nationality and subject discipline of authors; and the publishing history of authors. Analysis of these factors aimed to identify the extent to which the influence and longevity of publications could be predicted simply on the basis of their input characteristics. This analysis was based upon the construction of multiple regression models.

A number of important results emerged from the regression analysis. It highlighted the importance of input characteristics in the prediction of the level of influence of published management research. In particular, it pointed to the dominance of books within the dissemination of management research, and the central role played by North American authors in the development of this research. These findings were also reflected in the cluster analysis discussed in Chapter 9. Out of the 38 cases defined as being highly influential as a result of the cluster analysis, 36 were published in book form, and 34 were written by North American authors. None of the 38 cases were journal publications written by European authors. This suggests that the input characteristics of management publications have a strong impact upon their level of influence. As such, they may offer a partial explanation of why certain publications become influential within management research.

The regression analysis also revealed that input characteristics have a minimal impact upon the longevity of published items. Hence, it may be possible to predict which publications will become influential within management research simply from knowledge of their authoring details and publication media. However, predictions of the longevity of this influence are unlikely to be accurate if they are based solely upon these characteristics.

It was therefore necessary to seek alternative explanations for the disparity revealed in the longevity of management publications. The content of these publications, and how it may affect the longevity of influence associated with them, was therefore analysed. This was achieved using both quantitative and qualitative methods. Cluster analysis was employed to identify groups of cases for further analysis; while case studies were used to develop a greater understanding of the nature of the contribution of particular authors to the development of management research.

Various factors were identified which may affect the longevity of management literature. It was postulated that the initial popularisation of theories occurred because of their compatibility with prevailing social and political ideas. They could therefore be defined as being influential as a result of the fashionable nature of their theoretical content and resultant conclusions. The example offered to highlight this hypothesis was the Organisation Development movement, which was fashionable in the early part of the 1970s. Having become influential, various factors were identified which may mediate the length of time over which this influence continues. These include changes in the environment which originally led to the popularisation of a given management theory or technique; the susceptibility to falsification of this technique; and its similarity to other ideas which are prominent at the same time.

Comparisons with Previous Research

The results of the second stage in the empirical research identified the factors which may affect the influence and longevity of management literature. These results may be compared with previous analyses of the characteristics associated with management fashions. The discussion in Chapter 2 analysed the work of Abrahamson (1991, 1996) on management fashions in some detail. His work may be regarded as having a significant influence upon the theoretical framework of this project. It is therefore appropriate to study whether the results of this project match the hypotheses contained within his work.

Abrahamson (1996) offers a number of propositions regarding the factors which may be associated with the dissemination of management fashions. These propositions are based upon theoretical, rather than empirical analysis. Three of these propositions may be analysed on the basis of the empirical findings of this project.

> Proposition 1: There will tend to be more frequent and
> shorter lived management fashions in nations that have
> relatively stronger norms of rational management progress.

Abrahamson argues that this proposition applies chiefly to American management theories, since the USA is particularly concerned with management progress. In this project, the sample was divided into North American and European authors (see Chapter 5). The longevity and level of influence of the work of these two groups of authors was then analysed as part of the regression analysis (see Chapter 8). It was discovered that North American authors are more influential than their European counterparts. However, no evidence was discovered to support the idea that American theories have a shorter life cycle than those produced by European authors. As such, this evidence refutes the proposition put forward by Abrahamson.

> Proposition 2: If there exists unmet demand for a certain type
> of management technique, then one or more techniques
> belonging to this type will become fashionable if they are
> created, selected, processed, and disseminated by the
> management-fashion-setting community.

Abrahamson suggests that management techniques become fashionable because they are in accord with the demands of managers at a particular point in time. In turn, the demands of managers will be influenced by the economic conditions and social expectations made of them. The techniques which become fashionable will therefore tend to be those which reflect prevailing social and economic conditions and mores.

The empirical findings of this project offer support for this proposition. In Chapter 9, detailed analysis was undertaken into the patterns of citations received by the most influential publications within the development of management research during recent decades. These citation patterns were then compared with case studies of the work of the authors concerned. Evidence was discovered to support the idea that particular theories became fashionable because they reflected the prevailing ideas within society. For example, the post-war period of full employment saw general discontent with mundane jobs offering little interest to workers (Rose, 1988). This led to the development of a number of theories of motivation and job satisfaction, which were designed to overcome the dissatisfaction with the scientific management techniques prevalent at this time. A similar pattern may be identified with reference to the late 1960s and early part of the 1970s, defined by Rose (1988) as the 'protest peak' period. At this point in time, the role of existing social and economic institutions, and their effect upon the lives of individual workers, was increasingly being questioned. This was reflected in the prominence of authors who questioned traditional ideas (e.g. Gouldner, 1970; Braverman, 1974); along with theorists who placed significant importance upon the needs of individual workers (e.g. Bennis, 1966); and those offering economic alternatives to existing large scale organisations (Schumacher, 1973).

> Proposition 3: There will be more management fashions
> when managers' expectations are disappointed.

As discussed in Chapter 2, managers are often regarded as being dependent upon a succession of new management techniques to solve organisational problems. If these techniques do not produce the solutions that they promise, managers will seek alternative methods to solve their problems. The less successful particular techniques are in practice, the more rapidly managers will reject them. Hence, if managers are continually disappointed in the techniques that they employ, there is likely to be a steady stream of fashionable approaches to address organisational problems.

Indirect evidence was found in this project to support this proposition. Managers will tend to be disappointed when particular techniques do not fulfil the promises that they make. In other words, the promises are shown to be false to some degree. A parallel may be drawn here with management research. As discussed in Chapter 9, management theories appear to be particularly susceptible to pressures of fashion where their findings are falsified. The support for Abrahamson's proposition is therefore indirect, since it is based upon management research, rather than management practice. However, there does appear to be a relationship between the failure of management theories to achieve what they claim (whether in terms of research or practical applications), and the tendency for their influence to be relatively short-lived.

A further statement made by Abrahamson (1996) which is relevant to this project is that the popularity of particular management techniques will lead to an increase in interest in similar techniques. Evidence was found to support this contention. As discussed in Chapter 9, one of the factors which was regarded as a mediating factor upon the diffusion of management fashions was their similarity to other theories and techniques. Where theories were found to be similar, the peak of interest in them tended to be at around the same time, suggesting that their patterns of influence were related.

The results of the empirical work undertaken in this project may thus be regarded as offering support to a number of the hypotheses put forward in previous analyses of management fashions. On the basis of the findings of the empirical research undertaken in this project, and building upon previous research into management fashions, it is therefore possible to develop a theory of the operation of fashions in management literature. This theory is outlined below.

A Theory of Fashion in Management Research

This study of fashion in management research is based upon analysis of why particular patterns of influence may be associated with certain management publications. There are two aspects of this issue. The first of these addresses the reasons why some management fashions become more popular than others, with the result that publications on this subject tend to be more influential. A number of reasons for this may be located in previous research into management fashions.

Fashions may become influential because they are in accord with the prevailing requirements and mores of managers and their organisations. The way in which organisations operate changes over time (Lawrence and Lorsch, 1967). This may be the result of variations in environmental conditions, such as changing macroeconomic conditions (Barley and Kunda, 1992) or social and political ideas (Gouldner, 1970); alternatively it may emerge from inherent contradictions in their operation (Blau, 1971). These changes lead to the requirement for managers to employ different techniques to address their evolving needs, and therefore to a demand among managers for new methods to address organisational problems (Abrahamson, 1996). Specific management techniques emerge which are congruent with this change of emphasis. These techniques are selected and developed by management consultants and academics because they meet the demands of practising managers (Kieser, 1997). The techniques which become most influential will therefore tend to be those which most accurately reflect the requirements of the management community.

The second aspect of the study of fashions in management literature is why certain publications detailing a particular theory or technique become highly influential, while others are relatively disregarded. Management ideas are largely disseminated using published media, including books, academic journals and the popular management press. As these ideas are popularised, researchers attempt to analyse them in greater depth, in order to study their theoretical foundation and potential applications. The results of these later analyses are also often distributed through the published media. The management literature thus contains both publications in which techniques are formulated, and analyses of their application.

The results of the empirical analysis undertaken in this project reveal that the level of influence associated with different publications can be partially explained on the basis of their input characteristics. Specifically, the most influential published items tended to be books, especially those written by North American authors. This may reflect the dominance of American management research (Alvarez, 1993), and the importance of book publication in the development of social science disciplines (Bath University, 1980).

The extent to which particular publications become influential is therefore mediated by two factors. The first of these is the extent to which they are in accord with the demands of managers; the second is their input characteristics. However, once a publication is popularised, its input characteristics have a negligible impact upon how long it will remain influential. Hence, the longevity of the influence of management publications must be the product of other factors. A number of factors which may influence longevity were identified in this project.

The first of these factors is the social, economic and political environment. In the same way as changes in this environment lead to the popularisation of particular management theories and techniques, further changes may lead to a reduction in their influence. Hence techniques will tend to be more short lived where the environment in which organisations operate is rapidly changing. This explanation locates the reason for the fashionable nature of management publications outside the content of these publications.

It may also be possible to identify aspects of the content of published research which affect its longevity. The extent to which theories are disregarded will be partially dependent upon the ability of later researchers to reinterpret and build upon them. In turn, the potential for reinterpretation of theories may be dependent upon their susceptibility to falsification. Theories which are open to falsification by later researchers may suffer a lack of longevity, since it is possible to highlight shortcomings in their methods and conclusions. As a result, it is more difficult for later researchers to explicitly build upon these theories, since their methods and findings have been openly questioned. As noted by Meadows (1974), the most common response to research which is shown to be incorrect in some way is to ignore it.

Management ideas may thus be disregarded because they become out of step with prevailing organisational practices and mores; or because their content is falsified by the work of later researchers. The negative effect of these factors upon a particular area of management research will be particularly strong where the concerns within this area are similar, because the concepts and methods employed will tend to be more closely associated.

In conclusion, therefore, management techniques become fashionable because they meet the demands of practising managers. These demands are largely based upon existing social, economic and organisational norms and practices. A number of publications will detail the applications and benefits of these techniques, only a small number of which will become highly influential. These will tend to be those publications with certain input characteristics. Having been popularised, the length of time over which the publications remain influential will be mediated by the rate at which changes occur in the environment in which organisations operate; the extent to which the ideas contained within the publications may be falsified; and the similarity of these ideas with those forming the basis of other management publications. In (extremely) simplistic terms, this study suggests that the 'classic' example of a fashionable management publication is a book published by an American author, based upon research that is susceptible to falsification, which is one of a number of publications on a similar (constantly evolving) management issue.

A Final Note

This research has been based upon measuring the influence over time of management publications. A large part of this analysis has been concerned with the life cycles associated with published management research. However, the life cycle model fails to account for one important aspect of management research. The model suggests that the influence of a published item will eventually fade, to the point where it is virtually disregarded. It is then assumed that this publication has no further influence upon the management research community, since it is no longer being cited. Such a conclusion may be invalid for two reasons. The first is that management techniques are often 'recycled' by later writers under a different name (Kimberly, 1981). Hence, the influence of a particular technique may theoretically follow a cyclical pattern, as it is disregarded and then rediscovered. This may not be reflected in citation patterns, as theorists who have recycled the earlier technique may be unwilling to highlight its influence upon their work, for fear of appearing to lack originality.

A second problem may be identified with the assumption that the influence of a particular management fashion disappears after the fashion has been disregarded. This project has highlighted the fashionable nature of a number of theories, notably those associated with the Organization Development (OD) movement. Previous researchers have also highlighted the fashionable nature of quality circles (Lawler and Mohrman, 1985; Castorina and Wood, 1988). Both of these approaches have been identified as having clearly defined peaks of influence (OD in the early 1970s, and quality circles during the early 1980s). The life cycles calculated in this project suggest that the OD movement has little influence in the present day; while Abrahamson (1996) noted that the influence of quality circles was largely restricted to the 1980s. It could be concluded from this that these two approaches have little influence upon present day research.

Such a conclusion may be overly simplistic. It may be valid to argue that there is little research currently being undertaken directly into quality circles or OD. However, this does not necessarily mean that these approaches have no influence upon current research. As discussed in Chapter 9, OD theories were based upon the idea that organisations could be changed in order to offer employees more interesting and varied jobs. In this way, it was assumed, the productivity of these workers would be improved. These ideas may be located in a number of more recent theories. For example, human resource management is based upon the tenet that the human resource is the most important component of any organisation, and care should be taken with its management. Another current interest among researchers is that of empowerment. This involves devolving greater responsibility to individual workers in the design of their work, through modifications of their relationship with their supervisors and the organisation as a whole. Again, this idea is directly related to the concept of worker autonomy developed by OD theorists.

A similar pattern may be identified with regard to quality circles. Interest in their application in the early 1980s formed part of a wider concern with Japanese methods of production at that time, particularly those concerned with improvements in quality. The attention paid to Japanese management ideas may not be as intense now as it was during the 1980s. As a result of this, and also due to problems with their implementation, quality circles have been largely abandoned (Abrahamson, 1996). However, the concern with quality remains important within present day organisations. Management techniques must now not only point to improvement in the productivity of organisations, measured quantitatively, but also to the quality of the products or services developed (Kieser, 1997).

Hence, although particular publications may no longer be cited regularly, their influence on later research should not be dismissed. They may be recycled in their entirety, and so become influential again at some later date. Alternatively, their influence may be more indirect, in that their ideas are incorporated to some degree in later techniques.

Appendix 1
List of Publications in the Sample

VAR	AUTHOR	YEAR	PUBLICATION
1	ARGYRIS C	1957	Personality and Organization
2	ARGYRIS C	1960	Understanding Organizational Behavior
3	ARGYRIS C	1962	Interpersonal Competence and Organizational Effectiveness
4	ARGYRIS C	1964	Integrating the Individual and the Organization
5	ARGYRIS C	1965	Organization and Innovation
6	ARGYRIS C	1968	Psychological Bulletin 70: 185
7	ARGYRIS C	1969	American Psychologist 24: 893
8	ARGYRIS C	1970	Intervention Theory and Method
9	ARGYRIS C	1971	Management Science 17: 275
10	ARGYRIS C	1972	Applicability of Organizational Sociology
11	ARGYRIS C	1973	Administrative Science Quarterly 18: 141
12	ARGYRIS C	1974	Theory in Practice: Improving Professional Effectiveness
13	ARGYRIS C	1975	American Psychologist 30: 469
19	BAKKE E	1959	Modern Organizational Theory
20	BAKKE E	1970	Monthly Labor Review
26	BLAKE R / MOUTON J	1961	Management Science 7: 420
27	BLAKE R / MOUTON J	1961	Sociometry 24: 177
28	BLAKE R / MOUTON J	1964	Harvard Business Review 42: 133
29	BLAKE R / MOUTON J	1964	The Managerial Grid
30	BLAKE R / MOUTON J	1964	Managing Intergroup Conflict
31	BLAKE R / MOUTON J	1968	Corporate Excellence

VAR	AUTHOR	YEAR	PUBLICATION
32	BLAKE R / MOUTON J	1969	Building Dynamic Organizations
37	BOULDING K	1956	The Image
38	BOULDING K	1959	Journal of Conflict Resolution 3: 120
39	BOULDING K	1962	Conflict and Defense
41	BROWN W	1960	Exploration Management
42	BROWN W	1962	Piecework Abandoned
43	BROWN W / JAQUES E	1965	Glacier Project Papers
44	BROWN W	1971	Organization
46	JAQUES E	1956	Measurement of Responsibility
47	JAQUES E	1961	Equitable Payment
48	JAQUES E	1970	Work, Creativity and Social Justice
51	BURNS T / STALKER G	1961	The Management of Innovation
52	BURNS T / STALKER G	1963	New Society 18
53	BURNS T / STALKER G	1966	Operations Research 165
57	CHANDLER A	1962	Strategy and Structure
60	SLOAN A	1965	My Years with General Motors
61	CROZIER M	1963	The Bureaucratic Phenomenon
62	CROZIER M	1970	Societe Bloquee
63	CROZIER M	1971	The World of the Office Worker
64	CROZIER M	1973	Stalled Society
65	CROZIER M	1975	The Crisis of Democracy
72	DRUCKER P	1964	Managing for Results
73	DRUCKER P	1966	The Effective Executive
74	DRUCKER P	1968	The Age of Discontinuity
75	DRUCKER P	1973	Management: Tasks, Responsibilities, Practices
79	EDWARDS R	1975	Labor Market Segmentation

VAR	AUTHOR	YEAR	PUBLICATION
81	ETZIONI A	1960	Administrative Science Quarterly 5: 257
82	ETZIONI A	1961	A Comparative Analysis of Complex Organizations
83	ETZIONI A	1962	Hard Way to Peace
84	ETZIONI A	1964	Modern Organizations
85	ETZIONI A	1964	Winning Without War
86	ETZIONI A	1965	Organizational Control Structures
87	ETZIONI A	1965	Political Unification
88	ETZIONI A	1967	Public Administration Review 27: 385
89	ETZIONI A	1968	The Active Society
90	ETZIONI A	1969	Semiprofessions and their Organization
91	ETZIONI A	1971	American Sociologist 6: 8
99	FIEDLER F	1958	Leader Attitudes and Group Effectiveness
100	FIEDLER F	1964	Advances in Experimental Social Psychology 1: 149
101	FIEDLER F	1965	Harvard Business Review 43: 115
102	FIEDLER F	1967	A Theory of Leadership Effectiveness
103	FIEDLER F	1971	Psychological Bulletin 76: 128
104	FIEDLER F	1972	Organizational Dynamics 1: 3
105	FIEDLER F	1974	Leadership and Effectiveness
111	FREEMAN J	1973	American Sociological Review 38: 750
112	FREEMAN J	1973	Social Forces 52: 108
113	FREEMAN J	1975	American Sociological Review 40: 215
114	GALBRAITH JK	1958	The Affluent Society
116	GALBRAITH JK	1967	The New Industrial State
120	GOULDNER A	1957	Administrative Science Quarterly 2: 281

VAR	AUTHOR	YEAR	PUBLICATION
122	GOULDNER A	1960	American Sociological Review 25: 161
123	GOULDNER A	1968	American Sociologist 3: 103
124	GOULDNER A	1970	The Coming Crisis in Western Sociology
126	HANNAN M	1971	Aggregation and Disaggregation in Sociology
127	HANNAN M	1971	Causal Models in Social Science
128	HANNAN M	1974	American Sociological Review 39: 374
131	HERZBERG F	1957	Job Attitudes: A Review of Research
132	HERZBERG F	1959	The Motivation to Work
133	HERZBERG F	1966	Work and the Nature of Man
134	HERZBERG F	1968	Harvard Business Review 46: 53
136	PAUL WJ *et al*	1969	Harvard Business Review 47: 61
138	HOFSTEDE G	1967	Game Budget Control
141	KANTER RM	1968	American Sociological Review 33: 499
142	KANTER RM	1972	Commitment and Community
143	KANTER RM	1975	Another Voice
150	LAWLER E	1967	Industrial Relations 7: 20
151	LAWLER E	1967	Journal of Applied Psychology 51: 369
152	LAWLER E	1967	Organizational Behavior and Human Performance 2: 122
153	LAWLER E	1968	Journal of Applied Psychology 52: 462
154	LAWLER E	1969	Journal of Applied Psychology 53: 467
155	LAWLER E	1969	Personnel Psychology 22: 426

VAR	AUTHOR	YEAR	PUBLICATION
156	LAWLER E	1970	Journal of Applied Psychology 54: 305
157	LAWLER E	1971	Pay and Organizational Effectiveness
158	LAWLER E	1972	Organizational Behavior and Human Performance 7: 26
159	LAWLER E	1973	Journal of Applied Social Psychology 3: 49
160	LAWLER E	1973	Motivation and Work Organization
161	LAWLER E	1973	Organizational Behavior and Human Performance 9: 482
164	LAWRENCE P	1967	Administrative Science Quarterly 12: 1
165	LAWRENCE P/ LORSCH J	1967	Organization and Environment
166	LAWRENCE P/ LORSCH J	1969	Developing Organizations
167	LORSCH J	1973	Managing Diversity and Interdependence
168	LORSCH J / MORSE J	1974	Organizations and their Members
171	LIKERT R	1961	New Patterns of Management
172	LIKERT R	1967	Human Organizations: Their Management and Value
174	LINDBLOM C	1959	Public Administration Review 19: 79
175	LINDBLOM C/ BRAYBROOKE D	1963	A Strategy of Decision
176	LINDBLOM C	1965	The Intelligence of Democracy
177	LINDBLOM C	1968	The Policy Making Process
180	MARCH J / SIMON H	1958	Organizations
181	CYERT R / MARCH J	1963	A Behavioral Theory of the Firm
182	MARCH J	1965	Handbook of Organizations

VAR	AUTHOR	YEAR	PUBLICATION
183	COHEN M *et al*	1972	Administrative Science Quarterly 17: 1
184	COHEN M	1974	Leadership and Ambiguity
190	McGREGOR D	1957	Harvard Business Review 35: 89
191	McGREGOR D	1960	The Human Side of Enterprise
192	McGREGOR D	1966	Leadership and Motivation
193	McGREGOR D	1967	The Professional Manager
195	MILES R / SNOW C	1974	Industrial Relations 13: 244
196	MILES R / SNOW C	1975	Theories of Management
198	MINTZBERG H	1971	Management Science 18: 97
199	MINTZBERG H	1972	California Management Review 15: 92
200	MINTZBERG H	1973	California Management Review 16: 44
201	MINTZBERG H	1973	The Nature of Managerial Work
202	MINTZBERG H	1975	Harvard Business Review 53: 49
208	OUCHI W	1975	Administrative Science Quarterly 20: 559
213	PARKINSON C	1958	Parkinson's Law
214	PARKINSON C	1960	Law and Profits
217	PFEFFER J	1972	Administrative Science Quarterly 17: 218
218	PFEFFER J	1972	Administrative Science Quarterly 17: 382
219	PFEFFER J / LEBLEBICI H	1973	Administrative Science Quarterly 18: 449
220	PFEFFER J / SALANCIK G	1974	Administrative Science Quarterly 19: 135
221	SALANCIK G / PFEFFER J	1974	Administrative Science Quarterly 19: 453

VAR	AUTHOR	YEAR	PUBLICATION
229	PUGH D	1963	Administrative Science Quarterly 8: 289
230	PUGH D	1968	Administrative Science Quarterly 13: 65
231	PUGH D	1969	Administrative Science Quarterly 14: 91
232	HICKSON D	1969	Administrative Science Quarterly 14: 378
233	HICKSON D *et al*	1971	Administrative Science Quarterly 16: 216
234	PUGH D	1973	Organizational Dynamics 1: 19
235	HININGS CR	1974	Administrative Science Quarterly 19: 22
236	DONALDSON L	1975	Administrative Science Quarterly 20: 453
237	PENNINGS J	1975	Administrative Science Quarterly 20: 393
244	CHILD J	1969	British Management Thought
245	CHILD J	1972	Administrative Science Quarterly 17: 163
246	CHILD J	1972	Sociology 6: 1
247	CHILD J	1972	Sociology 6: 369
248	CHILD J	1973	Administrative Science Quarterly 18: 1
249	CHILD J	1973	Administrative Science Quarterly 18: 168
250	CHILD J	1973	Administrative Science Quarterly 18: 328
251	CHILD J	1974	Journal of Management Studies 11: 175
252	CHILD J	1975	Journal of Management Studies 12: 12
254	SCHEIN E	1965	Organizational Psychology
255	SCHEIN E	1965	Personal and Organizational Change
256	SCHEIN E	1968	Industrial Management Review 9: 1
257	SCHEIN E	1969	Process of Consultation

<u>VAR</u>	<u>AUTHOR</u>	<u>YEAR</u>	<u>PUBLICATION</u>
259	SCHEIN E	1971	Journal of Applied Behavioral Psychology 7: 401
262	SCHUMACHER E	1973	Small is Beautiful
264	SILVERMAN D	1970	Theory of Organizations
271	SIMON H	1956	Econometrica 24: 74
272	SIMON H	1957	Administrative Behavior
273	SIMON H	1957	Models of Man
274	SIMON H	1958	American Economic Review 48: 607
275	SIMON H	1959	American Economic Review 49: 233
276	SIMON H	1960	The New Science of Management
278	SIMON H	1964	Administrative Science Quarterly 9: 1
280	SIMON H	1965	The Shape of Automation for Men and Management
281	TANNENBAUM A	1956	American Journal of Sociology 61: 536
282	TANNENBAUM A	1961	American Journal of Sociology 67: 33
283	TANNENBAUM A	1962	Administrative Science Quarterly 7: 236
284	TANNENBAUM A	1964	American Journal of Sociology 69: 585
285	TANNENBAUM A	1966	Social Psychology of the Work Organization
286	TANNENBAUM A	1968	Control in Organizations
287	TANNENBAUM A	1974	Hierarchy in Organizations
291	THOMPSON J	1957	Administrative Science Quarterly 2: 325
292	THOMPSON J	1958	American Sociological Review 23: 23
293	THOMPSON J	1959	Comparative Studies in Administration

VAR	AUTHOR	YEAR	PUBLICATION
294	THOMPSON J	1962	American Journal of Sociology 68: 309
295	THOMPSON J	1967	Organizations in Action
297	RICE A	1958	Productivity and Social Organizations
298	TRIST E	1963	Organizational Choice
299	RICE A	1963	The Enterprise and its Environment
300	EMERY F / TRIST E	1965	Human Relations 18:1
301	RICE A	1965	Learning for Leadership
302	EMERY F	1969	Systems Thinking
303	EMERY F	1969	Form and Content in Industrial Democracy
304	EMERY F	1974	Futures We Are In
309	URWICK L / BRECH E	1956	Patterns of Management
313	VICKERS G	1965	The Art of Judgement
314	VICKERS G	1967	Towards a Sociology of Management
315	VICKERS G	1968	Value Systems and Social Processes
316	VICKERS G	1970	Freedom in a Rocking Boat
317	VICKERS G	1973	Making Institutions Work
318	VROOM V	1960	Some Personality Determinants of the Effects of Participation
319	VROOM V	1964	Work and Motivation
320	VROOM V	1966	Organizational Behavior and Human Performance 1: 212
321	VROOM V	1967	Methods of Organization
322	VROOM V	1968	Administrative Science Quarterly 13: 26
323	VROOM V	1971	Organizational Behavior and Human Performance 6: 36
324	VROOM V	1973	Leadership and Decision Making
325	VROOM V	1973	Organizational Dynamics 1: 66

VAR	AUTHOR	YEAR	PUBLICATION
329	WHYTE WH	1956	Organization Man
330	WILLIAMSON O	1963	American Economic Review 53: 1032
331	WILLIAMSON O	1964	The Economics of Discretionary Behavior
332	WILLIAMSON O	1966	American Economic Review 56: 810
333	WILLIAMSON O	1967	Journal of Political Economy 75: 123
334	WILLIAMSON O	1970	Corporate Control and Business Behavior
335	WILLIAMSON O	1971	American Economic Review
336	WILLIAMSON O	1975	Bell Journal of Economics
337	WILLIAMSON O	1975	Markets and Hierarchies
341	WOODWARD J	1958	Management and Technology
342	WOODWARD J	1960	The Saleswoman
343	WOODWARD J	1963	Management International Review 8: 137
344	WOODWARD J	1965	Industrial Organization: Theory and Practice
345	WOODWARD J	1970	Industrial Organization: Behavior and Control
347	BRAVERMAN H	1974	Labor and Monopoly Capital
349	ANSOFF I	1957	Harvard Business Review 35: 133
350	ANSOFF I	1965	Corporate Strategy
351	ANSOFF I	1967	Harvard Business Review 45: 71
352	ANSOFF I	1969	Business Strategy
353	ANSOFF I	1970	Long Range Planning 3: 1
354	ANSOFF I	1971	20 Years of Acquisition Behavior
355	ANSOFF I	1975	California Management Review 23: 21

VAR	AUTHOR	YEAR	PUBLICATION
357	HAYS R	1971	Journal of International Business Studies 2: 40
358	HAYS R	1974	Journal of International Business Studies 5: 25
359	BENNIS W	1966	Changing Organizations
360	BENNIS W	1968	The Temporary Society
361	BENNIS W	1969	Organization Development
362	BENNIS W	1956	Human relations 9: 415
363	BENNIS W	1961	The Planning of Change
364	DE BONO E	1967	The Use of Lateral Thinking
365	DE BONO E	1967	The 5 Day Course in Thinking
366	DE BONO E	1969	The Mechanism of the Mind
367	DE BONO E	1970	Lateral Thinking
368	DE BONO E	1971	Lateral Thinking for Management
370	HUMBLE J	1971	Management By Objectives in Action
371	JURAN J	1964	The Managerial Breakthrough
372	JURAN J	1964	The Handbook of Quality Control
373	LEVITT T	1960	Harvard Business Review
374	LEVITT T	1962	Innovation in Marketing
375	LEVITT T	1965	Harvard Business Review
376	LEVITT T	1969	The Marketing Mode
377	LEVITT T	1972	Harvard Business Review
378	LEVITT T	1975	Harvard Business Review
380	REVANS R	1958	Human Relationships
381	REVANS R	1964	Standards for Morale: Cause and Effect
382	REVANS R	1971	Developing Effective Managers
383	SELZNICK P	1957	Leadership in Administration
384	SELZNICK P	1969	Law, Society and Industrial Justice

VAR	AUTHOR	YEAR	PUBLICATION
385	MASLOW A	1962	Towards a Psychology of Being
386	MASLOW A	1971	The Farther Reaches of Human Nature
387	MASLOW A	1965	Eupsychian Management
388	MASLOW A	1966	The Psychology of Science
389	McCLELLAND D	1961	The Achieving Society
390	McCLELLAND D	1965	Journal of Personality and Social Psychology 1: 389
391	McCLELLAND D	1975	Power: The Inner Experience
393	McCLELLAND D	1965	American Psychologist 20: 321
394	McCLELLAND D	1969	Motivating Economic Achievement
395	McCLELLAND D	1971	Assessing Human Motivation
396	McCLELLAND D	1973	American Psychologist 28:1
397	JANIS I	1958	Psychological Stress
398	JANIS I	1959	Personality and Persuasibility
399	JANIS I	1972	Victims of Groupthink
400	JANIS I	1965	Journal of Personality and Social Psychology 1: 181
401	JANIS I	1967	Advances in Experimental Social Psychology 3: 166
402	BLAU P	1956	Bureaucracy in Modern Society
403	BLAU P	1956	Industrial and Labor Relations Review 9: 531
404	BLAU P	1960	American Sociological Review 25: 178
405	BLAU P	1962	Formal Organizations
406	BLAU P	1964	Exchange and Power in Social Life
407	BLAU P	1966	American Sociological Review 31: 179
408	BLAU P	1967	The American Occupational Structure
409	BLAU P	1968	American Journal of Sociology 73: 453
410	BLAU P	1970	American Sociological Review 35: 201

VAR	AUTHOR	YEAR	PUBLICATION
411	BLAU P	1971	The Structure of Organizations
412	BLAU P	1973	The Organization of Academic Work
413	BLAU P	1974	American Sociological Review 39: 615
414	BLAU P	1974	Change 6: 42
415	BLAU P	1974	On the Nature of Organizations
417	BLAU P	1956	American Sociological Review 21: 290
418	WALKER A	1968	Harvard Business Review 46: 129
419	KATZ D	1956	Human Relations 9: 27
420	KATZ D	1959	Psychology: A Study of Science 3: 423
421	KATZ D	1960	Public Opinion Quarterly 24: 163
422	KATZ D	1964	Behavioral Science 9: 131
423	KATZ D / KAHN R	1966	The Social Psychology of Organizations
424	KATZ D	1975	Bureaucratic Encounters
425	KAHN R	1960	American Journal of Psychiatry 117: 326
426	KAHN R	1957	Dynamics of Interviewing
427	KAHN R	1964	Organizational Stress
428	KAHN R	1975	Archives of General Psychiatry 32: 1569
429	KAST F	1972	Academy of Management Journal 15: 447
430	KAST F	1973	Contingency Views of Organization and Management
431	KAST F	1970	Organization and Management: A Systems Approach
432	GALBRAITH JR	1967	Organizational Behavior and Human Performance 2: 237
433	GALBRAITH JR	1973	Designing Complex Organizations

VAR	AUTHOR	YEAR	PUBLICATION
434	GALBRAITH JR	1974	Interfaces 4: 28
435	MITROFF I	1974	Subjective Side of Science
436	MITROFF I	1972	Management Science 19: 11
437	MITROFF I	1974	American Sociological Review 39: 579
439	MITROFF I	1974	Behavioral Science 19: 383
440	MECHANIC D	1961	American Sociological Review 26: 51
441	MECHANIC D	1962	Administrative Science Quarterly 7: 349
442	MECHANIC D	1962	Students Under Stress
444	MARGULIES N	1972	Organization Development: Values,Process and Technology
445	MARGULIES N	1973	Organization Change Techniques
446	CLARK B	1960	American Journal of Sociology 65: 569
447	CLARK B	1960	The Open Door College
448	CLARK B	1966	Colleges and Peer Groups
449	CLARK B	1970	The Distinctive College
450	CLARK B	1972	Administrative Science Quarterly 17: 178
451	PONDY L	1967	Administrative Science Quarterly 12: 296
452	PONDY L	1969	Administrative Science Quarterly 14: 47
453	PONDY L	1970	Power in Organizations

Appendix 2
Life Cycles and Influence of Management Publications

VAR	AUTHOR	INFLUENCE	LIFE CYCLE
1	ARGYRIS C	161.0	30.6
2	ARGYRIS C	43.3	29.4
3	ARGYRIS C	66.4	20.2
4	ARGYRIS C	97.3	18.6
5	ARGYRIS C	22.2	19.7
6	ARGYRIS C	22.3	21.7
7	ARGYRIS C	10.8	16.6
8	ARGYRIS C	47.1	18.0
9	ARGYRIS C	13.5	19.9
10	ARGYRIS C	20.5	17.8
11	ARGYRIS C	12.3	17.3
12	ARGYRIS C	18.3	15.5
13	ARGYRIS C	11.7	14.9
19	BAKKE E	10.5	16.9
20	BAKKE E	3.1	20.7
26	BLAKE R / MOUTON J	3.9	15.6
27	BLAKE R / MOUTON J	7.4	24.4
28	BLAKE R / MOUTON J	17.6	15.4
29	BLAKE R / MOUTON J	66.9	17.5
30	BLAKE R / MOUTON J	21.2	16.9
31	BLAKE R / MOUTON J	14.1	19.1
32	BLAKE R / MOUTON J	10.4	17.3
37	BOULDING K	80.5	38.0
38	BOULDING K	14.1	24.6
39	BOULDING K	84.1	23.4
41	BROWN W	24.8	21.1

VAR	AUTHOR	INFLUENCE	LIFE CYCLE
42	BROWN W	5.9	35.7
43	BROWN W / JAQUES E	4.5	17.1
44	BROWN W	1.7	16.4
46	JAQUES E	38.4	19.8
47	JAQUES E	43.6	33.2
51	BURNS T / STALKER G	166.0	28.1
52	BURNS T / STALKER G	1.8	20.1
53	BURNS T / STALKER G	3.8	22.7
57	CHANDLER A	125.0	32.0
60	SLOAN A	24.9	18.6
61	CROZIER M	147.0	20.1
62	CROZIER M	11.4	23.3
63	CROZIER M	5.3	22.1
64	CROZIER M	5.2	18.8
65	CROZIER M	13.4	18.6
72	DRUCKER P	19.2	17.8
73	DRUCKER P	17.2	17.9
74	DRUCKER P	66.6	23.1
75	DRUCKER P	64.0	22.7
79	EDWARDS R	31.2	18.4
81	ETZIONI A	29.7	32.7
82	ETZIONI A	190.0	24.2
83	ETZIONI A	14.5	22.0
84	ETZIONI A	109.0	18.1
87	ETZIONI A	34.6	14.0
88	ETZIONI A	15.0	25.0
89	ETZIONI A	101.0	18.5
90	ETZIONI A	38.5	25.0
91	ETZIONI A	7.5	11.8
99	FIEDLER F	40.5	15.1
100	FIEDLER F	31.0	14.9
101	FIEDLER F	12.8	16.1

VAR	AUTHOR	INFLUENCE	LIFE CYCLE
102	FIEDLER F	108.0	19.1
103	FIEDLER F	16.9	22.4
105	FIEDLER F	13.0	17.8
111	FREEMAN J	4.8	18.7
112	FREEMAN J	7.7	17.6
113	FREEMAN J	12.6	24.3
114	GALBRAITH JK	231.0	33.9
116	GALBRAITH JK	313.0	21.3
120	GOULDNER A	105.0	27.1
122	GOULDNER A	125.0	29.2
123	GOULDNER A	31.2	20.7
124	GOULDNER A	161.0	23.4
126	HANNAN M	12.9	18.3
127	HANNAN M	5.5	15.1
128	HANNAN M	6.7	20.4
131	HERZBERG F	95.8	28.1
132	HERZBERG F	219.0	31.7
133	HERZBERG F	109.0	22.2
134	HERZBERG F	37.1	20.2
136	PAUL WJ *et al*	16.6	12.5
138	HOFSTEDE G	13.8	20.1
141	KANTER RM	20.7	18.6
142	KANTER RM	43.9	27.1
143	KANTER RM	6.7	17.6
150	LAWLER E	17.2	22.4
151	LAWLER E	20.4	20.7
152	LAWLER E	20.4	178
153	LAWLER E	14.8	15.6
154	LAWLER E	11.7	16.1
155	LAWLER E	11.1	16.0
156	LAWLER E	20.5	21.1
157	LAWLER E	46.6	16.9

VAR	AUTHOR	INFLUENCE	LIFE CYCLE
158	LAWLER E	5.5	17.0
159	LAWLER E	8.3	21.2
160	LAWLER E	51.9	20.2
161	LAWLER E	9.9	18.0
164	LAWRENCE P	28.7	21.6
165	LAWRENCE P / LORSCH J	208.0	19.3
166	LAWRENCE P / LORSCH J	20.9	15.0
168	LORSCH J / MORSE J	12.8	19.5
171	LIKERT R	253.0	23.7
172	LIKERT R	162.0	17.7
174	LINDBLOM C	146.0	36.5
175	LINDBLOM C /BRAYBROOKE D	8.1	15.4
176	LINDBLOM C	66.2	18.7
177	LINDBLOM C	36.9	21.3
180	MARCH J / SIMON H	467.0	30.5
181	CYERT R / MARCH J	278.0	25.0
182	MARCH J	34.2	15.0
183	COHEN M *et al*	56.2	24.3
184	COHEN M	31.7	20.2
190	McGREGOR D	30.5	26.5
191	McGREGOR D	222.0	26.7
192	McGREGOR D	16.1	18.4
193	McGREGOR D	27.5	17.0
195	MILES R / SNOW C	8.8	20.1
196	MILES R / SNOW C	6.0	27.4
198	MINTZBERG H	4.4	22.2
199	MINTZBERG H	2.1	27.0
200	MINTZBERG H	13.8	21.3
201	MINTZBERG H	90.1	22.8
202	MINTZBERG H	22.4	21.7
208	OUCHI W	11.2	18.6

VAR	AUTHOR	INFLUENCE	LIFE CYCLE
213	PARKINSON C	79.3	29.4
214	PARKINSON C	4.9	22.0
217	PFEFFER J	18.8	25.7
218	PFEFFER J	10.5	21.1
219	PFEFFER J / LEBLEBICI H	14.6	27.6
220	PFEFFER J / SALANCIK G	19.5	22.6
221	SALANCIK G / PFEFFER J	15.1	22.0
229	PUGH D	23.1	15.9
230	PUGH D	61.9	23.2
231	PUGH D	71.4	20.7
232	HICKSON D	46.8	20.0
233	HICKSON D *et al*	40.2	21.9
234	PUGH D	0.8	15.1
235	HININGS CR	14.8	21.2
236	DONALDSON L	5.6	19.1
237	PENNINGS J	14.5	16.1
244	CHILD J	5.25	24.8
245	CHILD J	25.4	21.5
246	CHILD J	61.8	25.6
247	CHILD J	13.4	20.6
248	CHILD J	8.85	22.9
249	CHILD J	21.5	20.2
250	CHILD J	3.3	10.5
251	CHILD J	8.52	25.5
252	CHILD J	8.17	23.0
254	SCHEIN E	56.1	19.8
255	SCHEIN E	58.4	13.2
257	SCHEIN E	43.0	19.8
259	SCHEIN E	11.5	21.9
262	SCHUMACHER E	107.0	16.8
264	SILVERMAN D	49.9	27.7
271	SIMON H	33.5	34.5
272	SIMON H	199.0	32.2

VAR	AUTHOR	INFLUENCE	LIFE CYCLE
273	SIMON H	260.0	37.4
274	SIMON H	29.8	25.0
275	SIMON H	60.9	31.3
276	SIMON H	64.9	20.5
278	SIMON H	28.6	21.6
280	SIMON H	15.4	15.7
281	TANNENBAUM A	13.2	13.9
282	TANNENBAUM A	14.9	27.9
283	TANNENBAUM A	17.8	16.7
284	TANNENBAUM A	13.9	16.2
285	TANNENBAUM A	13.9	17.5
286	TANNENBAUM A	46.7	20.3
287	TANNENBAUM A	24.6	21.1
291	THOMPSON J	10.7	21.0
292	THOMPSON J	48.5	30.1
293	THOMPSON J	25.9	27.0
294	THOMPSON J	7.1	12.7
295	THOMPSON J	293.0	23.7
297	RICE A	38.5	40.9
298	TRIST E	36.6	22.4
299	RICE A	21.3	20.6
300	EMERY F / TRIST E	70.1	20.9
301	RICE A	20.1	18.5
302	EMERY F	26.7	18.2
303	EMERY F	16.1	22.6
304	EMERY F	8.4	16.7
309	URWICK L / BRECH E	11.3	20.1
313	VICKERS G	24.7	20.6
314	VICKERS G	3.0	29.2
315	VICKERS G	18.2	20.4
316	VICKERS G	12.6	26.9
317	VICKERS G	5.0	22.2
318	VROOM V	53.2	34.2
319	VROOM V	232.0	19.8

VAR	AUTHOR	INFLUENCE	LIFE CYCLE
320	VROOM V	22.3	20.1
321	VROOM V	4.5	12.0
322	VROOM V	6.6	20.3
324	VROOM V	52.1	30.2
325	VROOM V	1.9	18.7
329	WHYTE WH	340.0	20.5
330	WILLIAMSON O	14.8	19.7
331	WILLIAMSON O	59.8	19.4
332	WILLIAMSON O	22.5	16.9
333	WILLIAMSON O	18.1	30.2
334	WILLIAMSON O	38.2	24.0
335	WILLIAMSON O	18.8	22.6
337	WILLIAMSON O	260.0	22.7
341	WOODWARD J	25.4	24.0
342	WOODWARD J	1.3	21.5
344	WOODWARD J	124.0	20.4
345	WOODWARD J	17.7	19.6
347	BRAVERMAN H	226.0	20.9
349	ANSOFF I	2.8	20.6
350	ANSOFF I	63.6	21.6
351	ANSOFF I	9.7	38.7
352	ANSOFF I	8.7	34.4
353	ANSOFF I	6.6	14.7
354	ANSOFF I	4.3	30.6
355	ANSOFF I	5.0	29.9
357	HAYS R	1.3	19.7
358	HAYS R	2.0	14.6
359	BENNIS W	81.4	15.4
360	BENNIS W	43.7	13.8
361	BENNIS W	34.5	17.1
362	BENNIS W	38.9	23.2
363	BENNIS W	79.6	22.5

VAR	AUTHOR	INFLUENCE	LIFE CYCLE
364	DE BONO E	11.5	27.4
365	DE BONO E	3.8	30.3
366	DE BONO E	5.6	25.4
368	DE BONO E	4.2	23.9
370	HUMBLE J	7.5	16.5
372	JURAN J	5.7	22.1
373	LEVITT T	20.9	27.6
374	LEVITT T	8.9	20.0
375	LEVITT T	14.5	21.3
376	LEVITT T	2.8	24.1
377	LEVITT T	6.2	21.3
378	LEVITT T	5.3	28.7
380	REVANS R	6.0	17.5
381	REVANS R	22.8	17.1
382	REVANS R	3.6	13.1
383	SELZNICK P	115.0	32.3
384	SELZNICK P	25.0	24.1
385	MASLOW A	197.0	22.4
386	MASLOW A	58.4	24.5
387	MASLOW A	38.5	18.4
388	MASLOW A	35.1	25.7
389	McCLELLAND D	324.0	21.0
390	McCLELLAND D	5.9	22.6
391	McCLELLAND D	41.2	26.9
393	McCLELLAND D	24.9	17.2
394	McCLELLAND D	49.5	21.5
395	McCLELLAND D	5.1	21.9
396	McCLELLAND D	23.9	20.0
397	JANIS I	109.0	25.5
398	JANIS I	88.8	23.3
399	JANIS I	86.3	26.2
400	JANIS I	32.1	16.0

VAR	AUTHOR	INFLUENCE	LIFE CYCLE
401	JANIS I	16.5	18.7
402	BLAU P	64.8	20.8
403	BLAU P	34.9	26.3
404	BLAU P	40.3	21.8
405	BLAU P	233.0	23.1
406	BLAU P	207.0	18.2
407	BLAU P	18.6	19.3
408	BLAU P	257.0	22.3
409	BLAU P	13.0	19.0
410	BLAU P	43.2	24.7
411	BLAU P	75.7	30.5
412	BLAU P	25.9	19.5
413	BLAU P	7.3	16.8
414	BLAU P	6.1	21.1
415	BLAU P	9.5	18.3
417	BLAU P	34.4	27.0
418	WALKER A	2.6	25.0
419	KATZ D	19.2	20.5
420	KATZ D	34.8	23.6
421	KATZ D	51.3	23.1
422	KATZ D	8.0	18.9
423	KATZ D / KAHN R	293.0	23.2
424	KATZ D	13.2	24.3
425	KAHN R	52.9	31.1
426	KAHN R	58.3	23.8
427	KAHN R	149.0	23.9
428	KAHN R	20.1	23.5
429	KAST F	3.0	15.7
430	KAST F	7.7	14.4
431	KAST F	25.2	26.7
432	GALBRAITH JR	18.3	16.8
433	GALBRAITH JR	64.4	24.2
434	GALBRAITH JR	6.9	31.1
435	MITROFF I	29.1	24.2

VAR	AUTHOR	INFLUENCE	LIFE CYCLE
436	MITROFF I	10.2	28.0
437	MITROFF I	7.6	22.6
439	MITROFF I	8.6	23.4
440	MECHANIC D	45.5	25.5
441	MECHANIC D	21.6	30.5
442	MECHANIC D	24.4	27.3
444	MARGULIES N	8.0	12.4
445	MARGULIES N	4.0	10.6
446	CLARK B	30.4	35.3
447	CLARK B	43.5	30.0
448	CLARK B	20.5	20.8
449	CLARK B	13.3	31.9
450	CLARK B	10.6	20.0
451	PONDY L	19.2	29.9
452	PONDY L	20.3	18.2
453	PONDY L	5.9	17.1

Appendix 3
Results of Cluster Analysis

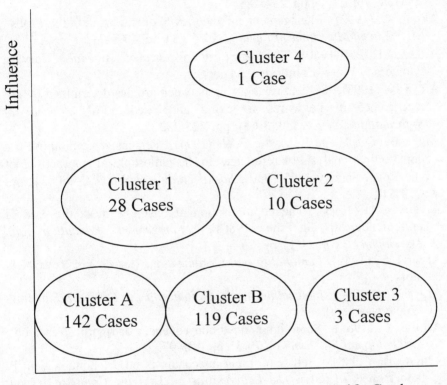

References

Abrahamson, E. (1991), 'Management fads and fashions: the diffusion and rejection of innovations', *Academy of Management Review*, vol. 16(3), pp. 586-612.

Abrahamson, E. (1996), 'Management Fashion', *Academy of Management Review*, vol. 21(1), pp. 254-285.

Aktouf, O. (1992), 'Management and theories of organization in the 1990s', *Academy of Management Review*, vol. 17(3), pp. 407-431.

Aitken, H.G. (1960), *Taylorism at Watertown Arsenal*, Harvard University Press, Cambridge, Mass.

Ali, S.N. (1993), 'Subject relationship between articles determined by co-occurrence of keywords in citing and cited titles', *Journal of Information Science*, vol. 19(3), pp. 225-232.

Allen, B., Qin J. and Lancaster F.W. (1994), 'Persuasive communities: a longitudinal analysis of references in the philosophical transactions of the Royal Society 1665-1990', *Social Studies of Science*, vol. 24, pp. 279-310.

Alvarez, J.L. (1993), 'The popularisation of business ideas: the case of entrepreneurship in the 1980s', *Management Education and Development*, vol. 24(1), pp. 26-32.

Argyris, C. (1957), *Personality and Organization*, Harper and Row, New York.

Argyris, C. (1964), *Integrating the Individual and the Organization*, John Wiley, New York.

Argyris, C. (1968), 'Some unintended consequences of rigorous research', *Psychological Bulletin*, vol. 70(3), pp. 185-97.

Arthur, B. (1988), 'Self-reinforcing mechanisms in economics', in P. Anderson *et al* (eds), *The Economy as an Evolving Complex System*, Addison-Wesley, Redwood City, Cal.

Aspinwall, K. (1992), 'Biographical research: searching for meaning', *Management Education and Development*, vol. 23(3).

Avramescu, A. (1979), 'Actuality and obsolescence of scientific literature', *Journal of the American Society for Information Science*, vol. 30, pp. 296-303.

Bailey, N. (1975), *The Mathematical Theory of Infectious Diseases*, Charles Griffin, London.

Baird, L.M. and Oppenheim, C. (1994), 'Do citations matter?', *Journal of Information Science*, vol. 20(1), pp. 2-15.

Barley, S.R. and Kunda, G. (1992), 'Design and devotion: surges of rational and normative ideologies of control in managerial discourse', *Administrative Science Quarterly*, vol. 37, pp. 363-399.

Baron, J.N., Dobbin, F.R. and Jennings, P.D. (1986), 'War and peace: the evolution of modern personnel administration in U.S. industry', *American Journal of Sociology*, vol. 92, pp. 350-383.

Barthes, R. (1983), *The Fashion System*, Hill and Wans, New York.

Bath University (1980), *The Design of Information Systems in the Social Sciences: Towards the Improvement of Social Science Information Systems*, Bath University Research Reports Series No.1, Bath.

Bavelas, J.B. (1978), 'The social psychology of citations', *Canadian Psychological Review*, vol. 19(2), pp. 158-163.

Bekavec, A., Petrak, J. and Buneta, Z. (1994), 'Citation behavior and place of publication in the authors from the scientific periphery: a matter of quality?', *Information Processing and Management*, vol. 30(1), pp. 33-42.

Bell, E. and Rothman, H. (1991), 'Some problematic aspects of using co-citation cluster time series to model the dynamics of research fields', *Research Evaluation*, vol. 1(3), pp. 155-159.

Bennis, W.G. (1966), *Changing Organizations*, McGraw-Hill, New York.

Berger, A.A. (1992), *Reading Matter: Multidisciplinary Perspectives on Material Culture*, Transaction, New Brunswick.

Beynon, H. (1988), 'Regulating research: politics and decision making in industrial organisations', in A. Bryman (ed), *Doing Research in Organisations*, Routledge, London.

Blake, R.R. and Mouton, J.S. (1964), *The Managerial Grid*, Gulf Publishing, London.

Blau, J. (1993), *The Shape of Culture: A Study of Contemporary Cultural Patterns in the United States*, Cambridge University Press, New York.

Blau, P. and Scott, W.R. (1962), *Formal Organizations*, Routledge, London.

Blau, P. (1964), *Exchange and Power in Social Life*, John Wiley, New York.

Blau, P. and Duncan, O. (1967), *The American Occupational Structure*, John Wiley, New York.

Blau, P. (1971), *The Structure of Organizations*, Basic Books, New York.

Bulmer, H. (1969), 'Fashion: from class differentiation to collective selection', *Sociological Quarterly*, vol. 10, pp. 275-291.

Bonzi, S. (1982), 'Characteristics of a literature as predictors of relatedness between cited and citing works', *Journal of the American Society for Information Science*, vol. 33(4), pp. 208-216.

Boulding, K.E. (1956), *The Image*, Michigan University Press, Ann Arbor.

Braverman, H. (1974), *Labor and Monopoly Capital*, Monthly Review Press, New York.

Broad, W. and Wade, N. (1982), *Betrayers of the Truth: Fraud and Deceit in Science*, Oxford University Press, Oxford.

Brookes, B.C. (1970), 'The growth, utility and obsolescence of scientific periodical literature', *Journal of Documentation*, vol. 26(4), pp. 283-94.

Brookes, B.C. (1975), 'Letter to the Editor', *Journal of Documentation*, vol. 31(1), pp. 46-7.

Brooks, T.A. (1985), 'Private acts and public objects: an investigation of citer motivations', *Journal of the American Society for Information Science*, vol. 36(4), pp. 223-229.

Brooks, T.A. (1986), 'Evidence of complex citer motivations', *Journal of the American Society for Information Science*, vol. 37(1), pp. 34-36.

Bryman, A. (ed) (1988), *Doing Research in Organizations*, Routledge, London.

Bryman, A. and Cramer, D. (1990), *Quantitative Data Analysis for Social Scientist'*, Routledge, London.

Buckland, M.K. (1972), 'Are obsolescence and scattering related?', *Journal of Documentation*, vol. 28(3), pp. 242-6.

Burns, T. and Stalker, G.M. (1961), *The Management of Innovation*, Tavistock, London.

Business Week (1986), 'Business fads: what's in and out', July 12, 52-56.

Campanario, J.M. (1993), 'Consolation for the scientist: sometimes it is hard to publish papers that are later highly cited', *Social Studies of Science*, vol. 23, pp. 342-62.

Carroll, G.R. and Hannan, M.T. (1989), 'Density dependence in the evolution of populations of newspaper organizations', *American Sociological Review*, vol. 54, pp. 524-541.

Carson, P.P. and Carson, K.D. (1992), 'Deming versus historical management theorists on the importance of goal-setting: can both be right?', *Proceedings of the Academy of Management*, pp. 144-148.

Castorina, P. and Wood, B. (1988), 'Circles in the Fortune 500: why circles fail', *Journal for Quality and Participation*, vol. 11, pp. 40-41.

Chandler, A.D. (1962), *Strategy and Structure*, MIT Press, Massachusetts.

Chubin, D.E. and Moitra, S.D. (1975), 'Content analysis of references: adjunct or alternative to citation counting', *Social Studies of Science*, vol. 5(4), pp. 423-441.

Clark, K.E. (1957), *America's Psychologists: A Survey of a Growing Profession*, American Psychological Association, Washington.

Clark, T. and Salaman, G. (1996), 'The management guru as organizational witch doctor', *Organization*, vol. 3, pp. 85-108.

Coe, R. and Weinstock, I. (1984), 'Evaluating the management journals: a second look', *Academy of Management Journal*, vol. 27, pp. 660-666.

Coghlan, A. (1991), 'Citation system may encourage 'banal' research', *New Scientist*, 11th May 1991.

Cohen, M.D., March, J.G. and Olsen, J.P. (1972), 'A garbage can model of organizational choice', *Administrative Science Quarterly*, vol. 17, pp. 1.

Cole, S. and Cole, J. (1967), 'Scientific output and recognition: a study in the operation of the reward system in science', *American Sociological Review*, vol. 32, pp. 377-90.

Cole, J. and Cole, S. (1971), 'Measuring the quality of sociological research: problems in the use of science citation index', *American Sociologist*, vol. 6, pp. 23-29.

Cole, J. and Cole, S. (1972), 'The Ortega Hypothesis: citation analysis suggests that only a few scientists contribute to scientific progress', *Science*, vol. 178, pp. 364-374.

Collin, S-O., Johansson, U., Svensson, K. and Ulvenblad, P-O. (1996), 'Market segmentation in scientific publications: research patterns in American vs. European management journals', *British Journal of Management*, vol. 7, pp. 141-154.

Colman, A.L., Dhillon, D. and Coulthard, B. (1995), 'A bibliometric evaluation of the research performance of British university politics departments: publications in leading journals', *Scientometrics*, vol. 32(1), pp. 49-66.

Cooper, R.A. and Weekes, A.J. (1983), *Data Models and Statistical Analysis*, Philip Allan, Oxford.

Cooper, R.B., Blair, D. and Pao, M. (1993), 'Communicating MIS research: a citation study of journal influence', *Information Processing and Management*, vol. 29(1), pp. 113-127.

Crane, D. (1972), *Invisible Colleges*, University of Chicago Press, Chicago.

Cronin, B. (1981a), 'Agreement and divergence on referencing practice', *Journal of Information Science*, vol. 3(1), pp. 27-34.

Cronin, B. (1981b), 'The need for a theory of citing', *Journal of Documentation*, vol. 37(1), pp. 16-24.

Cronin, B. (1982a), 'Invisible colleges and information transfer', *Journal of Documentation*, vol. 38(3), pp. 212-236.

Cronin, B. (1982b), 'Norms and functions in citation: the view of journal editors and referees in psychology', *Social Science Information Studies*, vol. 2(2), pp. 65-78.

Cronin, B. (1984), *The Citation Process*, Taylor Graham, London.

Cronin, B. and McKenzie, G. (1992), 'The trajectory of rejection', *Journal of Documentation*, vol. 48(3), pp. 310-317.

Cronin, B. (1996), 'Rates of return to citation', *Journal of Documentation*, vol. 52(2), pp. 188-197.

Crowther, J.G. (1952), *British Scientists of the Twentieth Century*, Routledge and Kegan Paul, London.

Crozier, M. (1963), *The Bureaucratic Phenomenon*, Tavistock, London.

Culnan, M.J. (1987), 'Mapping the intellectual structure of MIS, 1980-1985: a co-citation analysis', *MIS Quarterly*, vol. 11, pp. 341-354.

Cyert, R.M. and March, J.G. (1963), *A Behavioural Theory of the Firm*, Prentice-Hall, New York.

Darwent, C. (1988), 'Consultants after the party', *Management Today*, January, pp. 70-78.

Davies, D. (1970), 'Letter to the Editor', *Nature*, vol. 228, pp. 1356.

Delamont, S. (1989), 'Citation and social mobility research: self defeating behaviour?', *Sociological Review*, vol. 37(2), pp. 332-337.

De Queiroz, G. and Lancaster, F. (1981), 'Growth, dispersion and obsolescence of the literature: a case study in thermoluminescent dosimetry', *Journal of Research Communication Studies*, vol. 2, pp. 203-217.

De Stefano, D.A. (1987), 'Citation analysis and adaptive radiation', *Scientometrics*, vol. 2, pp. 43-51.

Diamond, A.M. Jr. (1986), 'What is a citation worth?', *Journal of Human Resources*, vol. 21, pp. 200-215.

Dieks, D. and Chang, H. (1976), 'Differences in impact of scientific publications: some indices derived from citation analysis', *Social Studies of Science*, vol. 6, pp. 247.

Dimaggio, P.J. and Hirsch, P. (1976), 'Production organizations in the arts', in R. Peterson (ed), *The production of culture*, Sage, Beverley Hills.

Dimaggio, P.J. and Powell, W.W. (1983), 'The iron cage revisited: institutional isomorphism and collective rationality in organizational fields', *American Sociological Review*, vol. 48, pp. 147-160.

Dogan, M. and Pahre, R. (1990), *Creative Marginality: Innovation at the Intersections of Social Sciences*, Boulder, San Francisco.

Doke, E.R. and Luke, R.H. (1987), 'Perceived quality of CIS/MIS journals among faculty: publishing hierarchies', *The Journal of Computer Information Systems*, pp. 30-33.

Doreian, P. and Fararo, T. (1985), 'Structural equivalence in a journal network', *Journal of the American Society for Information Science*, vol. 36(1), pp. 28-37.

Doreian, P. (1988), 'Measuring the relative standing of disciplinary journals', *Information Processing and Management*, vol. 24(1), pp. 45-56.

Doreain, P. (1994), 'A measure of standing for citation networks within a wider environment', *Information Processing and Management*, vol. 30(1), pp. 21-31.

Drucker, P.F. (1974), *Management: Tasks, Responsibilities, Practices*, Heinemann, London.

Duff, A.S. (1995), 'The 'information society' as paradigm: a bibliometric enquiry', *Journal of Information Science*, vol. 21(5), pp. 390-5.

Duncan, E.B. *et al.* (1981), 'Qualified citation indexing: its relevance to educational technology', *Proceedings of the First Symposium on Information Retrieval in Educational Technology*, 1st April, Aberdeen, pp. 70-79.

Dunkerley, D. (1988), 'Historical methods and organisational analysis: the case of a naval dockyard', in A. Bryman (ed), *Doing Research in Organisations*, Routledge, London.

Easterby-Smith, M., Thorpe, R. and Lowe, A. (1991), *Management Research: an Introduction*, Sage, Newbury Park.

Eccles, R.G. and Nohria, N. (1992), *Beyond the hype*, Harvard Business School Press, Cambridge, Mass.

The Economist, 11th March 1995, pp. 106.

Edwards, R. (1979), *Contested Terrain*, Basic Books, New York.

Egghe, L. (1993), 'On the influence of growth on obsolescence', *Scientometrics*, vol. 27(2), pp. 195-214.

Egghe, L. and Rao, I.K.R. (1992), 'Citation age data and the obsolescence function: fits and explanations', *Information Processing and Management*, vol. 28(2), pp. 201-217.

Ellis, D., Cox, D. and Hall, K. (1993), 'A comparison of the information seeking patterns of researchers in the physical and social sciences', *Journal of Documentation*, vol. 49(4), pp. 356-369.

E.S.R.C. (1994). *Report of the Commission on Management Research*.

Etzioni, A. (1961), *A Comparative Analysis of Complex Organizations*, Free Press, New York.

Etzioni, A. (1964), *Modern Organizations*, Prentice Hall, New York.

Etzioni, A. (1968), *The Active Society: A Theory of Societal and Political Processes*, Free Press, New York.

Everitt, B. (1980), *Cluster Analysis*, Heinemann, London.

Extejt, M.M. and Smith, J.E. (1990), 'The behavioral sciences and management: an evaluation of relevant journals', *Journal of Management*, vol. 16, pp. 539-551.

Fiedler, F.E. (1967), *A Theory of Leadership Effectiveness*, McGraw-Hill, New York.

Folly, G., Hajtman, B., Nagy, J. and Ruff, I. (1981), 'Methodological problems in ranking scientists by citation analysis', *Scientometrics*, vol. 3, pp. 135-147.

Franke, R.H., Edlund, T.W. and Oster, F. (1990), 'The development of strategic management: journal quality and article impact', *Strategic Management Journal*, vol. 11, pp. 243-253.

Freeman, J. (1986), 'Data quality and the development of organizational social science: an editorial essay', *Administrative Science Quarterly*, vol. 31, pp. 298-303.

Frost, C. (1979), 'The use of citations in literary research: preliminary classification of citation functions', *Library Quarterly*, vol. 49(4), pp. 399-414.

Galbraith, J.R. (1980), 'Applying theory to the management of organizations', in W.M. Evan (ed), *Frontiers in organization and management*, Praeger, New York.

Gapen, D.K. and Miller, S.P. (1981), 'Obsolescence', *Library Trends*, vol. 30(1), pp. 107-24.

Garfield, E. *et al* (1964), *The Use of Citation Data in Writing the History of Science*, Institute for Scientific Information, Philadelphia.

Garfield, E. (1970), 'Citation indexing for studying science', *Nature*, vol. 227, 15 Aug, pp. 669-71.

Garfield, E. (1972), 'Citations-to divided by items-published gives the impact factor', *Current Contents*, vol. 15, pp. 6-7.

Garfield, E. (1979), 'Is citation analysis a legitimate evaluation tool?', *Scientometrics*, vol. 1, pp. 359-375.

Garvey, W.D., Lin, N. and Nelson, C.E. (1971), 'A comparison of scientific communication behaviour of social and physical scientists', *International Social Science Journal*, vol. 23(2), pp. 256-272.

Gaston, J. (1971), 'Secretiveness and competition for priority of discovery in physics', *Minerva*, vol. 9(4), pp. 472-492.

Gilbert, G.M. (1977), 'Referencing as persuasion', *Social Studies of Science*, vol. 17, pp. 113-122.

Gill, J. and Whittle, S. (1992), 'Management by panacea: accounting for transience', *Journal of Management Studies*, vol. 30(2), pp. 281-295.

Gillett, R.T. (1987), 'Serious anomalies in the UGC comparative evaluation of the research performance of psychology departments', *Bulletin of the British Psychological Society*, vol. 40, pp. 42-49.

Glänzel, W. (1996), 'A bibliometric approach to social sciences. Natural research performances in 6 selected social science areas 1990-1992', *Scientometrics*, vol. 35, pp. 291-307.

Glänzel, W. and Schoepflin, V. (1995), 'A bibliometric study on aging and reception processes of scientific literature', *Journal of Information Science*, vol. 21(1), pp. 37-53.

Glenn, N.D. and Villemez, W. (1970), 'The productivity of sociologists at 45 American universities', *American Sociologist*, vol. 5, pp. 244-252.

Gomez-Meija, L.R. and Balkin, D.B. (1992), 'Determinants of faculty pay: an agency theory perspective', *Academy of Management Journal*, vol. 35, pp. 921-955.

Gottfredson, S.D. and Garvey, W.D. (1980), 'Review of 'Citation Indexing' by Eugene Garfield', *Behavioral and Social Sciences Librarian*, vol. 1(4), pp. 289-294.

Gouldner, A.W. (1970), *The Coming Crisis of Western Sociology*, Basic Books, New York.

Granovetter, M. (1978), 'Threshold models of collective behavior', *American Journal of Sociology*, vol. 83, pp. 1420-1443.

Granovetter, M. (1979), 'The idea of 'advancement' in theories of evolution and development', *American Journal of Sociology*, vol. 85, pp. 489-515

Griffith, B., Servi, P., Anker, A. and Drott, M. (1979), 'The aging of scientific literature: a citation analysis', *Journal of Documentation*, vol. 35(3), pp. 179-196.

Gupta, D.K. (1984), 'Periodical literature of exploration geophysics: obsolescence factors and patterns', *Library Science*, vol. 21(4), pp. 205-226.

Gupta, B.M., Sharma, L. and Karisiddappa, C. (1995), 'Modelling the growth of papers in a scientific specialty', *Scientometrics*, vol. 33(2), pp. 187-201.

Hackman, J.R. (1975), 'Is job enrichment just a fad?', *Harvard Business Review*, Sept-Oct, pp. 129-138.

Hannabus, S. (1987), 'Collaborating over meanings in management: Drucker looks at effectiveness', *Personnel Review*, vol. 16(5), pp. 34-39.

Harter, S., Nisonger, T. and Weng, A. (1993), 'Semantic relationships between cited and citing articles in library and information science journals', *Journal of the American Society for Information Science*, vol.

44(9), pp. 543-552.

Harvard Business Review (1991), *Business Classics: Fifteen Key Concepts for Managerial Success*, Harvard Business School Publishing, Boston.

He, C. and Pao, M.L. (1986), 'A discipline-scientific journal selection algorithm', *Information Processing and Management*, vol. 22, pp. 405-416.

Heisey, T.M. (1988), 'Paradigm agreement and literature obsolescence: a comparative study in the literature of the Dead Sea Scrolls', *Journal of Documentation*, vol. 44(4), pp. 285-301.

Herzberg, F., Mausner, B. and Snyderman, B. (1959), *The Motivation to Work*, John Wiley,New York.

Herzberg, F. (1968), 'One more time: how do you motivate employees?', *Harvard Business Review*, vol. 46, pp. 53-62.

Hirst, G. (1982), 'Discipline impact factor: a method for determining core journal lists', *Journal of the American Society for Information Science*, vol. 29, pp. 171-172.

Hodgson, A. (1987), 'Deming's never ending road to quality', *Personnel Management*, July, pp. 40-44.

Huczynski, A.A. (1993), *Management gurus*, Routledge, New York.

Hulin, C.L. and Smith, P.A. (1967), 'An empirical investigation of two implications of the two-factor theory of job satisfaction', *Journal of Applied Psychology*, vol. 51, pp. 396-402.

Johnes, G. (1988), 'Research performance indicators in the university sector', *Higher Education Quarterly*, vol. 42, pp. 54-71.

Johnson, J.L. and Podsakoff, P.M. (1994), 'Journal influence in the field of management: an analysis using Salancik's index in a dependency network', *Academy of Management Journal*, vol. 37(5), pp. 1392-1407.

Institute for Scientific Information (1988), *Journal Citation Reports: A Bibliometric Analysis of Social Science Journals in the ISI Database*, ISI Press, Philadelphia.

Kaplan, E. (1965), 'The norms of citation behavior: prolegomena to the footnote', *American Documentation*, vol. 16(3), pp. 179-184.

Katz, D. and Kahn, R.L. (1964), *The Social Psychology of Organizations*, John Wiley, New York.

Kennedy, C. (1991), *Guide to the Management Gurus*, Business Books, London.

Kessler, M.M. (1965), 'Comparison of results of bibliographic coupling and analytic subject indexing', *American Documentation*, vol. 16, pp. 223-233.

Kidd, J.S. (1990), 'Measuring referencing practices', *Journal of the American Society for Information Science*, vol. 41(3), pp. 157-163.

Kieser, A. (1997), 'Rhetoric and myth in management fashion', *Organization*, vol. 4(1), pp. 49-74.

Kimberly, J.R. *et al* (1980), *The Organizational Life Cycle*, Jossey-Bass, San Francisco.

Kimberly, J.R. (1981), 'Management innovation' in P.C. Nystrom and W.H. Starbuck (eds), *Handbook of Organizational Design*, Oxford University Press, Oxford.

Kochan, C.A. and Budd, J.M. (1992), 'The persistence of fraud in the literature: the Darsee case', *Journal of the American Society for Information Science*, vol. 43, pp. 488-493.

Kroeber, A.L. (1919), 'On the principle of order as exemplified by changes of fashion', *American Anthropologist*, vol. 21, pp. 235-263.

Krohn, R. (1980), 'Introduction: towards the empirical study of scientific practice', in K.D. Knorr *et al* (eds), *The social process of scientific investigation*, Reidel, Dordrecht.

Kuhn, T.S. (1968), 'The history of science', *International Encyclopaedia of the Social Sciences*, vol. 14, pp. 74-83.

Kuhn, T.S. (1970), *The Structure of Scientific Revolutions*, University of Chicago Press, Chicago.

Lancaster, F. *et al* (1986), 'Factors influencing sources cited by scientists: a case study for Cuba', *Scientometrics*, vol. 10, pp. 243-257.

Lancaster, G. and Massingham, L. (1993), *Essentials of Marketing*, McGraw Hill, Maidenhead.

Lasch, C. (1991), *The True and only Heaven: Progress and its Critics*, Norton, New York.

Latour, B. and Woolgar, S. (1979), *Laboratory Life: The Social Construction of Scientific Facts*, Sage, Beverley Hills.

Latour, B. (1987), *Science in Action: How to Follow Scientists and Engineers through Society*, Open University Press, Milton Keynes.

Lauer, J.C. and Lauer, R.H. (1981), *Fashion Power: the Meaning of Fashion in American Society*, Prentice Hall, New Jersey.

Lawler, E.E. and Mohrman, S.A. (1985), 'Quality circles after the fad', *Harvard Business Review*, Jan-Feb, pp. 65-71.

Lawrence, P.R. and Lorsch, J.W. (1967), *Organization and Environment*, Harvard, Cambridge, Mass.

Leach, D. (1981), 'Re-evaluation of the logistic curve for human populations', *Journal of the Royal Statistical Society A*, vol. 144(1), pp. 94-103.

Lee, D. and Evans, A. (1984), 'American geographers rankings of American geography journals', *Professional Geographer*, vol. 36(3), pp. 292-300.

Leydesdorff, L. (1994), 'The generation of aggregated journal-journal citation maps on the basis of the CD-ROM version of the science citation index', *Scientometrics*, vol. 31(1), pp. 59-84.

Liebowitz, S.J. and Palmer, J.P. (1984), 'Assessing the relative impacts of economics journals', *Journal of Economic Literature*, vol. 22, pp. 77-88.

Likert, R. (1961), *New Patterns of Management*, McGraw-Hill, New York.

Likert, R. (1967), *The Human Organization: Its Management and Value*, McGraw-Hill, New York.

Line, M.B. (1970), 'The 'half-life' of periodical literature: apparent and real obsolescence', *Journal of Documentation*, vol. 26(1), pp. 46-54.

Line, M.B. (1974), 'Does physics literature obsolesce?', *BLL Review*, vol. 2, pp. 84-91.

Line, M.B. and Carter, B. (1974), 'Change in the use of sociological articles with time: a comparison of diachronous and synchronous data', *BLL Review*, vol. 2, pp. 124-29.

Line, M.B. and Sandison, A. (1974), ''Obsolescence' and changes in the use of literature with time', *Journal of Documentation*, vol. 30(3), pp. 283-350.

Lipetz, B.A. (1965), 'Improvement of the selectivity of citation indexes to science literature through the inclusion of citation relationship indicators', *American Documentation*, vol. 16(2), pp. 81-90.

Liu, M. (1993a), 'The complexities of citation practice: a review of citation studies', *Journal of Documentation*, vol. 49(4), pp. 370-408.

Liu, M. (1993b), 'A study of citing motivation of Chinese scientists', *Journal of Information Science*, vol. 19(1), pp. 13-23.

Macmillan, I.C. and Stern, I. (1987), 'Delineating a forum for business policy scholars', *Strategic Management Journal*, vol. 8, pp. 183-186.

Macroberts, M.H. and Macroberts, B.R. (1988), 'Author motivation for not citing influences: a methodological note', *Journal of the American Society for Information Science*, vol. 39(6), pp.432-433.

Mann, S.J. (1992), 'Telling a life story: issues for research', *Management Education and Development*, vol. 23(3).

March, J.G. and Simon, H.A. (1958), *Organizations*, Wiley, New York.

March, J.G. and Olsen, J.P. (1976), *Ambiguity and Choice in Organizations*, Universitesforlaget, Bergen, Norway.

Maslow, A. (1954), *Motivation and Personality*, Harper and Row, New York.

Maslow, A. (1962), *Towards a Psychology of Being*, Van Nostrand Press, New York.

Maslow, A. (1970), *Motivation and Personality*, Harper, New York.

Matricciani, E. (1994), 'Shannon's entropy as a measure of the 'life' of the literature of a discipline', *Scientometrics*, vol. 30(1), pp. 129-145.

May, K.O. (1967), 'Abuses of citation indexing', *Science*, vol. 156, pp. 890-892.

Mayo, E. (1933), *The Human Problems of an Industrial Civilisation*, Macmillan, London.

McCain, K.W. (1984), 'Longitudinal author cocitation mapping: the changing structure of macroeconomics', *Journal of the American Society for Information Science*, vol. 35, pp. 351-359.

McCain, K.W. (1986), 'Co-cited author mapping as a valid representation of intellectual structure', *Journal of the American Society for Information Science*, vol. 37(3), pp. 111-122.

McClelland, D.C. (1953), *The Achievement Motive*, Appleton-Century-Crofts, New York.

McClelland, D.C. (1961), *The Achieving Society*, Van Nostrand, New York.

McClelland, D.C. (1969), *Motivating Economic Achievement*, Free Press, New York.

McGregor, D. (1960), *The Human Side of Enterprise*, McGraw-Hill, New York.

Meadows, A.J. (1974), *Communication in Science*, Butterworths, London.

Medawar, P.B. (1964), 'Is the scientific paper fraudulent?', *Saturday Review*, August 1st, pp. 42-43.

Menard, H.W. (1971), *Science, Growth and Change*, Harvard Press, Cambridge, Mass.

Merton, R.K. (1968), 'The Matthew effect in science: the reward and communication systems of science are considered', *Science*, vol. 159, pp. 56-63.

Merton, R.K. (1973), *The Sociology of Science: Theoretical and Empirical Investigations*, Chicago University Press, Chicago.

Meyer, J.W. and Rowan, B. (1977), 'Institutionalized organizations: formal structure as myth and ceremony', *American Journal of Sociology*, vol. 83, pp. 364-385.

Miller, R.G. (1974), 'The jackknife: a review', *Biometrika*, vol. 61, pp. 1-15.

Mintzberg, H. (1979), *The Structuring of Organizations*, Prentice-Hall, New York.

Miquel, J. *et al* (1995), 'World science in 18 disciplinary areas: comparative evaluation of the publication patterns of 48 countries over the period 1981-1992', *Scientometrics*, vol. 33(2), pp. 149-167.

Mitra, A.C. (1970), 'The bibliographic reference: a review of its role,

Annals of Library Science, vol. 17(3/4), pp. 117-123.

Mitroff, I.I. (1972), 'The myth of subjectivity or why science needs a new psychology of science', *Management Science*, vol. 18, pp. 613-618.

Mitroff, I.I. and Mohrman, S. (1987), 'The slack is gone: how the United States lost its competitive edge in the world economy', *Academy of Management Executive*, vol. 1, pp. 65-70.

Moed, H.F., Burger, W., Frankfort, J. and Van Raan, A. (1985), 'The use of bibliometric data for the measurement of university research performance', *Research Policy*, vol. 14, pp. 131.

Moed, H.F. (1989), 'Bibliometric measurement of research performance and Price's theory of differences among the sciences', *Scientometrics*, vol. 15, pp. 473-485.

Moed, A.F. and Vriens, M. (1989), 'Possible inaccuracies occurring in citation analysis', *Journal of Information Science*, vol. 15(2), pp. 95-107.

Moravcsik, M.J. and Murugesan, P. (1975), 'Some results on the function and quality of citations', *Social Studies of Science*, vol. 5, pp. 86-92.

Narin, F. (1976), *Evaluative Bibliometrics*, Computer Horizons Inc., Cherry Hill, New Jersey.

Nelson, A. (1996), 'Best footnote forward', *Times Higher Education Supplement*, 12 April.

Oliver, M.R. (1971), 'The effect of growth on the obsolescence of semiconductor physics literature', *Journal of Documentation*, vol. 27(1), pp. 11-17.

Oppenheim, A.N. (1992), *Questionnaire Design, Interviewing and Attitude Measurement*, Pinter, London.

O'Reilly, C.A. (1991), 'Organizational behavior: where we've been, where we're going', *Annual Review of Psychology*, vol. 42, pp. 427-458.

Owen, F. and Jones, R. (1990), *Statistics*, Pitman, London.

Paul, W., Robertson, K. and Herzberg, F. (1969), 'Job enrichment pays off', *Harvard Business Review*, vol. 47, pp. 61-78.

Peters, T. and Waterman, R.H. (1982), *In Search of Excellence*, Harper and Row, New York.

Peters, H. and Van Raan, A. (1994), 'On determinants of citation scores: a case study in chemical engineering', *Journal of the American Society for Information Science*, vol. 45(1), pp. 39-49.

Peters, H., Hartmann, D. and Van Raan, A. (1988), 'Monitoring advances in chemical engineering', in L. Egghe and R. Rousseau (eds), *Informetrics 87/88*, Elsevier, Amsterdam.

Peterson, R.A. (1979), 'Revitalising the culture concept', *Annual Review of Sociology*, vol. 5, pp. 137-166.

Pettigrew, A. (1985), 'Contextualist research and the study of organizational change processes', in E. Lawler *et al* (eds), *Doing Research that is Useful for Theory and Practice*, Jossey-Bass, San Francisco.

Pichappan, P. (1993), 'Identification of mainstream journals of science speciality: a method using the discipline-contribution score', *Scientometrics*, vol. 27(2), pp. 179-193.

Polanyi, M. (1958), *Personal knowledge*, University of Chicago Press, Chicago.

Popper, K.R. (1959), *The Logic of Scientific Discovery*, Hutchinson, London.

Porter, A.L., Chubin, D.E. and Jin, X.Y. (1988), 'Citations and scientific progress: comparing bibliometric measures with scientist judgements', *Scientometrics*, vol. 13, pp. 103-24.

Prabha, C.G. (1983), 'Some aspects of citation behavior: a pilot study in business administration', *Journal of the American Society for Information Science*, vol. 34(3), pp. 202-206.

Price, D.J. de S. (1963), *Little Science, Big Science*, Columbia University Press, New York.

Price, D.J. de S. (1965), 'Networks of scientific papers', *Science*, vol. 149, pp. 510-515.

Price, D.J. de S. (1970), 'Citation measures of hard science, soft science, technology and non-science', in C.E. Nelson and D.K. Pollock (eds), *Communication amongst Scientists and Technologists*, Heath, Lexington.

Pugh, D.S. and Hickson, D.J. (1989), *Writers on Organizations*, Penguin, London.

Punch, M. (1986), *The Politics and Ethics of Fieldwork*, Sage, Newbury Park.

Raisig, L.M. (1960), 'Mathematical evaluation of the scientific serial', *Science*, vol. 131, pp. 1417.

Ravetz, J.R. (1971), *Scientific Knowledge and its Social Problems*, Penguin, Harmondsworth.

Rice, A.K. (1958), *Productivity and Social Organization*, Tavistock, London.

Rinia, E.J., De Lange, C. and Moed, H. (1993), 'Measuring national output in physics: delimitation problems', *Scientometrics*, vol. 28(1), pp. 89-110.

Rip, A. and Courtial, J-P. (1984), 'Co-word maps of biotechnology: an example of cognitive scientometrics', *Scientometrics*, vol. 6(6), pp. 381-400.

Robinson, D.E. (1976), 'Fashion in shaving and trimming of the beard: the men of the Illustrated London News 1842-1972', *American Journal of Sociology*, vol. 81, pp. 1133-1141.

Roche, T. and Smith, D.L. (1978), 'Frequency of citations as criterion for the ranking of departments, journals and individuals', *Sociological Enquiry*, vol. 48(1), pp. 49-57.

Rogers, E.M. (1983), *Diffusion of Innovation*, Free Press, New York.

Rose, M. (1988), *Industrial Behaviour*, Penguin, London.

Sandison, A. (1971), 'The use of older literature and its obsolescence', *Journal of Documentation*, vol. 17, pp. 184-189.

Sandison, A. (1975), 'References/citations in the study of knowledge', *Journal of Documentation*, vol. 31(3), pp. 195-8.

Sandison, A. (1983), 'Thematic analysis and obsolescence', *Journal of the American Society for Information Science*, vol. 34, pp. 295.

Sandison, A. (1987), 'Studies of citations and of obsolescence', *Journal of Information Science*, vol. 13, pp. 371-372.

Sandison, A. (1989), 'Thinking about citation analysis', *Journal of Documentation*, vol. 45, pp. 59-64.

Sapir, E. (1937), 'Fashion', *Encyclopaedia of the Social Sciences*, vol. 3, pp. 139-144.

Schneider, B. (1985), 'Organizational behavior', *Annual Review of Psychology*, vol. 36, pp. 573-611.

Schubert, A. and Braun, T. (1993), 'Reference standards for citation based assessments', *Scientometrics*, vol. 26(1), pp. 21-35.

Schumacher, E.F. (1973), *Small is Beautiful*, Blond and Briggs, London.

Science, Vol. 260, 14/5/93, pp. 884.

Seglen, P.O. (1994), 'Causal relationship between article citedness and journal impact', *Journal of the American Society for Information Science*, vol. 45(1), pp. 1-11.

Selznick, P. (1957), *Leadership in Administration: A Sociological Interpretation,* Harper Collins, Scranton PA.

Shafritz, J.M. and Whitbeck, P.H. (1979), *Classics of Organization Theory*, Moore, New York.

Shadish, W.R., Tolliver, D., Gray, M. and Gupta, S.K.S. (1995), 'Author judgements about works they cite: three studies from psychology journals', *Social Studies of Science*, vol. 25(3), pp. 477-98.

Shaw, J.G. (1987), 'Article-by-article citation analysis of medical journals', *Scientometrics*, vol. 12, pp. 101-110.

Simmel, G. (1904), 'Fashion', *International Quarterly*, vol. 10, pp. 130-55.

Reprinted in *American Journal of Sociology* (1957), vol. 62, pp. 541-48.

Small, H. (1976), 'Structural dynamics of scientific literature', *International Classification*, vol. 3(2), pp. 67-74.

Small, H. (1977), 'Co-citation model of a scientific specialty. Longitudinal study of collagen research', *Social Studies of Science*, vol. 7(2), pp. 139-166.

Small, H. (1978), 'Cited documents as concept symbols', *Social Studies of Science*, 8, 327-340.

Small, H. (1980), 'Co-citation context analysis and the structure of paradigms', *Journal of Documentation*, vol. 36(3), pp. 183-196.

Snyder, H., Cronin, B. and Davenport, E. (1995), 'What's the use of citation? Citation analysis as a literature topic in selected disciplines of the social sciences', *Journal of Information Science*, vol. 21(2), pp. 75-85.

Institute for Scientific Information, *Social Sciences Citation Index*, ISI Press, Philadelphia.

Spencer, H. (1888), *The Principles of Sociology Volume 2*, Appleton, New York.

Sperber, I. (1990), *Fashions in Science*, University of Minnesota Press, Minneapolis.

Stahl, M.J., Leap, T.L. and Wei Z.Z. (1988), 'Publication in leading management journals as a measure of institutional research productivity', *Academy of Management Journal*, vol. 31, pp. 707-720.

Starr, S.L. (1983), 'Simplification in scientific work: an example from neuroscience research', *Social Studies of Science*, vol. 13(2), pp. 205-228.

Staw, B.M. (1984), 'Organizational behavior: a review and reformation of the field's outcome variables', *Annual Review of Psychology*, vol. 35, pp. 627-666.

Stinson, E.R. and Lancaster, F.W. (1987), 'Synchronous versus diachronous methods in the measurement of obsolescence by citation studies', *Journal of Information Science*, vol. 13(2), pp. 65-74.

Sullivan, D., White, D.H. and Barbioni, E.J. (1977), 'Co-citation analyses of science: an evaluation', *Social Studies of Science*, vol. 7, pp. 223-240.

Swales, J.M. (1990), *Genre Analysis: English in Academic and Research Settings*, Cambridge University Press, Cambridge.

Swanson, D.R. (1987), 'Two medical literatures that are logically but not bibliographically connected', *Journal of the American Society for Information Science*, vol. 38(4), pp. 228-233.

Taylor, F.W. (1911), *The Principles of Scientific Management*, Reprinted: Harper Collins, New York, 1947.

Thomas, K.S. (1992), 'The development of eponymy', *Scientometrics*, vol. 24, pp. 405-417.

Thomas, P.R. (1995), 'Size effects in the assessment of discipline-contribution scores: an example from the social sciences', *Scientometrics*, vol. 33(2), pp. 203-220.

Thomas, P.R. and Watkins, D.S. (1995), 'Peer review versus bibliometric analysis as indicators of research excellence', *British Academy of Management Conference*, Sheffield, September.

Thompson, J.D. (1967), *Organizations in Action*, McGraw-Hill, New York.

Thompson, P. and Davidson, J.O. (1994), 'The continuity of discontinuity: management rhetoric in turbulent times', *Strategic Direction of Human Resource Management Conference*, Nottingham, December.

Tijssen, R. and Van Leuwwen, T.N. (1995), 'On generalising scientometric journal mapping beyond ISI's journal and citation databases', *Scientometrics*, vol. 33(1), pp. 93-116.

Valency, M. (1973), 'Fashion', *Encyclopaedia Americana*, vol. 11, pp. 40-41.

Van Raan, A. and Tijssen, R. (1993), The neural net of neural network research: an exercise in bibliometric mapping', *Scientometrics*, vol. 26(1), pp. 169-192.

Vinkler, P. (1987), 'A quasi-quantitative citation model', *Scientometrics*, vol. 12(1-2), pp. 47-72.

Vladutz, G. and Cook, J. (1984), 'Bibliographic coupling and subject relatedness', in B. Flood *et al* (eds), *1984: Challenges to an Information Society*, Proceedings of the 47th ASIS Annual Meeting.

Voos, H. and Dagaev, K.S. (1976), 'Are all citations equal? Or did we *op.cit.* your *idem?*', *Journal of Academic Librarianship*, vol. 1(6), pp. 19-21.

Vroom, V.H. (1964), *Work and Motivation*, John Wiley, New York.

Wallace, D.P. (1986), 'The relationship between journal productivity and obsolescence', *Journal of the American Society for Information Science*, vol. 37(3), pp. 136-145.

Walpole, R.E. (1974), *Introduction to Statistics*, Collier Macmillan, London.

Watson, T.J. (1993), 'Managing, crafting and researching: words, skill and imagination in shaping management research', *British Academy of Management Conference*, September.

Weber, M. (1930), *The Protestant Ethic and the Spirit of Capitalism*, Allen and Unwin, London.

Weinstock, M. (1971), 'Citation indexes', *Encyclopaedia of Library and Information Science*, vol. 5, pp. 16-40.

Westin, S., Roy, M. and Kim, C. (1994), 'Cross-fertilization of knowledge: the case of MIS and its reference disciplines', *Information Resources Management Journal*, vol. 7(2), pp. 24-34.

White, H.D. and Griffith, B.C. (1981), 'A co-citation map of authors in judgement and decision research', in B.F. Anderson *et al* (eds), *Concepts in Judgement and Decision Research: Definitions, Sources, Interrelationships, Comments*, Praeger, New York.

Whittington, R. (1992), 'Putting Giddens into action: social systems and managerial agency', *Journal of Management Studies*, vol. 29(6), pp. 693-712.

Whyte, W.H. (1956), *The Organization Man*, Simon and Schuster, New York.

Wiberley, S.E. (1982), 'Journal rankings from citation studies: a comparison of national and local data from social work', *Library Quarterly*, vol. 52(4), pp. 348-359.

Wickens, P. (1995), 'Getting the most out of your people', *People Management*, 9th March, pp. 28-30.

Williamson, O.E. (1975), *Markets and Hierarchies*, Free Press, New York.

Woodward, J. (1965), *Industrial Organization: Theory and Practice*, Oxford University Press, Oxford.

Xhignesse, L.V. and Osgood, C.E. (1967), 'Bibliographical characteristics of the psychological journal network and 1950 and in 1960' *American Psychologist*, vol. 22, pp. 778-795.